CAPITAL HORSE COUNTRY

Not every polo player receives a plaque from a U.S. Senator, but the horses and riders in the D.C. area are a "capital" lot.

CAPITAL HORSE COUNTRY

A Rider's and Spectator's Guide

Jackie C. Burke

EPM Publications, Inc.
McLean, Virginia

Library of Congress Cataloging-in-Publication Data

Burke, Jackie C.
    Capital horse country : a rider's and spectator's guide / Jackie
C. Burke.
        p.   cm.
    ISBN 0-939009-80-3
    1. Horse sports—Virginia—Guidebooks.   2. Horse sports—Maryland—
Guidebooks.   3. Horse racing—Virginia—Guidebooks.   4. Horse
racing—Maryland—Guidebooks.   I. Title.
    SF294.26.V8B87   1994
    798.2'4'09752--dc20   94-6658
                                                                                    CIP

EPM Publications, Inc., 1003 Turkey Run Road
    McLean, VA   22101
Printed in the United States of America

First Printing, April 1994

Cover and book design by Kimberley Roll
Cover photo by Douglas Lees

In special memory of
Steve Roll

About Using This Book

The vast majority of events in this book, with the exception of a half dozen, are staffed by volunteers. In some cases, contacts change yearly. In others, club officers may remain the same for a decade. It is regrettable if the reader is inconvenienced by a changed phone number, but unavoidable.

Most of the events in this book are free, but those with admission charges are subject to change also. Every effort has been made to explain that event dates can vary, too. Extra weekends in a month set off the regular pattern of dates, as does Easter and other holidays.

The *Fauquier-Democrat* in Virginia carries extensive, up-to-date calendars of horse events. The *Washington Post*'s "Weekend" section carries some information about horse-related activities in the area. Horse magazines do also, and a number of those that serve Maryland and Virginia are listed in Chapter XII.

J.B.

CONTENTS

Jackie Onassis has ridden frequently in Virginia's Hunt Country since her days as First Lady. Here she enjoys a day hunting with Piedmont, the nation's oldest pack.

Credit: Douglas Lees

I

HORSING AROUND HUNT COUNTRY

The Whys and Wherefores of This Book

Some people like to watch horses; some like to ride them. Those who like to ride them, like to watch them, too, and those who don't like either attend an occasional horse event with friends. If you fit into any of the above categories, this guide will put you on the inside track for a winning trip to Pimlico Race Track, the Virginia Gold Cup or the local point-to-point. It can surely make your first trip to the Upperville Horse Show a blue ribbon experience. If your goal is to see top polo, or dressage, or carriage driving, or combined training events, you must read on.

For newcomers who want to feel like insiders, the jargon is decoded. You'll come to understand how jousting became Maryland's state sport. There are listings for the mega-riding centers that dot the area as well as state and county fairs that feature draft horses and mules. Spectators wishing to turn their interest active will be put on the right trail. And, finally, for riders who are also readers, a listing of outstanding library collections of horse lore has been included.

The countryside just beyond the Washington and Baltimore beltways teems with horses and horse events. In fact, one doesn't have to leave Washington D.C. proper to see first-rate polo (played on Sundays right on Lincoln Mall) or to see a horse show or take a hack. Historically, a hack or hackney was a horse for hire. Today the term is applied to an informal trail ride, like the one through Rock Creek Park. Many of the events listed in this book are free, and all feature beautiful horses and scenery.

With few exceptions, the events are located within an hour's drive of the Washington Beltway. Directions are generally cued to the Washington Beltway, I-495, and the Baltimore Beltway, I-695. This book clears the path for finding equine events that are held down beautiful but scantily marked lanes. It also includes tips on how early one really needs to leave home in order to see the first horse on course.

Many of the events are held in Virginia's legendary hunt country. The term "hunt country" was not designed to make ritzy Middleburg sound even ritzier, but rather is a title of respect used by generations of horsemen who have found that the Piedmont region of northern Virginia is as good as it gets for horse sports. The very fine book, Kitty Slater's *Hunt Country of America*, is devoted almost entirely to the hunting around Middleburg, which may offend Marylanders whose forebears brought the very first foxhounds to the New World way back in 1650.

Maryland hosts some pretty fine horse events, including the second jewel of the Triple Crown, the Preakness Stakes, held the third Saturday in May at Pimlico Race Track just north of Baltimore. The first subscription racing trophy in North America was awarded at Annapolis back in 1743. When George Washington, the father of our country, attended this race, which was sponsored by the Maryland Jockey Club, the event was already almost 20 years old. Racing has since moved from Annapolis, but is flourishing at Pimlico, and at Laurel, which is an easy run from Washington. Some of the earliest steeplechases, as races over jumps are called, were staged at Pimlico as early as 1873. On the Virginia side of the line, steeplechases were held at Fauquier Springs near Warrenton before 1820, according to some accounts, but this effort was discontinued when the old hotel there burned during the Civil War. The bulk of events described here are located in northern Virginia and the verdant valleys around Baltimore, but the border lines have oozed a bit to include a few choice plums beyond.

This book, which supplies an easy-to-follow guide for the novice horse enthusiast, also includes interesting bits of history which underscore the importance of horses to the economy and heritage of the area. The history, unearthed mostly from original sources, should fill in some blanks among even the most ardent and long-lived devotees. Because riding is very much an insider's

The Annapolis Subscription Plate, first run in 1743, is racing's second oldest trophy.
Credit: Reprinted by permission of the Baltimore Museum of Art. Gift of Mrs. Sarah Steuart Hartshorne and Mrs. Alice Key Montell. BMA 1936.45.

activity, details about types of competition and the criteria for each are included, so as to bring those attending their first horse event up to speed. This will help spectators to appreciate the quality of both horses and riders. Events, ranging from steeplechases to polo to horse shows, to jousting tournaments (competitors aim at rings, not one another), are included in this guide. All provide "G" rated entertainment for all ages and all stages of life.

As in days of yore, equine events continue to bring together local gentry, visiting horsemen from all over the countryside and urbanites from D.C. These diverse groups are all drawn to the beautiful scenery and excitement of the competition. Friends and families gather to socialize, perhaps to place informal wagers on the competition and to share food and refreshment.

Racing weekends offer fine opportunities to pack the picnic hamper and pull out the horsey tweeds. These, along with horse shows, polo, and other special events all combine to offer a wide range of equine activities. While the rules of the game vary and the objectives of competition differ for the various horse sports, by their nature each requires a large track of grass, almost guaranteeing beautiful pastoral settings. Backdrops are often palatial estates that trace ties to colonial land grants, with brick houses where Washington or Lafayette is claimed to have spent the night or come to dinner.

Virginia has more steeplechases (23) than any other state, and Maryland (11) has the second most. These include two of steeplechasing's most prestigious prizes, the Maryland Hunt Cup and the Virginia Gold Cup. The $250,000 Breeder's Cup, the nation's richest steeplechase, has been held in Fair Hill, MD, four of its first six years.

Upperville, the nation's oldest horse show, continues to be held under the same venerable oak trees that shaded its proceedings back in 1853. During summer there are scads of horse shows in the area surrounding D.C., held virtually every day of the week during summer, with multiple choices on Wednesdays, Saturdays and Sundays. Showing moves indoors during fall with the Washington International Show. The Washington International, with the New York National and Royal Winter Fair in Toronto, is a showcase for international show jumping and a glittering gem on the social calendar.

Toss in some very good polo, the occasional combined training event, lots of dressage, annual stable tours in Upperville and Maryland, along with jousting—the state sport of Maryland—and you have as many reasons for planning a picnic as you have recipes for potato salad.

Any equine event selected for an outing gives one an excuse to drive down charming country lanes or rural byways. Even getting lost enroute holds a promise of discovering some beautiful sites, which might feature stately stone manor houses surrounded by boxwoods the size of buildings, and fields covered by centuries old turf. Sleek, young stock and contented broodmares graze in paddocks bound by black board fences or rock walls. These idyllic scenes are made even more beautiful in many areas by a backdrop of the Blue Ridge Mountains.

Besides seeing champion horses and beautiful scenery, each event offers a good opportunity for people watching, too. A long list of celebrities, some outgoing and others quiet and reclusive, frequent the horse events. Recent sightings include Senator John Warner, himself a fox hunter, Redskins owner Jack Kent Cooke, who owns champion steeplechasers and flat horses, and Redskins legend Sam Huff, who now organizes the West Virginia Breeder's Classic at the Charles Town Race Track. Comedian Richard Smothers and his wife Lorraine are both proficient show riders. Marilyn Quayle, wife of the former vice-president, and her daughter hunt with Casanova. Robert Duval, who owns jumpers, frequents local horse shows and the streets of Middleburg looking like a native. Former local Kelly Klein, champion show rider and wife of designer Calvin Klein, returns to Middleburg where her dad owns a shop on the main street, and sometimes shows in competitions. Talented sports commentator

Horses hurdle for total purses of almost $90,000 at the International Gold Cup Races.
Credit: Betsy Branscome

17

Charlsie Cantey, who once galloped horses at the Middleburg Training Track, is likely to surface, also. Weathercaster Willard Scott frequently prognosticates against backdrops of his own farm in Delaplane. Middleburg farm owner Pamela Harriman, named Ambassador to France under Clinton, and once married to Winston Churchill's son Randolph, to Broadway producer Leland Hayward and to the late Averell Harriman, entertained well-heeled Democratic contributors at the local pub in Middleburg. "Bo" Derek, a perfect "10," is a member of the Washington Horse Show board and is sometimes around Middleburg to ride Andalusian horses. Jackie Onassis, the First Lady of her generation, hunts with Orange County and Piedmont. Onassis also shows up at horse events where the participants and spectators would not dream of gawking or staring—at most they might emit a "pip, pip, well done" when Jackie "O" puts in a winning round in a local hunter trials.

Best-selling author Dick Francis, who writes those wonderful mysteries about steeplechasing, occasionally nips in to Middleburg to sign a wagonload of books and to watch a steeplechase. It is said that one day while Francis was out with the Orange County Hounds, Ms. Onassis rode up to the car in which the author was following the hunt and signaled for him to roll down the window. She said, "Mr. Francis, I've always wanted to meet you. I really enjoy your books." After the famous First Lady rode away, Francis turned to a companion and asked who that woman was. All the way around, celebrities can achieve a comfortable anonymity with the low-key horsey sorts.

Queen Elizabeth and Prince Philip visited the Middleburg Training Center in 1957. In separate trips both Anne, the Princess Royal, and her brother Prince Charles, when he was still accompanied by Lady Di, have stopped by to pay their respects to philanthropist and champion horse breeder Paul Mellon and to view his private art collection. Prince Rainier and the late Grace Kelly have visited Middleburg, as did the late Duke and Duchess of Windsor, the Duchess having attended Foxcroft School, one of the horsiest of girls' prep schools. Each hunt country hostess has her own story about famous visitors and each venerable old house its own list of famous and infamous guests, with presidents and heads of state placed near the top of the rundown.

What with the number of retired ambassadors, foreign service officers, authors, artists, English and Irish types, and generals and admirals around, the locals who are not first-degree famous are interesting enough in their own right to liven up a good afternoon of people watching. At horse events local chaps are earmarked by proper tweeds and twills, well-worn caps, carefully trimmed mustaches and burnished bench-made shoes and hunting boots. Leading ladies turn out in hats for protection against sun or cold, vintage Chanel suits and sensible shoes.

True devotees of equestrian sport, whichever particular discipline one favors, can glut on viewing super stars, either picking up their horse blankets at Fauquier Laundry or winning local competitions on their way to the next Olympics. Heroes of the eventing world include Capt. Mark Phillips, formerly married to Anne, Britain's Princess Royal, along with double world champion and Olympic Gold Medal winner Bruce Davidson, and Three Day coach Jack LeGoff, who trained the gold medal winning team. So might Upperville resident Jimmy Wofford, former President of the American Horse Shows Association and also an Olympic medal winner. Rodney Jenkins, who may be the best grand prix jumper rider of all times, has retired from active competition but still judges many of the shows and now trains successful race horses. Other biggies in terms of talent are grand prix jumping star Katie Monahan, gold medal winner Torrance Watkins and many times national champion Karen Lende, and Olympians Phyllis Dawson and Stephen Bradley.

Of course, the horses are the real champions. In 1993, the winners of both the Kentucky Derby, Sea Hero, and the Belmont Stakes, Colonial Affair, were Virginia-breds, an amazing record for a state that lacks the incentive of parimutuel tracks that support lucrative state-bred races. The area's tradition for breeding champion horses was brought from England and has been nurtured since the time of the first settlers. Early race champions in Maryland were sons and daughters of the root stock of the thoroughbred breed, chiefly the Darley Arabian and the Godolphin Arabian. One of the latter's most famous daughters, the great broodmare Selima, is memorialized by a stakes bearing her name run annually at Laurel. (A stakes is a major race with a big money purse; owners pay fees to enter, and this was once put in a winner-take-all stake.) The third thoroughbred foundation stallion was a Barb; American settlers were importing horses from the Barbary coast before the thoroughbred was even a registered breed.

Centuries of selective breeding have produced the likes of Gallant Fox, Omaha and Nashua, raised by the Woodward family, former owners of the Belair estate, which is now home of the Bowie training center. One doesn't have to read the *Daily Racing Form* to have heard of some of Virginia's best, such as Triple Crown winning Secretariat, Hansel, winner of the Preakness and Belmont, and Virginia-bred Mill Reef, who won all the classic races in England and France, then in retirement became the cornerstone for the National Stud in England. Northern Dancer, surely the most influential stallion of the century, stood at Windfields Farm in Maryland. The region's proud tradition of racing has produced three steeplechase champions, Battlefield, Jay Trump and Ben Nevis, that have gone on to win the world's toughest jump race, the English Grand National.

Beside the fresh air, atmosphere, and sheer physical beauty of events, there is another subtler element that comes to play which adds to the enjoyment of equestrian events, namely the appeal they hold for such a wide range of ages and economic groups. Traditionally, jockeys' own offspring appear in the paddock bundled on their mothers' backs within days of their births. Four generations removed from these tykes are the great grandfathers, leaning on the paddock fence or propped on a seat stick, remembering the day when a horse they owned, bred or rode won the Virginia Gold Cup or local point-to-point. Between these age extremes are a sea of college students, who meet their friends for a day of general carousing, young families picnicking with their contemporaries, and chic empty nesters who meet and greet in corporate tents over canapes at the Gold Cup. Multimillionaires brush shoulders with Irish grooms, and members of the President's cabinet come together with shop owners.

A survey done in 1991 by insurers who wrote policies for the horse industry showed that people listed the following as reasons they enjoyed riding and being around horses: (1) enjoyment of nature and being out of doors; (2) the challenge of training and riding horses; (3) the softness, gentleness and grace of horses; (4) the beauty, strength and mystique of horses; (5) the exercise and physical fitness derived from riding; (6) sociability with others who like horses.

The allure of horses goes far beyond snaring only those who like to ride, as the survey demonstrates. The earliest settlers came to Virginia and Maryland and surrounds brought an innate love of horses with them to the New World. Those centuries of knowledge and care, selective breeding and training will be easy to spot at any of the horse events listed in this book. Only an allergy to horses could stand in the way of making a day in the country at an equine event enjoyable, and this condition can be managed by taking an antihistamine beforehand and staying upwind of the paddock.

II

TAILGATES AND THE POINT OF THE POINT-TO-POINT

Steeplechasing, Stirrup Cups and Other Mystifying Terms

During Colonial times, everyone rode or drove. Those who didn't, walked. But in Maryland and Virginia, horses have always been more than just a source of transportation. Settlers from the British Isles brought with them a love of horses, racing and foxhunting.

Ships' dockets show that foxhounds arrived in Maryland in 1650, providing the essential element for fox hunting in the New World. Horse races were probably held as soon as enough trees were cleared to permit a short track.

When organized racing moved to Annapolis in the early 1700s, records showed that winners hailed back to the bloodlines of the thoroughbred foundation stock. American thoroughbreds, many of which are still raised in Maryland and Virginia, were then and continue to be a precious commodity in the world market.

In the field of thoroughbred racing, Maryland has always had reason to hold its head up proudly. Venerable Pimlico Race Course hosts the Preakness, second jewel in the Triple Crown.

Horse competitions have always provided a good excuse for a tailgate party. Riders and spectators gather (overleaf) for a hunter trials near The Plains, VA.
Credit: © **The Washington Post.** *Reprinted by permission of the* **D.C. Public Library.**

24

Laurel Racetrack, circa 1911, hosts the International Turf Festival. Add to these Timonium and Marlborough, remnants of Maryland's colorful half-mile tracks and its unique parimutuel steeplechase track, Fair Hill, and you have some of the nation's best and most diverse racing.

One of the most famous steeplechases in the world, the Maryland Hunt Cup, has been run over the Green Spring Valley hunt country near Baltimore annually since 1894. The Grand National has coursed through the Elkridge-Harford Hunt Country since 1898, as has My Lady's Manor, begun in 1909. Down in Virginia, harder hit by the Civil War, modern-day steeplechasing started later with Middleburg in 1921 and the Virginia Gold Cup in 1922.

Horse showing, an important diversion in rural life, predated the Civil War. First held in 1853, the Upperville Show stakes a legitimate claim to being the oldest horse show in the nation. A number of shows in Virginia are 100 years old or more.

Competitions continue spring, summer and fall. Then comes winter and with it, foxhunting. Of the 157 recognized hunts in the United States, Virginia is home to the most, 19, and Maryland has the third most, 11. Second most are in Pennsylvania, 15, with all but three huddled on the Maryland/Delaware line. Virginia Hunt Country, together with that in Maryland, forms the center of horse activities in the Capital area.

Foxhunting first came to America when Robert Brooke brought foxhounds, along with his family and household, to Maryland in 1650. Tradition has it that red foxes were imported from the British Isles to the Eastern Shore in 1730 to improve the sport, as the indigenous grey fox runs shorter courses when chased and goes readily to ground when provoked by the sight of large numbers of hounds. Lord Fairfax brought hunting in "the English fashion" to Virginia in the 1740s. George Washington greatly admired Lord Fairfax, whom he emulated by forming his own pack of foxhounds. The oldest American pack surviving to the modern day is Piedmont Hunt (Upperville), founded in 1840 by the Dulany family.

The Washington Hunt was organized by the British minister in 1828. The kennels were located at the corner of 14th Street and Pennsylvania Avenue, across from the Willard Hotel. The history of the Potomac Hunt reports that foxhunters roamed the open territory of the Mall from Rock Creek on the west to the junction of Florida and New York Avenues on the east.

In Virginia Deep Run (Richmond) and Warrenton were both begun in 1887, Blue Ridge (Clarke Co.), in 1888, Loudoun, 1894 and Keswick in 1896. Of the Maryland hunts in existence today, the oldest is Green Spring Valley (Glyndon), 1894.

The area's first recognized polo club was the now-defunct Washington Club, founded in 1896. The club never listed many playing members, but rather an organizer, who presumably drew from visiting diplomats and military officers to make up games. The Army Polo Club, founded 1902 at West Point, moved its address to D.C. in 1939 as war clouds brewed and top brass moved closer to the base of power. Officers continued to play polo on or around the Mall through the war. Today, civilians keep the tradition going on a beautiful field just across the street from the Lincoln Memorial.

Whether for polo or racing, foxhunting or horse showing, horses were always an important part of the Cavalier Society in what is now the Capital area. A slim, valuable volume printed earlier in this century entitled *Unison Farmer's Hunt* by Charles S. Monroe, points out that the riding and showing of horses rated right up there with skating and sledding parties, drama clubs, musical societies and Friday night dances as favorite diversions in the country . The privately published tract put it this way: "Old McDonald had a farm and on this farm there were good horses. Every farmer was a horseman."

If horsemen in the Capital area have enjoyed riding, racing and raising horses since early on, they have also held an equal affinity for watching horses perform. Eating, drinking, and socializing against the backdrop of equestrian events have evolved into a number of specialized forms. Several of these are associated with hunting. For instance, before setting off for a day in the field, stirrup cups are sometimes served to the riders. These jigger-size containers of port and brandy are so named because they were traditionally passed up to the riders from stirrup height. Some of the handsome and collectable cups used for this purpose had fanciful handholds shaped like foxes or hounds. After the contents were emptied, the cups were set back on trays rim down.

The most festive day of the hunt year is opening day, the first day of the formal hunt season. This generally occurs in

October or November. Some of the hunts invite a local clergy to bless the hounds. In a brief religious service, the cleric always takes the opportunity to also say prayers for the wildlife, countryside, farmers and riders. A big feed is always part of the day.

Big spreads of grits, Virginia ham and other delicacies served on polished hunt boards (hence the name) served before the hunt or anytime up into early afternoon are tagged hunt breakfasts. Buffets, longer on cocktails and joints of meat than breakfasts, are served from dining tables and can last past dark even though they are called hunt teas.

Winter in hunt country begins the whirl of hunt balls. To these, the swells wear scarlet tailcoats and white tie (plainer gents, tuxedos), and ladies don ball gowns of white or black so as not to distract from or clash with the proud cocks whose lapels display the distinctive colors of their local hunts.

For polo, steeplechasing, coaching, and to some degree horse showing and other competitions, a tailgate is certainly in order. Unlike hunting parties, which may be limited to participants and neighboring farmers, tailgates are open to all comers. It has been suggested that the first Virginia tailgate picnic occurred during the First Battle of Manassas, because the gentry drove their carriages out from Washington to view the battle and to see what all the excitement was about. The seats really weren't very good. Spectators, who followed confident Union troops out from Washington, parked in Centreville. That was four miles from the battle line, even farther away from the action than the back row of general parking at today's Virginia Gold Cup. The camp followers could see nothing more than smoke from the battle. Those who stayed behind in Washington got better reports on the action than those sitting in Centreville and wondering. It was one of those "you could see it better on television" events, but before the age of electricity. The tailgaters, unfortunately, did participate in and inhibit the retreat. Carriages clattered and petticoats flapped in the wind as the gallery joined and impeded the Union soldiers in their hasty retreat back to Washington. This sojourn to the First Battle of Manassas was the only such happening during the Civil War. For Washingtonians, the home team had not won. Worse, men were wounded and killed.

The idea of venturing into the verdant Virginia and Maryland countryside on fine weekends did have its merit, however.

The pilgrimage from D.C. to see men dashing about on horses was revived and continues to this day. Steeplechasing, the ultimate thoroughbred sport of daring do, offers an especially good excuse for a tailgate. The first steeplechase occurred, according to the hackneyed tale, when two hunting gentlemen raced 4½ miles from one steeple to another in County Limerick, Ireland.

Well, you see how this sort of thing could happen among raucous members of the hunting fraternity. After all, when the foxes and hounds did not yield the requisite amount of exercise on a given day, young bloods and their fit-to-the-minute mounts were left with steam to blow. Church spires made handy start and finish points for this natural phenomenon.

Jumping was a major part of the game from early on. When agricultural practices turned from keeping stock on commons, farmers began staking off their fields with hedgerows, timber fences, ditches and, where materials were available (most of Ireland), stone walls. To cross the country from one spot to another, therefore, required a mount capable of leaping what-ever manmade obstacles stood in the way, in addition to natural elements such as streams and brooks. These "steeplechases" came to be more organized due in part to enterprising owners of public houses, like Thomas Coleman, proprietor of the Turf Hotel in St. Albans, England. In 1830, Coleman orchestrated a four-mile 'chase from Harlington Church to finish near his hotel at West Park, offering an excellent reason for patrons to line up to cheer the winner while ringing up the house profits.

What is interesting to note is that the much documented and heralded event that took place in St. Albans may have been a Johnny-come-lately by Virginia terms. In the not very well documented annals of American sporting history, Fauquier White Sulphur Springs Hotel near Warrenton, Virginia, is re-ported to have held races over jumps even earlier. (Certainly a much advertised steeplechase was held there in 1875).

The first well documented steeplechase in North America was held in London, Ontario, in 1843, with Paterson, NJ, hosting a steeplechase in 1865. Pimlico Race Course carded a steeple-chase as an experiment on October 28, 1873, and liked the results enough to keep a jump race on the cards every day until the 1950s. In the 1880s, hunt clubs started holding steeplechases on a regular basis.

In England, the sport, with its emphasis on speed, jumping ability and daring, was an instant hit with sportsmen but not the turf racing authorities, who held no sway over these free-for-all dashes across the countryside. To bring some consistency and to quell charges of race fixing and other skullduggery, the National Hunt Committee was formed in 1862 to bring a set of rules and standardization to the sport. The National Hunt Committee came under the stead of the British Jockey Club in 1875.

By 1895, America had formed its own regulatory body to oversee steeplechasing, the National Steeplechase, Hunt and Pony Racing Association. Still in existence, it is now known as the National Steeplechase Association or NSA. This American cousin of the National Hunt Committee has not merged with flat racing authorities, though the NSA cooperates with respective state racing associations where parimutuel gambling is permitted on steeplechases.

A dig through the NSA archives shows on its 1910 card that race meets were hosted by the Warrenton Hunt Club, Virginia Race and Horse Show Association (now Strawberry Hill), and Maryland United Hunts. The races on Warrenton's card that year were for hunters owned and ridden by members of a recognized hunt, for half-bred hunters, and for farmers or their sons over whose property the Warrenton Hunt Club hunts. The fictional Mr. Sponge, a creation of 19th century author Robert Surtees, noted that steeplechasing led to use of horses "neither hunter nor hacks nor yet exactly race-horses."

The United Hunts included in its 1923 list of autumn race meetings both the Blue Ridge Hunt at Berryville and Virginia Gold Cup at Warrenton. By 1939, six of the top moneyed steeplechase meets were held in Virginia and Maryland. The lion's share of purses in those days were being doled out by parimutuel tracks, with Pimlico leading the list at $35,080, followed by Delaware Park, $32,100, and then Laurel and Timonium, which, like Pimlico, are both in Maryland. Montpelier in Virginia and the Virginia Gold Cup offered sizeable amounts compared with other hunt meets.

Steeplechasing in England and America both had its heyday in the '20s and '30s. During the '30s, Paul Mellon, patron saint of the National Gallery and a Cambridge graduate, became enthralled by English steeplechasing. Mellon went on to make contributions to racing through his husbandry in the matings that created such influential stallions as Mill Reef, accomplishments which match the mark he has made on the art world. It was during this era that Mellon began developing Rokeby, his spread in Upperville, VA.

It was also during this golden age that American sportsmen sent out their best to try for England's chief steeplechase prize, the Grand National. Billy Barton, who in 1926 was the last horse to win both the Maryland Hunt Cup and Virginia Gold Cup, made a valiant effort in the Grand National in 1928. Two years later, Battleship, owned by Mrs. Marion DuPont Scott of Mont-pelier Station, VA, won the race. The feat has been matched in recent years by not one but two Marylanders, Charles Fenwick on Ben Nevis and Tommy Smith on Jay Trump. All the American winners, and most of the connections were bred, raised, and/or trained in Maryland or Virginia.

After World War II, the picturesque sport of steeplechasing found less favor at the parimutuel tracks. Steeplechasing took a severe body blow when New York and Maryland all but elimi-nated steeplechasing from their schedules in the 1960s. It then came to the hunt meet to keep the sport alive, something of an irony. From its earliest days on this shore, two minds of thinking were in operation regarding hunt racing. One view was that steeplechasing should approximate the natural hazards of the hunt field, ergo—conditions that did not permit speedballs from the race track to defeat the steadfast, sure-footed hunters capable of negotiating challenging terrain and substantial fences. The opposing view saw steeplechasing as a promising spectator sport and began standardizing racing conditions.

Those in the steeplechases-should-be-for-hunters school de-veloped the solid timber fence, which remains unique to Amer-ican racing. The other branch favored brush fences, which are American equivalents of the gorse hurdles and larger steeple-chase fences used in England and Ireland.

These two patterns of thinking perhaps best explain how point-to-points became point-to-points and steeplechases be-came steeplechases, and why the two continue to carry these respective names even to this day. From this somewhat con-voluted description of the history of the earliest steeplechases, the analytical reader might think, Aha! So, steeplechases are held on an oval track over brush jumps and point-to-points, limited to hunting horses, travel in a more or less straight line over timber jumps. Alas, no. Both nowadays have a start and finish point in view of spectators and feature a prescribed track. Steeplechases are run over brush, but may also offer timber racing. Point-to-points do feature races over timber, but most also offer races over brush to round out the race card. In England, all riders in point-to-points must be amateurs. In America, professionals may ride at point-to-points and often do to sharpen their skills. In England, horses at point-to-points shall have been fairly hunted. In America, some of the series at point-to-points carry this requirement, but not all.

Other differences between point-to-points and steeplechases are perhaps too subtle for all but the initiated to perceive. Generally, steeplechases, which often offer large money prizes, come under the authority of the NSA. Point-to-points, which lack this temptation to breech good sportsmanship, do not.

The point-to-point circuits that operate in the Virginia/Maryland area do come under central authority for the purpose of promotion, standardization of conditions assigned to challenge trophies given for year-end awards, and general support to fellow races. The associations themselves give one quick access to a bank of information about a large number of races. (See listings at the end of this chapter.) The Virginia Point-to-Point Council consists of representatives from each of the 12 races listed in its condition book. The Virginia circuit, which started operating as a coalition in the early '70s, has given rise to an excellent series of point-to-points, very professional in conduct. Attention to detail in planning, officiating and course preparation has attracted to the circuit the very best horses, trainers and riders, who will later in the year be prominent in the major moneyed races on the NSA circuit. The Maryland Governor's Cup Point-to-Point Series includes five races. Trophies for the circuit were first offered in 1976. A committee was formed and a trophy was awarded for the leading rider of the series. The job of keeping up with such things came more and more to Sissy Finley Grant, who then wrote about horses and point-to-point racing for the old *Washington Star*. Grant, who wrote under the name of Finley, remembers that when the Maryland series was formed, Virginia was already going great guns and that she was

31

seeking some credit for riders who raced on the "right side of the Potomac." For a while, though, there were fewer and fewer races in Maryland, not more and more, as in Virginia. The Governor's Cup series all but disappeared, but is now back on thanks to monetary sponsorship of awards provided by Prince George's Equestrian Center. The races now on the series include original participants Howard County, Elkridge-Harford, Marlborough and Potomac Hunts, and the series is once again growing. Unlike most point-to-point series, the Governor's Cup now includes My Lady's Manor, which is also recognized by NSA. Furthermore, Maryland's Grand National, also an NSA race, will soon join the series. The reason for this duality is to make certain an outstanding horse that excels in these two classic timber tilts has an opportunity to win the series prizes.

In America, as in England, point-to-points are sponsored by local hunts and are major fundraisers for the same. In England and Ireland, all steeplechases are held at regular tracks, not dissimilar in physical facilities from Laurel or Pimlico. In America, steeplechases, like point-to-points, are held in grassy fields yielding the requisite terrain and turf cover, but lacking paved parking lots and indoor toilets.

Steeplechases here are often run for the benefit of local charities such as hospitals, historic properties, and non-profit cultural endeavors. In order to maximize such contributions, businesses are sought to sponsor the sometimes hefty purses offered as incentives to competitors. This gives rise to corporate tents which lend visibility to generous sponsors such as BMW, Continental Airlines, and Tiffany & Co., which in turn use these oases of creature comforts to woo favored customers or to lobby important suppliers or politicians. Guests may expect such luxuries as a grand piano, jazz trio, vintage champagne and exquisite luncheon menus, but port-a-pots are the order of the day.

Tents aren't unheard of at point-to-points, but picnic venues lean towards tailgates in the family station wagon or Range Rover. In America, as in England and Ireland, point-to-points tend to be a bit more rough-hewn than their slightly more uptown cousin, the steeplechases. Point-to-points in England and Ireland are viewed by ruddy-faced farmers in caps and coarse tweeds and green Wellington boots. Here in America the knowledgeable spectator may be garbed in the same. After all, the season over there, as well as here, starts in February when weather can easily be cold and rainy.

Dates for the races vary each year, but they follow the same pattern. The Virginia race calendar works backwards from the Virginia Gold Cup, always held the first Saturday in May. Lest ye forget, the Virginia Gold Cup shares the same day with the Kentucky Derby. Up in Maryland, everything works off the Maryland Hunt Cup, which is the last Saturday in April, always one week before the Virginia Gold Cup. It is of course wise to double check dates before packing up the station wagon. Generally, though, if you get out your calendar and turn to the first Saturday in May and start marking back from there, you will have a good idea of when a particular race will occur. Fall race chairmen are generally bound to dates they have used in previous years. Should September or October have five Saturdays, that can throw things askew, however.

SPRING RACE CALENDAR

Grand National Steeplechase, Butler, MD one Saturday before Maryland Hunt Cup
Middleburg Spring Race Meet, Middleburg, VA usually third Sunday in April
Foxfield Spring Race Meet, Charlottesville, VA last Saturday in April
My Lady's Manor Race Meet, Monkton, MD two Saturdays before Maryland Hunt Cup
Maryland Hunt Cup, Glyndon, MD last Saturday in April
Middleburg Hunt Point-to-Point, Middleburg, VA Sunday before first Saturday in May
Virginia Gold Cup Race Meet, The Plains, VA first Saturday in May
Kentucky Derby, Louisville, KY first Saturday in May
Bull Run Hunt Point-to-Point, Middleburg, VA Sunday after first Saturday in May
Winterthur Point-to-Point, Wilmington, DE Sunday after first Saturday in May
Potomac Hunt Races, Seneca, MD second Sunday after first Saturday in May
Marengo Race Meet, New Kent County, VA third Saturday in May
Preakness, Pimlico Race Track, MD third Saturday in May
Georgetown Race Meet, Leesburg, VA third Sunday in May

Fair Hill Steeplechase, Fair Hill, MD	last Monday in May, Memorial Day
Pimlico Special Handicap, Pimlico Race Track, MD	second Saturday in May
Casanova Hunt Point-to-Point, Warrenton, VA	ten Saturdays before Virginia Gold Cup
Rappahannock Hunt Point-to-Point, Sperryville, VA	nine Saturdays before Virginia Gold Cup
Blue Ridge Hunt Point-to-Point, Berryville, VA	eight Saturdays before Virginia Gold Cup
Warrenton Hunt Point-to-Point, Warrenton, VA	seven Saturdays before Virginia Gold Cup
Howard County-Iron Bridge Race Meet, Glenelg, MD	four Saturdays before Maryland Hunt Cup
Piedmont Fox Hounds Point-to-Point, Upperville, VA	six Saturdays before Virginia Gold Cup
Orange County Hunt Point-to-Point, Middleburg, VA	five Saturdays before Virginia Gold Cup
Elkridge-Harford Hunt Point-to-Point Races, Monkton, MD	three Saturdays before Maryland Hunt Cup
Old Dominion Hunt Point-to-Point, Ben Venue, VA	four Saturdays before Virginia Gold Cup
Marlborough Hunt Races, Davidsonville, MD	three Sundays before Maryland Hunt Cup
Strawberry Hill Race Meet, Richmond, VA	three Saturdays before Virginia Gold Cup
Loudoun Hunt Point-to-Point, Leesburg, VA	three Sundays before Virginia Gold Cup
Fairfax Hunt Point-to-Point, Leesburg, VA	generally third Saturday in April

FALL RACE CALENDAR

Fair Hill Steeplechase, Fair Hill, MD Labor Day
Shenandoah Race Meeting, Mt. Jackson, VA first Saturday after Labor Day, also on a Sunday, mid-October
Fairfax Race Meet, Leesburg, VA third Saturday in September
Foxfield Fall Race Meet, Charlottesville, VA last Sunday in September
Virginia Fall Race Meet, Middleburg, VA first weekend in October, generally with races on Saturday and Sunday
Morven Park Race Meet, Leesburg, VA second Saturday in October
International Gold Cup Race Meet, The Plains, VA third Saturday in October
Montpelier Race Meet, Montpelier Station, VA first Saturday in November

RACE ASSOCIATIONS

VIRGINIA
POINT-TO-POINT CIRCUIT
William O'Keefe
P.O. Box 4096
Leesburg, VA 22075

Phone: 703-777-2575

The Virginia Point-to-Point Circuit consists of a coalition of 12 point-to-points sponsored by area hunts. Most are located in Fauquier and Loudoun Counties, two are in Rappahannock County. The circuit was formed in the early '70s, though a number of the races have been around considerably longer.

Races operate with a high degree of professionalism, apparent in course preparation, officials, riders, trainers and horses. Course preparation is a year round concern for sponsoring hunts, and horse preparation, a task that takes a minimum of three months for participating trainers.

The actual countdown for competitors race week starts when entries are phoned in on Monday preceding each race. Some Monday mornings over 200 entries are received. With few exceptions, all entries are permitted to run causing races to be split to keep the number of starters to a manageable level. Virginia Beach, who is racing secretary, makes this call on race day. To get the 10 or more races that can be required to accommodate up to 150 plus starters completed on winter-shortened afternoons, she runs a tight ship in the paddock. Beach, herself a veteran of the ladies' races, and the paddock judge can send runners out on a 20-minute time schedule.

Once the race starts, the race call is made by veteran announcer Will O'Keefe. O'Keefe and his sidekick Michael Hughes, who handles public service announcements, are excellent assets of the entire Virginia Circuit, including steeplechases. They also announce some of the races in Maryland. Other officials, too, tend to serve multiple times each year, bringing experience to the circuit.

Some of the trophies offered pre-date the series. Riders earn points for series trophies by winning points in the division for which the prize is offered. Not every meet offers races that carry points for each series. What races each meet offers is determined in part by the terrain. Rappahannock, for instance, which has some real terrain (the Blue Ridge Mountains, to be precise), has scrapped its brush race, because the pell-mell pace in these is better suited for flatter courses.

Besides offering services to races and trophies to winners, the Point-to-Point Council annually produces a racing seminar. The seminar is held in the dead of winter, generally around the first of February, at the Middleburg Community Center. It is free and features speakers and topics of interest to experienced and inexperienced. For details call Peter Winants at 703-687-6542.

MARYLAND GOVERNOR'S CUP POINT-TO-POINT SERIES

c/o Edward L. Coffren
2817 Crain Highway
Upper Marlboro, MD 20772

Phone: 301-627-2298

The Governor's Cup Series includes Howard County-Iron Bridge, a fairly new race that is growing rapidly as well as Elkridge-Harford, located north of Baltimore. Also included are My Lady's Manor, a full-fledged NSA event with large money prizes and Marlborough and Potomac, both near D.C. and both very large in terms of entries and numbers of spectators.

Series awards carry generous money prizes thanks to sponsorship by Prince George's Equestrian Center. These awards are presented at the conclusion of the Potomac Races, the final event on the circuit.

DELAWARE VALLEY
POINT-TO-POINT ASSOCIATION
P.O. Box 97
Unionville, PA 19375

The Delaware Valley Point-to-Point Association recognizes five races in the Delaware Valley. All are a pretty good hike from D.C. Four of the races are in the foxhunting country of southeast Pennsylvania and can be classified as old-style point-to-points, with fairly small crowds, cross country style courses and excellent competition. Winterthur Races, held the first Sunday in May on the grounds of the Winterthur Museum near Wilmington, DE, stands apart as a well-attended steeplechase with a slick presentation. Special events in the spectacle include a large parade of carriages. The museum and gardens are open the morning of the race, with shuttle service offered from the race course to permit patrons to arrive early, thus avoiding traffic, and view Winterthur's azaleas, generally in full bloom at that time of the year.

Winterthur's proximity to Longwood Gardens, the Brandywine Museum, the Hagley Museum and the Delaware Art Museum make this race a possibility for the centerpiece of an overnight sightseeing trip to the area. Convenient lodging possibilities range from charming bed and breakfasts to country inns to the elegant Hotel duPont in Wilmington. For details about the races, call Ms. Nancy Miller at 302-888-2310.

VIRGINIA STEEPLECHASE ASSOCIATION
P.O.Box 1158
Middleburg, VA 22117

Phone: 703-687-3455

The Virginia Steeplechase Association exists apparently for the purpose of giving awards and having parties. Membership in the organization costs $25 for individuals, $40 for families and $15 for juniors. Members receive a badge and are invited to several nice parties each year, some free and some for a modest fee. In March, prizes are awarded to the leading hurdle horse, timber horse, jockey, trainer, owner and breeder on the circuit. The after-dinner speaker at that affair is historically more entertaining than most, and the recipients are too, as Virginia horsemen are typically a colorful lot. Officials, riders, owners, and trainers on the circuit are more or less the same lot seen at the Virginia Point-to-Points, with a contingent from Pennsylvania and Maryland thrown in for good measure.

NATIONAL STEEPLECHASE ASSOCIATION
400 Fair Hill Drive
Elkton, MD 21921

Phone: 410-392-0700

The National Steeplechase and Hunt Association was founded as, and continues to be, the rules-making body for steeplechases in America. Patterned after the National Hunt Committee, which performs the same function in England, this American cousin obtained its charter in 1895. Races on the NSA circuit carry money prizes, from a few thousand for the least flat race, to $250,000 for the Breeder's Cup Steeplechase. Through the years, purses have tended to be very fair across the board in steeplechasing.

The NSA keeps track of the performance records of horses for the purpose of determining eligibility for various race conditions. It also tracks wins by riders, who receive weight allowances based on number of wins. Those who get a full ten pounds off have never won a NSA race. These non-winners carry three asterisks by their name in the race programs. Two asterisks means that the rider has one to three wins, and receives a seven pound weight allowance. One "bug" riders have won three to ten races and receive a five-pound allowance. The NSA also gives year-end trophies to the leading timber horse, brush horse, rider and trainer.

Membership in the NSA costs $100. Privileges of membership include free admission to meets, including 11 in Virginia and five or more in Maryland, depending on how many meets Fair Hill holds each year. Also, members receive a discount toward the purchase of *American Steeplechasing,* a hardbound annual review of NSA races, and distinctive badges for members and their guests.

III

THE VIRGINIA POINT-TO-POINTS

A Guide to Parking and Particulars

A great many inhabitants of the towns, villages and hamlets of northern Virginia simply live for the point-to-point season. For riders in the area, winter does not encourage out-of-door activities beyond foxhunting, and those participants are galloping across the countryside with not much time for chatting and tailgating, two activities favored at point-to-points.

This is why the locals, joined by friends from the city and suburbia, flock to the races, come hail or high water. It was once thought that no day was too foul for ruddy race-goers and hardy horsemen, but there have been exceptions like the Blizzard of '93. For the most part, if you are planning to attend a race and the weather turns bad, you just pile on more clothes. The horses don't mind, nor do spectators who turn out in knee-high mud boots, ankle-long Australian drover coats, and stockmen hats that keep snow and rain off the neck. Folks like to put on their best spring bonnets for the Virginia Gold Cup, but guests at an early Spring point-to-point should not let style stand in the way of comfort.

Part of the fun of the point-to-points, compared with races like the Gold Cup, is their laid-back, easy-going atmosphere. You will not have to arrive two hours early to avoid traffic jams, and because the crowds are smaller, you will have easy access to the paddock for close-up views of the magnificent horses. You

Bundled-up crowds cheer competitors up the home-stretch at the Rappahannock Point-to-Point. The hilly race course lies at the foot of the Blue Ridge Mountains.
Credit: Douglas Lees

will certainly see winners of the Gold Cup or other top moneyed races make their Spring debuts at the point-to-points.

CASANOVA HUNT
POINT-TO-POINT
Mt. Sterling Farm
Casanova, VA

When: February, generally the fourth Saturday

Time: First race at NOON, with frequent race splits, resulting in a card of nine or ten races most years.

Contact: Casanova Hunt
　　　　　Casanova, VA 22017

Phone: 703-347-5863

Directions: I-66 west from Washington to Route 29 south at Gainesville. South on Route 29 for 12 miles to Route 605 east; the course three miles on right. From Warrenton, Route 29 north to Route 605 east.

Casanova is the first race on the circuit, and therefore met with great enthusiasm in spite of the fact the weather conditions can be deplorable. Sam Richards, retired Casanova MFH, remembers at least two years when it snowed. Though no one could tell who was in the lead on the far side of the course, the show went on. Casanova Point-to-Point runs in February because it was not begun until 1957, making it a junior member of the circuit. Richards said the hunt took that date rather than tagging on at the end of the circuit. The early date and horror stories about the weather have not deterred large numbers of spectators from attending the race.

Though general admission parking is a short walk from the course and viewing areas are ample and well placed, you might want to spring for a reserved space so you can huddle in your car or use it for a wind break. Reserved parking goes on sale around the first of February.

The course itself is fair enough for the first of the season. The timber fences are low, inviting, and forgiving should a horse make a miscue from lack of experience or over-eagerness. The track of the course is without tricks for the flat and hurdle races.

45

Virginia Racing Sites

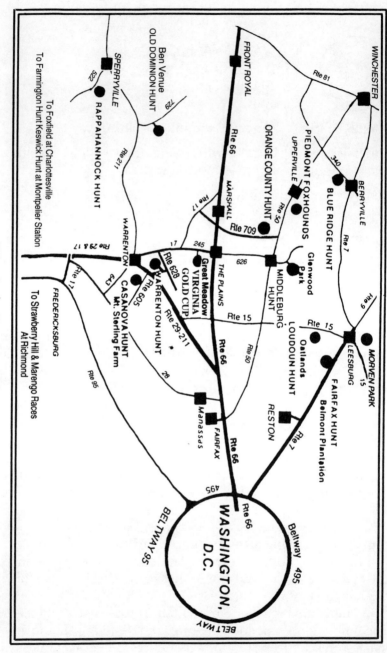

Scads of horses enter each year, usually more than 100, and racing is always competitive and sometimes dramatic.

In 1992 Bay Cockburn, leading rider of the circuit, won the owner-rider timber in other-than-your-usual manner. His mount popped him off with an unusually bad jumping effort: but Cockburn, who had been in the lead, vaulted back into the saddle and was back stalking the horses that had passed him, running down his final rival at the wire. Back in the early days, MFH Richards remembers when a competitor from Maryland won both the first and second division of the flat race—on the same horse.

As winners go, no one has put his name on more trophies than Randy Rouse, MFH of Fairfax Hunt and chairman of its races. While Rouse no longer pilots his own entries, honors at Casanova are still claimed by horses ridden by his wife Michele.

Admission: Patron parking, which includes front row parking, with all occupants admitted at no additional charge, is $75. Reserved parking at $50 features a numbered parking space on the second row. Four occupants are admitted at no charge, with additional tickets available for $3. Recreational vehicle parking costs $50. Subscriptions are $25, which admits a vehicle and two occupants to subscriber parking area on third row. General admission costs $5. Viewing areas for the public are on the slope between the second and third rows, and in the infield, which affords a good view of the course, particularly the backside and final turn. Prices quoted are for advanced reservations. Some areas sell out, so it is advisable to call around the first of February.

RAPPAHANNOCK HUNT POINT-TO-POINT
Thornton Hill Farm
Sperryville, VA

When: First Saturday in March, generally, or last Saturday in February

Time: First race starts at NOON

Contact: Rappahannock Hunt
P.O. Box 315
Sperryville, VA 22740

Phone: 703-547-2810

Directions: From Washington, I-66 to Route 29 at Gainesville. Route 29 to Warrenton, then 211 west to Sperryville. Turn south toward Culpeper on 522. Course is one mile east of Sperryville.

Rappahannock is the second race on the circuit, and as such is early and subject to winter weather patterns—in other words, it can be very cold. Though Casanova is most famous for its weather stories, what really sets Rappahannock apart is its terrain. Set right at the foot of the Blue Ridge Mountains, it is in view of some spectacular climbs, including Old Rag Mountain.

The scenery for spectators is no more breathtaking than the jumps are for the competitors. One expects to see Heidi and her goats standing across the meadow on the summit of the course to cheer on riders as they face the most daunting drop fence en route to the final turn. Not only does the course test the courage of riders and the stamina of horses, it requires right- and left-handed turns. The flat course travels clockwise, and this can make a difference in some cases to horses accustomed to running the standard counter-clockwise course prevalent in America.

Rappahannock Huntsman and Clerk of the Course Oliver Brown admits that their drop fence coming down the hill has caused riders to be catapulted from here to eternity. Their course nevertheless accounts for fewer falls than others on the circuit. The jumps are a step up from Casanova's but not so big as to be discouraging. The terrain itself holds down the raw speed which often causes bad spills. Interestingly, these factors have prevented any one rider from dominating at Rappahannock as has sometimes been the case at other meets.

The mountain may take a few entries away from his meet, Brown figures, but he notes that good horsemen have always been willing to send their horses to Rappahannock. The list of previous winners proves his point. On it are the best stables in Pennsylvania and Maryland as well as Virginia. The names on the junior race trophy are especially significant in terms of previous winners. Champions who cut their racing teeth at Rappahannock include Ricky Hendricks and J.L. "Chuck" Lawrence, who have both earned leading rider title of the NSHA circuit; champion lady rider Dawn Dugan; Gus Brown, champion owner/rider in the hurdles division of the Virginia circuit; Charles Fenwick II, a top flat rider at Laurel and Pimlico, and

Patrick Worrall, winner of the Maryland Hunt Cup and multiple winner of the Virginia Gold Cup.

Another special feature of the Rappahannock races is the hound race. More than 50 foxhounds are turned loose following the final horse race of the day, and in theory the hounds follow a line dragged with fox scent. The race has been uproarious at times. More than once the entire lot of entries has found the line of a live fox. The race, whatever the results, has become a favorite part of the card, a case of the tail wagging the dog in a very real sense.

General parking is located across from the course, not a long walk but refer to notes on Casanova and consider splurging for a reserved spot here, too, as insurance against bitter cold. The entire course can be viewed from the reserved parking area.

Admission: Options for reserved parking include the infield, which costs $50, always a sellout, and patrons parking, $60, in an area kept exclusive from the throngs of spectators. The subscriber area behind the paddock costs $35, and admits two. General admission is $5 per person, plus $5 per car.

BLUE RIDGE HUNT POINT-TO-POINT
Woodley Farm
Berryville, VA

When: March, generally the second Saturday

Time: First race at 12:30 P.M., nine races, generally with several splits

Contact: Blue Ridge Hunt
Caveland Farm
Boyce, VA 22620

Phone: 703-837-2077

Directions: Route 50 west, past Middleburg and Upperville, over the Blue Ridge Mountains and Shenandoah River. Turn right on Route 723 to Millwood, admiring the old mill and browsing in antique shops, if desired; then right on Route 255 to Route

340. Turn right on Route 340 toward Berryville. Signs pointing to the course will be ¾ of a mile on the right.

Blue Ridge Point-to-Point equals a medium size steeplechase in terms of attendance and also in regard to numbers and quality of entries. Race co-chairman Peter Dunning said that the race draws spectators from a geographic area roughly within an hour and a half of the course, with a good draw from Washington and Baltimore. Horses and competitors come from even farther away, with the best stables in Maryland and Pennsylvania's hunt country represented. The weather can be good or, like the other early race meets, it can be bad. Blue Ridge has had a pretty good run of weather in recent years and there are few prettier or better spots for race viewing than their hillside.

At risk of discouraging reserved parking, general admission here is not bad on a good day. The walk from the general admission lot is not far, and unusual rock outcroppings below the paddock and reserved parking provide unique bleachers. In spite of this interesting natural feature, reserved parking has been expanded by 15 to 20% each year for the past five. The lines just stretch farther and farther across the hill, but every seat in the house is good. People who have been coming a long time tend to get territorial, Dunning says. Some patrons have had the same spot for 20 years and want the same people next to them. Newcomers should apply for reserved spaces early in February.

Out-of-state entries keep things on the race course stirred up and interesting. The large number of high quality entries keep any one rider or owner from dominating. Dunning figures horsemen usethe timber course as a step up from the first two meets of the year. The bigger, straighter fences give entries a chance to get their flaps up a notch higher before they meet the really big fences in Maryland.

Speaking of flaps up, Dunning recalls that Sally Roszel, one of the best riders he ever saw go around the course, had such long legs she is said to have kept the heels worn off her boots clicking over the top rail. Roszel, since retired from active race riding, now serves as an official at Blue Ridge and other races on the Virginia Circuit. Race officials like Roszel bring an air of professionalism to their posts that Dunning says is only fitting, given the quality and numbers of horses entered (more than 100 starters). Beside Roszel other great riders that Dunning has admired are the Randys, Rouse and Waterman, that is.

Skill and experience both help on this course. Inexperienced riders or those on recalcitrant horses can end up in the woods rather than at the finish line if they don't ride the tight final turn just so. Many races are won and lost right there. Another challenge is a pair of jumps set in a line fence. The takeoff and landing on these are at different heights, causing a sharp jolt for those who haven't ridden their line just right.

Blue Ridge traces its current point-to-point back to 1949, but NHSA records report that the hunt held a fall race meet on the regular steeplechase circuit as early as 1923. Blue Ridge has sponsored a horse show even longer, since 1892.

WARRENTON HUNT POINT-TO-POINT RACES
Airlie Race Course
Warrenton, VA

When: March, generally the third Saturday

Time: First race at 1:00 P.M.

Contact: Warrenton Hunt
P.O. Box 972
Warrenton, VA 22186

Phone: 703-349-3048

Directions: I-66 west, south on Route 17 at Marshall. Travel 7.5 miles to Route 628; turn left. In just a few hundred yards, turn right on Route 605.

Are these race meets coquettish about their age? Warrenton does admit to being the oldest on the circuit, claiming to have been born in 1934. Warrenton actually held a meet in 1910 so that it could be even older. Master of Foxhounds Sally Tufts knows a family who possess a race trophy from the Warrenton Races that bears the date 1900.

A charming description of the race in 1934, written by top local historian, the late Francis Greene, may explain the disparity in dates. Back in 1910, the NSHA year book shows that the races carded were for Warrenton Hunt members, for members of any recognized hunt, for members of any recognized hunt on half-breds, and for farmers and the sons of farmers who lived in Warrenton Hunt territory. By 1934, the NSHA had moved its emphasis to lightweight races for professional jockeys. Perhaps it was to bridge the gap and give hunting people a chance to participate again that Warrenton staged a six mile point-to-point of the old style, starting at one point in the hunt country and ending in another. The event, *Polo Magazine* reported, was great fun and the finish after all that distance very close, with the late Bill Streett besting Old Dominion MFH Sterling Larrabee by three lengths. Other hunts in the area, including Middleburg, Orange County, Old Dominion, and Piedmont, followed suit. Soon, Warrenton's race evolved to a two point affair with start and finish at the same location. Then a third point was added. Finally, to follow the local trend, Warrenton began running over a roughly circular track, bringing it full circle back to where it was started from in the '20s. Today professionals are permitted to ride, but some races are written for foxhunters and owner/riders.

Not only has the shape of the course changed through the years but also the location of the race. From 1966 until 1988 the hunt used the wonderful old Broadview course, so long the site of the Virginia Gold Cup. When developers started erecting houses there, the point-to-point relocated to Airlie Conference Center at the invitation of Dr. Murdoch Head. Hunt members and friends raised money, and actually performed the labor, to build the course. Mrs. Tufts said that with Airlie Conference Center's strong support for open space the race should be able to stay at this location.

The course itself is a classic. The timber course is a full mile-and-a-half, so that even in the long timber races it is only necessary to travel two circuits. Over some of the shorter courses on the circuit a lap counter is required for spectators and competitors to keep track of how many more turns of the course till the finish. The Warrenton course has wonderful turf, a flowing sweep to the turns and enough up and down to challenge a horse's fitness. A horse with the stamina to go the distance and jumping ability to handle the stiff fences has the class and talent to win on down the line in recognized NSHA meets.

At times, you can see the course; at other times, you can't. This is because viewing is from a hill smack dab in the center of the course. There is a way to catch all the action, however. One needs only to scurry from one side of the narrow ridge top to the other to view all the action.

Admission: The top dollar patron's ticket, at $75, gets a choice of a spot on top of the hill or along the finish line. For $50, one can split the difference with a subscriber's pass, which entitles the holder to park on the hillside between the hilltop and finish line. Although general admission spectators can shuffle across the hilltop right alongside of the carriage trade, reserved parking is probably a good idea, because general admission parking is a hike away. Price of general admission is $4 per person in advance, $5 at the gate.

PIEDMONT FOX HOUNDS POINT-TO-POINT
Salem Course
Upperville, VA

When: March, generally the fourth Saturday

Time: First race 1:30 P.M.

Contact: Piedmont Fox Hounds
P.O. Box 1877
Middleburg, VA 22117

Phone: 703-687-6067

Directions: I-66 west to Route 50 west. The course is located about eight miles west of Middleburg on the right or north side of Route 50, just east of Upperville.

The Piedmont Point-to-Point was begun in 1939 by Paul Mellon, benefactor of the National Gallery of Art and former master of Piedmont. The race was held on Mellon's Farm until 1956, when he built his jet air strip on what was once the race course. Some of the jumps used for that course, which was five miles long, still stand on Atoka Farm, which is now owned by Sen. John Warner. Dr. Joe Rogers, who won the feature race over that course, and also over the new course, said that Mellon set the standards for point-to-points in America when he started the Piedmont races in 1939. Rogers remembers that Mellon's course was magnificent, with fences broad of face and bigger than most so that a number of horses could jump next to one another. Then Mrs. A.C. Randolph, who continues to serve as Piedmont's joint master, moved the race to her farm. Like Mellon, Mrs. Randolph laid the course over natural hunt country. No jumps are repeated, and everything is in its natural state, so horses see just what they would face out hunting.

The feature race of the day is the Rokeby Bowl. The trophy for the race is donated by Mr. Mellon, who has it crafted expressly for that purpose by English silversmiths. The challenge trophy is held by the winner for a year, and those who can win the trophy three times get to keep it. The valuable prize has been

The Rokeby Bowl, one of the most sought-after awards of the circuit, is presented to Donnie Yovanovich (center) for the fifth time by Piedmont Master Randy Waterman (left) and its donor, art patron Paul Mellon (right).
Credit: Douglas Lees

retired several times, first by owner/rider Cyrus Manierre, winner in 1950, 1951 and 1954 over the Rokeby course, and by Mrs. H.R. Fenwick, who won three years in a row with three different horses, all ridden by Crompton Smith, Jr., and by Dr. Joe Rogers, who has cost Mr. Mellon two trophies and is well on his way to keeping a third Rokeby Bowl.

The Rokeby Bowl is unique not just for its fine trophy. Rather than following a more or less standard oval as most races on the circuit do, this race weaves over hill and dale, covering very natural hunt country. The course goes out of sight of the crowd, then comes past the spectators, over a stone wall and into the country again, around Mrs. Randolph's barn, across a lane and back to the main course for the finish. The course, the trophy itself and the fact that the winner is often crowned timber horse of the year (this honor bestowed by vote of a special committee of journalists) make the Rokeby Bowl especially coveted.

Don Yovanovich, who has ridden the winner five times, four of those wins in a five year period, has the race very much in mind before the season even starts when he plans a campaign for his best horses. Yovanovich said the trick to winning the Rokeby Bowl is to analyze the course when walking it beforehand, to form a plan and stick to that plan. The course has both right- and left-hand turns, and some are sharp. Which side is the inside must be taken into account when riding into those turns, Yovanovich says. No one steals the Rokeby Bowl by running out to the front and pumping iron to stay there; it's too long a distance. Moving too early can cost the race, too. When the riders come into sight of the crowd the final time, the push is on, but Yovanovich claims the time to move is not until three furlongs from home.

Hurdle races and flat races are also held at Piedmont, these being over an oval course in full view of the spectators. The two courses are tight, so the horses are always on the turn. It's a good place to bet on a horse a little closer in size to a polo pony than to a rangy, long-strided steeplechaser.

Admission: Rail spots are sold for $125 front row, $100 second row and $75 third row. The front row always sells out, but since the parking is on a hillside, all viewing is equally good, and each year new spots are added to accommodate the demand. Here general admission parking ($10) is a hike from the course and the weather can be very bad, even though spring, at least by the calendar, is near. Viewing for general admission is in the infield, plentiful and very good.

ORANGE COUNTY HUNT POINT-TO-POINT
Locust Hill Farm
Middleburg, VA

When: March, generally the final Saturday

Time: First race 1:00 P.M.

Contact: Orange County Hunt
Route 1, Box 8
The Plains, VA 22171

Phone: 703-364-1831

Directions: I-66 west from Washington, exit Route 50 west through Middleburg. Turn left on Route 709 south. Course is one mile from Route 50 on the right.

Orange County was on the circuit for a time, then wasn't, and now is again. First its point-to-point was held over farm fields near The Plains, later at Glenwood Race Course in Middleburg. When the race lapsed from lack of a race chairman and that problem was resolved, it lacked a racing date. Orange County came back onto the circuit, however, in 1988, with a double dose of good luck. First, they were given a prime date due to a change in Middleburg's point-to-point date; second, they were not granted permission to run any series races and that proved to be a bonanza, according to Orange County Master of Foxhounds James Young.

Young originally carded a lightweight timber race to give ladies, lacking a ladies race, an opportunity to compete. The way the race has shaped up, top trainers from Pennsylvania and Maryland as well as Virginia have used the race as a tune-up for Middleburg Spring, the Virginia Gold Cup and other NSHA races on the circuit. Top trainers like the course, so they bring along their most promising brush horses to give them a spin, too. Winners there in 1992 included Push and Pull, winner of the Gold Cup that year, and Lonesome Glory, undefeated in a string of six starts and two-time winner of an Eclipse Award, one of thoroughbred racing's highest national honors.

The turf on the race course is carefully tended, and the timber course provides a wide variety of jumps of the sort one would find "over fair hunting country," and is not too large or hard on the horses. The jumps on the timber course are named for famous and favorite hunters and race horses owned by Orange County Hunt members. Members were asked to sponsor jumps when the new course was built at Locust Hill Farm. The timber course goes this way and that, making viewing of the entire course from one point impossible. The brush course is unusual because it goes clockwise. This configuration was used according to Young to allow a straight run-in at the finish. Even so, the home stretch is short. After seeing horses like Push and Pull and Lonesome Glory pull away from the field (other horses in the race) in the straight, one could predict they would chalk up big wins later in their careers. (Push and Pull won a Gold Cup; Lonesome Glory, Eclipse awards and Breeder's Cup.)

Admission: Parking on the hillside, which gives the best view, is $100. Parking at the finish line, which is convenient to the paddock and a fine place to party, costs $75; and parking without a view but convenient to the paddock is $50. General admission is $5 a person. The walk from the general admission lot is not too far, and since no one has a perfect view, those taking this option can huddle here or there and see as well as anyone else.

 OLD DOMINION HUNT POINT-TO-POINT
Ben Venue Farm
Ben Venue, VA

When: April, generally the first Saturday

Time: First race, NOON

Contact: Old Dominion Hunt
P.O.Box 39
Orlean, VA 22128

Phone: 703-347-0603

Directions: Take Route 211 west from Warrenton 16 miles to Route 729. Turn right. Course is ¼ mile on the right.

Old Dominion started holding a point-to-point back in the '70s when the late William Brainard became Master. Until then, the hunt had been headed by Col. Hinkley, who was interested only in hunting and who picked up most of the expenses. Brainard, a brilliant organizer with a different idea of funding, started the hunter trials, hunt ball and point-to-point, with David L. "Zeke" Ferguson serving as chairman of the latter. The first couple of years the hunt was permitted to hold their race at the Glenwood Race Course in Middleburg. After one particularly cold afternoon of racing, Thomas Eastham, whose family estate, Ben Venue, lies in the Old Dominion Hunt Country, approached the masters and suggested that the race be held at his farm. Ben Venue has been the location of the race since 1980, and a more breathtaking location could hardly be found. The drive past the Eastham ancestral home itself is worth the trip. The original log cabin, built in 1805, where Tommy Eastham's great-great-great-grandfather once lived, still stands near the brick manor house.

The course occupies a natural amphitheater. Viewing is wonderful for everyone, and conditions are very fair for the horses. Brainard, Ferguson and horse trainer Ridgely White laid out the course, and the Easthams have lavished fertilizer and other care on it ever since. The result is magnificent turf, which traditionally turns brilliant blue-green in time for the races. Though everything is in a concentrated area, the timber and flat courses have a classic sweep. The brush course has one tight turn, but that is going up hill away from the start and trailers, so horses handle it all right.

Admission: Parking for sponsors used to cost $60, but prices were expected to rise. These spaces occupy the front two rows, with subscriber parking behind this selling for $45, (also expected to rise). Another option is tents, which command the view from the uppermost portion of the open hillside, like a feudal castle. Tent prices include the tent, table and chairs, along with two parking spaces. They are of adequate size to entertain a large number of guests. (Prices are in the $1,000 range.) General admission is $5 a head. It's a bit of a walk for those carrying coolers, chairs and blankets, but there is plenty of room for viewing: on the hillside in front of the tents, behind reserved parking and around the official's pavilion.

LOUDOUN HUNT POINT-TO-POINT
Oatlands
Leesburg, VA

When: April, usually the second Sunday

Time: First race 1:30 P.M.

Contact: Loudoun Hunt
P.O. Box 902
Leesburg, VA 22075

Phone: 703-777-9519

Directions: Take I-66 west from Washington. Exit onto Route 50 west to Route 15 north. Turn right into the drive to Oatlands Mansion. From Route 7 west, turn left (south) just before Leesburg onto Route 15. Oatlands Mansion will be on the left.

The Loudoun Point-to-Point was founded to provide more opportunities to race, according to Dr. Joe Rogers. Rogers called on his good friend Crompton "Tommy" Smith, who had just won the Grand National Steeplechase in England, to design the course. The course, like that of the Rokeby Bowl, goes over hill and dale and looks like it has always been there, though it was actually an engineering feat. Much earth was moved and tiles installed for drainage so the footing would be good, even in wet weather. A real variety of jumps was built to prepare horses for things to come in sanctioned steeplechases. The jumps and the turf, carefully nurtured since 1966 when the race was first held, encourage a high quality of entries. Those who enter the four-mile featured Eustis Cup are often being fitted for the Virginia Gold Cup. Three of Rogers' own horses have gone that route, winning the Eustis Cup, then the Gold Cup. There is a definite correlation between winners of the Eustis Cup and the Rokeby Bowl at the Piedmont races also. Eight of the first 26 winners of the Eustis Cup also won the Rokeby Bowl the same year. Rogers, a double winner three times himself, said that this is no coincidence, because both races are longer than average and both have a wide variety of jumps. The contestants are some times in view and some times drop out of sight behind a hill.

Hurdle races are more visible, though that course goes around the crown of a hill and finishes down a groove, so from any vantage point the horses are some times out of sight. The jump placement is good, as is the footing. Given the good racing conditions and the Sunday date, the race draws entries from far.

Wins by local entries and support early on by Bet Phillips, editor of the local paper, assured the popularity of the race. An extra attraction at Loudoun is Oatlands itself. Not only is it a beautiful setting, but the museum shop, historic house and gardens are open that day. The house is owned by the National Trust for Historic Preservation. The point-to-point is just one of the numerous events held at Oatlands designed to bring in the public. The gardens were originally designed and planted by George Carter, who built Oatlands in the early 1800s. Restorations of the gardens in recent years have been true to the early Virginia landscape designs, and original boxwoods and other bushes are the size of trees. Spring bulbs generally flower for the races.

Admission: All parking options are well filled. Patron parking costs $125, which includes two parking spots, one on each side of the driveway in the finish line area. For $45, subscriber parking permits a car and four passengers to park in the area near the paddock. This is not the spot for viewing the race, but it is only steps away from the main portion of the race course. A goodly number take the general admission at $5 a head. Those who go this route lug their picnic and blankets to the crown of the hill in the middle of the course, enjoy the spring afternoon and as good a view of the entire course as possible (not in range of the paddock or the finish).

FAIRFAX HUNT
POINT-TO-POINT
Belmont Plantation
Leesburg, VA

When: April, generally the third Saturday

Time: First race 1:30 P.M.

Contact: Fairfax Hunt
P.O. Box 902
Great Falls, VA 22066

Phone: 703-787-6673

Directions: From the beltway, travel west on Route 7 toward Leesburg to Belmont Plantation, which will be on the left approximately 15 miles from I-495.

Back in 1977 Fairfax MFH Randy Rouse had the idea that yet another point-to-point would go. He remembers thinking that it was a sport growing in popularity and he thought he could draw a crowd. He did. Picnickers, party goers and day trippers come in large numbers, mostly from the territory between the race course and Washington. Fairfax snares more corporate sponsors than most point-to-points. Sponsors entertain important clients under festive tents.

The hunt had always crossed Belmont Plantation, which was once owned by a hunt member. When IBM bought the historic property to put into their land bank, Rouse, a persuasive fellow, talked Big Blue into letting him build a race course there, which he leased on a year-to-year basis. The corporation came to like the event, and now plans to preserve the race course when the land is eventually developed into an office park. The exterior of the house has been recently restored, but the inside is currently in disarray. The land on which Belmont was built was acquired by Thomas Lees of Stafford, England, through a royal grant. It descended through the family, which included two signers of the Declaration of Independence. The house was built during the American Revolution in the Federalist style. President Madison took refuge there after the British burned the

White House during the War of 1812, and Lafayette was a guest during his tour of America in 1824–25.

If it rains for Fairfax, the bottom side of the course can be deep. The course, with a long downhill run to an uphill finish, is entirely visible, and is interesting enough with its unique clockwise track, tricky right hand turns and a long uphill finish. The triangular shape of the track puts a premium on a rider who can set a horse up for the turns and a horse that is well schooled to do his rider's bidding. The crowd, which seems more interested in the party than the racing, does stop feasting long enough to form informal pools, giving each his own champion to cheer to the finish.

The races do not draw the horses that start at Casanova, according to Rouse. In fact, some championship divisions can be a bit lean, as horses that have made a number of early starts may not need a race, and some owners have determined that their horses are just plain slow. Maiden and open hurdle races and the flat races can fill with fresh horses aimed at the Gold Cup or later NSHA races. Loudoun race chairman Joe Rogers and his wife, Donna, also an owner and trainer, have dominated the timber division in recent years.

Admission: Patrons' spaces close to the finish line are $90 on the rail, $60 across the driveway from the course. Sponsors parking further down the hill goes for $50 on the rail and $25 off. The viewing is good from any of the rail spots. General admission is $5 in advance and $10 day of the races. The general admission parking is not an unreasonable distance from the course, and there is plenty of viewing area in the infield. Patron parking sells out, so does everything on the rail. Those hoping for a prime spot are advised to make reservations two months in advance.

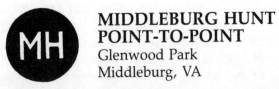

MIDDLEBURG HUNT POINT-TO-POINT
Glenwood Park
Middleburg, VA

When: Generally the final Sunday in April

Time: First race 1:00 P.M.

Contact: Middleburg Hunt
P.O.Box 61
Middleburg, VA 22117

Phone: 703-338-4366

Directions: From Washington, travel west on I-66 to Route 50 west to Middleburg. At the first and only traffic light turn right (north) to the course, about two miles on the right.

Middleburg's loss of its racing date was Orange County's gain. Previously held near the end of March, Middleburg was moved to near the end of the season when Glenwood Park declared that no other race meets should precede the important Middleburg Spring Races, which hosts two major stakes on the NSHA circuit. Well, it's not all bad for Middleburg Point-to-Point because series championships are often decided there. In 1992, the ladies' championship went to the wire, resulting in an interesting match race between Jill Waterman and Michele Rouse. Michele hung on, literally, to get a very inexperienced horse over the course. This gave Michele enough points to win the championship, though she lost the race to Waterman. Waterman, just 17 at the time, is sure to figure big in the future.

The owner/rider hurdle series was even closer, as the lead and wins were swapped around from week to week. In the end, John Branscome, who had been in the lead for the last part of the season, sat helplessly by, sidelined with a broken collarbone sustained the week before. He watched Gus Brown, his nearest rival, finish second, earning Brown enough points to win the championship. In a demonstration of sportsmanship that is admirable and standard to the sport, Brown piloted Branscome's horse to a win a few weeks later.

Feature race of the day, the Middleburg Hunt Cup, was once in the league with the Eustis Cup and Rokeby Bowl, and considered premier on the circuit. It has suffered in recent years due to the date change. With its date in the midst of NSHA races, the top competitors are out racing for checks. The point-to-points include owner/rider types or horses late in developing that did not peak in time to be Gold Cup contenders. To fill its race card and assure competitive races, Middleburg offers a number of races for riders who have not won an NSHA race, or five point-to-points. To gain proficiency requires racing experience, and opportunities are few and far between for the new guys. In open races trainers use the most experienced riders they can engage, so this gives a number of up-and-comers a chance to gain some seasoning.

Admission: Parking spaces are $150 for patrons, which includes prime spots on the front row near the finish line. Parking II, which sells for $100, is in the same area, but on the second row. Subscriber parking, at $50, features front row parking along the final turn. The view from this area, and every other area at Glenwood, is good, and also handy to the paddock, if not to the finish line. General admission is $5 per person and $5 per car. It's a good walk from the general admission parking area, but there are plenty of nice spots from which to watch. A deluxe option and one growing in popularity is the Middleburg Jockey Club, where for $75 per head, one is treated to lunch, drinks, parking and viewing from the party tent on top of the hill.

BULL RUN HUNT POINT TO POINT
Glenwood Park
Middleburg, VA

When: Sunday following the first Saturday in May

Time: NOON

Contact: James G. Kincheloe Jr.
4084 University Drive, Suite 202
Fairfax, VA 22030

Phone: 703-503-8286

Directions: See Middleburg Point-to-Point.

Amazing though it seems, the day after the mother-of-all steeplechases, the Virginia Gold Cup, there is yet another point-to-point. But there you are.

The Bull Run races, long on flat races and contests for novice horses and riders, fill to the brim with late comers who need one start before the spring ends, or who have been saved for a campaign in summer. In 1991, for example, the Worrall family, who had captured the Virginia Gold Cup the day before, came back to Virginia from their home in Maryland to give another potential champion a little seasoning.

A delightful feature is the Great Manassas Mule Race. It is filled with real jockeys on mules which are not real race horses. The mules cannot understand why they are being asked to sustain such a furious pace. The results can be side-splitting to watch. Other novelty races include a contest for Arabian horses, for ponies and for teams of fox hunters.

Admission: Call ahead.

IV

SPRING STEEPLECHASES IN VIRGINIA

Bring out the Benz and the Flowered Hats

Steeplechases, in Virginia or elsewhere, tend to be slicker renditions of their country cousins, the point-to-points. Mind you, the point-to-points are conducted with ultimate polish from a racing standpoint, but with a few exceptions they do not "put on the dog" quite like steeplechases.

The difference is most simply explained by the size of the cash prizes. Steeplechase meets like the Virginia Gold Cup offer $100,000 and upward in race purses. Much of this money is obtained through corporate sponsorship. A desire on the part of the races to give the companies their money's worth brings out a lot of the hooray. Sponsorship often includes the perk of a special tent, which the company bedecks with spreads of fine food and wine and important guests.

Gents at corporate parties usually wear coats and ties, and ladies take the opportunity to bring out new spring outfits, including often fetching hats. Hats are not bad ideas for either sex in sunny weather. Knowledgeable Virginia spectators carry along outdoor gear, such as rubber boots or grandmother's old fur coat, should the weather turn tough.

Pony races provide the warm-up act for the Virginia Gold Cup.
Credit: Douglas Lees

Younger spectators, who seem always to cluster together, don their Ivy League best, or shorts and other abbreviated wear. Wishing to quell any tendency toward the second option, the Gold Cup thoughtfully spells out what it considers appropriate race attire and sends this information along with tickets. Wherever the people gather, their mood will be festive, the spectacle fine and the racing very good.

 ## STRAWBERRY HILL RACES
State Fairgrounds
Richmond, VA

When: Generally the second Saturday in April

Time: First race 1:30 P.M.

Contact: Atlantic Rural Exposition
P.O. Box 26805
Richmond, VA 23261

Phone: 804-228-3238

Directions: From Washington, travel south on I-95. Take Exit 17, follow signs to the fairgrounds.

The Strawberry Hill Races, the first NSHA race meet in Virginia each year, are held on the Virginia State Fair Grounds. Unlike most state fairs, Virginia's is not held on state-owned grounds. The site is owned by the private, not-for-profit Atlantic Rural Exposition (ARE), which was originally founded by cattlemen who wanted to hold the eastern equivalent of the cattle exposition in Denver. The agricultural exhibits which have developed over the years are different from those in the West.

The Strawberry Hill Races were originally sponsored by the Deep Run Hunt Club. Among the older races in the United States, they date from 1895. Held first at Ginter Park, then on the site of the current Country Club of Virginia, the races moved to the current location in 1947, not long after ARE purchased Strawberry Hill Farm. After years of funding the race purses out of their own pockets, Deep Run Hunt members gave the entire project over to ARE whose board decided the race was in keeping with its mission to promote agriculture, namely the fine thoroughbred horses raised in Virginia. Up to that time it had certainly met the not-for-profit criteria of the ARE.

In 1980, the wise Exposition board sought out and found an ideal charitable beneficiary for the race, the Historic Richmond Foundation. With the high-powered, hard-working members of that organization handling advertising, ticket sales and promotions, the race was able to attract an enviable stable of corporate sponsors, and start generating real profits, which benefited the Historic Richmond Foundation. The partnership has inspired several innovative twists, not the least of which is the large carriage drive, that attracts teams to Richmond from Pennsylvania, New York, New Jersey, Kentucky, Tennessee and from all over Virginia. The afternoon before the race, patrons who pay $100 per ticket are treated to a preview of carriages and the race course, trim and ready for the big day. Later the patrons attend a black-tie dinner dance, held in a large cattle barn. The hall is large enough to permit a carriage drive, including four-in-hands, around the dance floor. Now, how's that for a floor show? Race day, the carriages travel to the state capital building for a stirrup cup, then proceed to the race course in time to put on an impressive parade before the first race.

A recent innovation was party tents for participating universities. Ten schools accepted the invitation the first year, and two came in too late to be included. The horses in the final race wore saddle cloths in the colors of the participating schools. This added to the enthusiasm of the already well-oiled crowd. Trailing the field was a lone rider on a mule, wearing the colors of the University of Virginia, one of the schools that missed the deadline for securing a tent.

All this led to a record crowd in 1992 of 21,000. While a high water mark was set in this area, it must be reported that the race course itself was in such bad shape that the race was almost canceled by officials of the NSHA. Other race courses have been carefully nurtured to produce the safest racing surfaces possible for the contestants; but Strawberry Hill, with its mission to serve many interests, had had to be used previously as a parking lot for NASCAR races with disastrous results. Sue Mullins, who manages horse events there, said the board had made a new commitment to bringing the course up to standards. Though the purses aren't the fattest at Strawberry Hill, the race in years past has attracted some of the best horses, including Virginia Gold Cup winners Von Csadek, Constantine and Private

70

Gary, and Uptown Swell, a hurdler who is near the top of the list for all-time money winners.

Admission: The race is a sell-out in terms of reserved parking, so call early. The deluxe ticket is the $100 a head VIP pass, which includes admission to the races and parking, a ticket to the formal ball, food and drink plus a race view from a divine oasis landscaped by the Horticultural Society. Reserved parking ranges from $50 to $100 per space, plus $12 per person in advance, $20 per head race day.

MIDDLEBURG SPRING RACES
Glenwood Park Course
Middleburg, VA

When: April, generally the third Sunday

Time: First race 2:00 P.M.

Contact: Middleburg Spring Race Association
P.O.Box 1173
Middleburg, VA 22117

Phone: 703-687-6545

Directions: From D.C., take I-66 west. Exit on Route 50 west to Middleburg. At the town's only light, by the Red Fox Tavern, turn right (north) to the course, about two and one half miles on the right.

Founded in 1921, Middleburg is the oldest continuous race held in Virginia. It is held at beautiful Glenwood Park, known for its attractive old stonework box seat area, spectacular views of the Blue Ridge Mountains, rolling terrain, good turf and good viewing from any point on the course. The park was a gift of the late F.R.S. Fred, and is now maintained by the Glenwood Park Trust, which is a beneficiary of the race. Glenwood Park is not the only steeplechasing legacy left by Fred, a major landowner in the Middleburg area. He was the father of Mrs. D. M. Smithwick, a top horsewoman and steeplechase trainer, who is also the mother of D.M. "Speedy" Smithwick, a top amateur rider in his day, good steeplechase trainer and currently head of Jack Kent Cooke's California racing stable.

Glenwood Park is one of those places that grows on you. The good news for newcomers to the course is that every seat and parking place offers good viewing. Horsemen hold the course in high esteem, running their very best horses there each spring. Though the purse doesn't match the $100,000 stakes held in other locales, few races can boast a better field than that of the featured brush race, the $40,000 Temple Gwathmey. The horse that ends the year as the Eclipse Champion almost invariably makes an appearance at Middleburg.

Paul Fout, the race's co-chairman and himself a race horse trainer, describes Glenwood as a horsemen's course, and that is why he figures trainers are willing to send their best for less. The hills and lush turf prevent the racing from being an all-out speed fest, and show off conditioning and horsemanship instead. Fout was responsible for nabbing the prestigious Temple Gwathmey trophy for the race, and for creating the unique co-feature, the Alfred Hunt Memorial. The Temple Gwathmey, first given in 1924, was initially run in New York, then at Rolling Rock, PA. When Rolling Rock threw in the towel, Fout asked the Temple Gwathmey foundation if he could run the race at Middleburg, and was granted the right by agreeing to adhere to a certain purse structure. One of the two iron jockey statues at the Red Fox Inn in Middleburg wears colors of the Temple Gwathmey winner.

The Alfred M. Hunt Steeplechase also is rooted in the Rolling Rock Races, once held at the beautiful country club of the same name in western Pennsylvania. Hunt was an integral part of that race and, following his death, his family came to his old friend Paul Fout, seeking a worthwhile memorial for the sportsman. On a suggestion from his wife, Eve Fout, he proposed creating a race in Hunt's name and building a special course for the race. The course is unlike any ever seen before, featuring every sort of obstacle, from open water ditches to brush hedges placed only strides apart to large timber jumps. Fout said the obstacles created were based on jumps he had seen on his travels to England, France and Australia.

"Eve and I figured," Fout explains, "that there are horses that can run over the National fences, and then there is the Maryland Hunt Cup type of horse. Not every horse fits one of those two molds, so we created something else." The something elses that won the first two years of the race included Topeador, one of the kindest and best owner/rider horses on the Virginia

Point-to-Point Circuit, and Bruce Miller's My Dear Judge, the family foxhunter of a famous Pennsylvania steeplechasing clan. So from the standpoint of winners to date, the race has been interesting. Topeador, for one of the only times in his career, was ridden by a pro, but My Dear Judge was ridden by his owner's son. Fout said the race attracted 26 entries its first year, proving his point that there is another kind of horse out there. The race has also been a favorite with the crowds, not only for the variety of fences but for three changes in direction configured in such a manner to prevent any rider from grabbing the inside and holding it.

Middleburg does offer good timber racing. The committee chose not to go head-to-head with the neighboring Virginia Gold Cup, which has three or four timber races, including the $50,000 Gold Cup. Middleburg's timber course rolls up and down hill, holding back the kind of blazing speed seen at the Gold Cup. The fences at Middleburg are stout enough, and require a good jumper. Also there is variety to the jumps, which keeps the horse on the alert and careful.

Admission: Parking spaces range from $60 for Row Two and Three on the final turn (good viewing but a distance from the finish) to $2,000, paid by sports council members for rail spots near the finish. A popular option is the $500 clubhouse box package, which includes lunch for four in the Tiffany's tent, and viewing from a covered clubhouse, with open bar all day. At $200, the member box seats are also a good deal, with admission for five and private boxes in the old stone stands overlooking the finish line and nearby parking. Parking on the rail away from the finish line costs $150, with prices increasing incrementally as one approaches the finish area. Because it doesn't offer general admission in the spring, Middleburg attracts a good size crowd but not a mob, a plus to those who truly came to see the horses, not just to see and be seen.

FOXFIELD RACES
Foxfield Race Course
Charlottesville, VA

When: Last Saturday in April
Time: First race 1:00 P.M.

Contact: Foxfield Racing Association
P.O.Box 5187
Charlottesville, VA 22905

Phone: 804-293-9501

Directions: The course is located 4½ miles west of Charlottesville at the junction of Route 29 and Barracks Road. From Warrenton, take Route 29 south to Charlottesville. After Route 250 and Route 29 merge, turn west on the by-pass to Route 654 west, 4½ miles to Foxfield, which will be on the left.

Foxfield Racing Association hosts two NSHA steeplechases each year, spring and fall. The spring race is a near sell-out, with large contingents from northern Virginia, the Lynchburg-Roanoke area, and Virginia Beach joining locals and hordes of UVA students.

Students muster in the Orange section of the infield. "They like to be together and we like them to be together," says Foxfield executive secretary Bobbi Wells. The event became a must-do for UVA students, Wells figures, because police and university officials were closing down the rollicking Easter weekend blowouts at the same time Foxfield was cranking up. The student body just moved their out-of-doors blast from one venue to another, joined by like-minded students from other area colleges. Those from James Madison University and Washington and Lee set up their own sections in the infield. Students in graduate and the professional schools at UVA huddle in the Green area in the infield. Wells said patrons in this section are expected to "act more grown up." It is in this section that newcomers to the race are most likely to get railside parking spaces.

The backside of the course drops behind a hill encouraging speed on the part of the horses and resulting in daunting jump placement on the descending ground. The final turn, on rising ground, sorts out those lacking in fitness, and the long straight over good turf assures exciting run-ins to the finish line.

Admission: Parking along the finishing straight is $200, which includes four tickets and four lunches. Racing members also have on-the-rail parking. Admission for four and parking on the second tier of the finishing straight is $95 per car. Railside parking in the student area in the infield, is $80, with off-rail parking

74

$65. Reserved parking on the hillside by the first turn, which affords excellent viewing but is a distance from the finish and the paddock, costs $85. General admission is $12 per person in advance, $15 at the gate, with an additional $5 charged per car. General admission parking is a pretty good hike, but those with friends who have sprung for a railside can probably muster the strength to walk over to join them.

VIRGINIA GOLD CUP RACES
Great Meadow
The Plains, VA

When: First Saturday in May

Time: First race 1:30 P.M.

Contact: Virginia Gold Cup Association
P.O. Box 840
Warrenton, VA 22186

Phone: 703-347-2612

Directions: From Washington, travel west on I-66. Exit at The Plains, Route 245 south, for north parking area. Exit at Marshall, Route 17 south, for south parking. Course is several miles south of I-66. Just follow the traffic.

If you want to be where "everyone" will be on the first Saturday in May, you must attend the Virginia Gold Cup. You can expect to see a handful of cabinet members, a gaggle of ambassadors, a near quorum of senators and congresspersons, a flight of generals, a flotilla of admirals, along with recognizable celebrities of every sort—all in sun glasses. Wheelers, dealers, and lobbyists will be jockeying for position among the latter, as well as the large contingent of powerful business types. The farther you get away from the prestigious Member's Hill, the more you see attractive members of the under forty crowd. Jostling all around and professing to dislike the intensity of the large crowds are the cool horse people who, in truth, would not miss the event for anything because the Virginia Gold Cup is one of the major races on the circuit.

Jack Kent Cooke gives pointers to Loki van Roijen (left), Marlene, (his wife at the time) and Molly Paget. The Cookes' marriage ceremony took place on the morning of the 1990 Gold Cup.
Credit: Scott Ferrell

Winning the Virginia Gold Cup is the Virginia equivalent of winning the Maryland Hunt Cup in Maryland. The two races, along with the Breeder's Cup Steeplechase and a handful of $100,000 hurdle races, are the best America has to offer.

The Gold Cup has existed since 1925, and has been run in a number of venues, settling at Great Meadow in 1984. Great Meadow replaced the popular Broadview course, which fell to developers. Newspaper magnate Arthur W. Arundel formed the Meadow Outdoors Foundation, dedicated to holding open spaces for field sports. The race course is fairly flat and features very good turf, carefully nurtured by Great Meadow's ground keepers and watered when necessary by an extensive underground watering system. The turns are fair, the fences stout but not excessively high. The distance of the race is four miles, a long way by American standards, but is kept interesting by the fact that the horses never jump any of the 22 fences twice.

Like great races, the Gold Cup has produced some unforgettable performances. Race announcer Will O'Keefe, who calls races at every point-to-point and steeplechase in Virginia, and some in Maryland, has been to more races than most, and he counts Von Csadek's Gold Cup wins as the most thrilling he has witnessed. Ridden by young Patrick Worrall, then only 17, Von Csadek first laid down a stunning 100-length victory in 1988. Von Csadek came back in 1990 to smash 1989 winner and national champion Call Louis. That year the more seasoned Worrall, by then a senior in high school, rated the big brown gelding right behind Call Louis, ridden by Jack Fisher. Every time Fisher glanced over his shoulder, he saw the flaring nostrils of Von Csadek and must have felt the hot breath on his sleeve. When Worrall finally gave the go-ahead, Von Csadek switched into overdrive, blowing past Call Louis with such force it must have taken some skill for Fisher to stay aboard. The tables turned in 1992, when Von Csadek, after finally winning the Maryland Hunt Cup and a favorite to win a third Gold Cup, which would make him the first horse to win both races in the same year since 1926, shied at a falling horse and lost his rider. That year Fisher, aboard Push and Pull, won the Gold Cup with no horse near but the riderless Von Csadek.

If you plan to attend the Gold Cup by all means make reservations early, say February, and plan to arrive early on race day. Gates open at 10:00 A.M. and entertainment commences shortly thereafter. It's a pity so many miss the pre-race demonstrations. They are very good, including such acts as a drill ridden by the mounted U.S. Park Patrol and trained sheep dogs herding live sheep.

Admission: Reserved parking spaces, which include admission for four plus four tickets to Member's Hill, start at $150 and range to $530 for party spaces, which are triple-size rail spaces generally claimed by organizations and businesses for party tents. The Gold Cup sells many more tickets than any other area race, and its prices aren't out of line, but premium spaces are hard to come by. For instance, the Broadview Boxes, the best seats in the house, cost $450 but are not available. One goes up

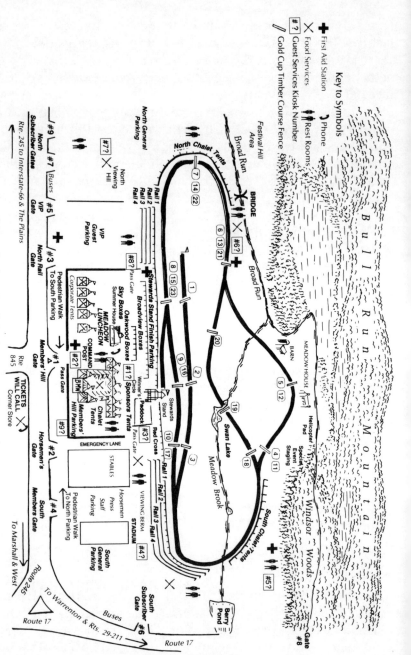

Virginia Gold Cup at Great Meadow

Key to Symbols

✚ First Aid Station
✗ Food Services
🕭 Phone
🛉 Rest Rooms
🍴 Guest Services Kiosk Number
#?
Gold Cup Timber Course Fence

Bull Run Mountain

Windsor – Woods

for sale every few years, but the waiting list is long and carries over from year to year. Only one or two of the next-best Steward's Stand boxes ($400) become available each year, and these spaces are given to newcomers who submit their checks first as soon as spaces go on sale. Other reserved spaces are assigned to newcomers in the same manner, with more spaces becoming available as the distance from Member's Hill and from the rail lengthens. Be advised, no tickets are sold race day. Even general admission tickets are sold only in advance. The general admission parking is a long walk from the course, and to have convenient access to the paddock one must pay $30 a head for Member's Hill badges (these may be purchased the day of the race at $40). Unless you have been invited to one of the many private parties or you have a friend with a reserved space, by all means send your money early to get a reserved space. The rail spaces on the north are slightly closer to D.C. because of the access routes, and they are on the final turn. On the other hand, they are extra crowded. The south rail is handier to the paddock area. From time to time the race sells a special area, usually a distance from Member's Hill, for a cost of more than general admission and less than reserved parking. Though away from the hubbub, these areas tend to be a good buy for those who want to enjoy a less hectic afternoon with friends and family. Parking prices for all these options tend to rise annually, so best check with the number listed above.

THE RACES AT MARENGO
Marengo Plantation
New Kent County, VA

When: Third Saturday in May

Time: First race 1:00 P.M.

Contact: Historic Richmond Foundation
2407 East Grace Street
Richmond, VA 23223

Phone: 804-643-7407

Directions: Marengo is located 30 minutes east of Richmond and 30 minutes west of Williamsburg. From Richmond, travel east on I-64 to the Talleysville exit. Turn left onto Route 106 to Talleysville. Cross Route 249 and continue on 106 to Route 609. Bear left. Cross the railroad tracks. The gate to Marengo is one mile past Routes 619 and 608, which intersect with Route 609.

An interest in racing in New Kent County came about when a proposal was submitted to build a parimutuel track there. The Historic Richmond Foundation, which had been associated with the Strawberry Hill Races for ten years, came aboard as the sponsoring charity. A large crowd, no doubt drawn by the high powered HRF (and a deep appreciation of a good party) came in 1993, the inaugural year.

The setting is beautiful, but course visibility is very low. The terrain is flat, and the course goes around the outside of Marengo Plantation and its admirable, large old trees. Only three jumps at most can be seen from any one spot. The spectators who filled the corporate tents and special parties barely seemed to care. They leaned out to cheer as the horses galloped by, then went back to the party.

Admission: General admission tickets may be purchased for $13 in advance, $20 at the gate, children 7–12 $5, under 7, free. General admission parking is $5 per car. Tailgate parking ranges from $100 to $350, depending on location. Box seating for six costs $300 (box lunches included). Table options include umbrella seating at $20 per person, up to pavilion tent seating at $150 per person (includes lunch and beverages).

GEORGETOWN RACES
Morven Park
Leesburg, VA

When: Third Sunday in May

Time: First race 1:30 P.M.

Contact: Georgetown University Medical Center
4000 Reservoir Road, NW
Washington, D.C. 20007

Phone: 202-687-3866

Directions: From D.C., travel to Leesburg on Route 7, turning north on the Route 15 by-pass. Where Route 15 narrows, turn left into the course. From the north, the course will be on your right before entering Leesburg. From the south, take the Route 15/7 by-pass around Leesburg, continuing on Route 15 after the two split. The course will be on your left where Route 15 narrows.

Fall steeplechases have been held at Morven Park since 1979. The idea to hold a spring race there came not from race management but from fund-raisers at Georgetown Hospital. Morven Park's Ed Maurer said he and race chairman Joe Rogers had long had a spring race in mind, but the Georgetown Race was the brain-child of Georgetown Hospital's Jennifer Goins. Maurer and Rogers, who were appointed the event's directors of racing, have just sat back (well, not really) and marveled at the job Georgetown volunteers and staff have done. The reserved spaces were sold out the inaugural year. Those who attend the well-managed races take comfort in knowing that ticket dollars go to the hospital. Donations are specifically ear-marked for Georgetown's perinatal unit.

The course at Morven Park is relatively flat, lush thanks to good turf management and irrigation, and features reasonable turns and a long run-in to the finish, which is straight and wide. So that spectators would be able to see, tons and tons of dirt were hauled in to make a hill. The race has not existed long enough to gauge what sort of horses run there, and why. Winners to date seemed to be horses that had raced in the spring, some a lot, some lightly. The trend for close finishes seen at Morven Park, its sister race in the fall, seems to be holding for Georgetown. Horses round the graceful sweep towards home, jump another hurdle right in front of the crowd for good measure, then flatten out for some inspiring runs to the wire, with only whiskers and ears often separating the winner from the runner up.

V

RACING OVER JUMPS IN MARYLAND

Land of the Tall Timbers

Maryland's steeplechase season is restricted to spring, with a few exceptions, and timber racing is featured. Though some meets are recognized by the National Steeplechase and Hunt, most of them retain the feeling of old-time point-to-points.

The centerpiece of the season, the Maryland Hunt Cup, consists of one race over huge jumps on a course that cannot be seen in its entirety from any one spot. Generations of Maryland horsemen have dreamt of winning the Hunt Cup, and steeplechase trainers always have that goal in mind. The winner of the race automatically qualifies for the English Grand National. The Maryland Hunt Cup and English Grand National are universally acknowledged as the toughest jump races in the world.

Spectators at the timber classics in Maryland resemble the point-to-point crowds in Virginia, in terms of dress and informal air. A few of the men wear neckties and jackets, and some of the women, tailored tweed suits; almost all wear sensible footwear. In general, slacks and wool trousers predominate. Timber fans tend to be knowledgeable, and also hardy enough to sprint from one vantage point to the next to follow the progress of the race. Warmer weather that comes with its later date brings forth tasteful spring outfits at the Maryland Hunt Cup, but not the high heels and big hats seen at Virginia's biggest steeplechase, the Gold Cup. Marlborough and Potomac, which are very like

The Maryland Hunt Cup is one of the most difficult jump races in the world. Many of the jumps top five feet in height.
Credit: Douglas Lees

Virginia steeplechases in course configuration, race card and crowd size, draw a dressier group of fans from the suburbs.

Parimutuel steeplechasing, both at the Maryland tracks and at Fair Hill, round out the season. The Maryland tracks offer a few steeplechases as special features, and Fair Hill presents a full card of parimutuel steeplechases twice a year.

HOWARD COUNTY-IRON BRIDGE RACE MEET
Meriwether Farm
Glenelg, MD

When: Generally the third Saturday in March

Time: First race at 1:00 P.M.

Contact: Harvey Goolsby
The Greyhouse
Glenwood, MD 21738

Phone: 410-442-1813

Directions: From D.C., take Georgia Avenue from town. Georgia Avenue becomes Route 97. The course is approximately 35 minutes beyond the Beltway. From Route 97, turn right on Roxebury Road. The race course will be on the right.

Howard County is the first Maryland jump race of the season. Racing secretary Harvey Goolsby describes it is "a low key affair featuring high class entries." Most Maryland Hunt Cup winners, he adds, have their first start over timber at Howard County. That is because the course resembles, on a smaller scale, the vertical and "airy" fences of the Maryland Hunt Cup. Most timber courses have slope to the fence. In considering the arc a horse makes when it jumps, this slope gives the animal some margin of error, be it ever so small; the horse that misses his ideal take off spot gets an opportunity to curl up his knees on his way up over the fence. "Airy" fences, such as those at the Maryland Hunt Cup, are made of rails that permit the horses to see the ground beyond; they are more difficult to judge than solid ones. The fences at Howard County are lower than the normal, only 2 feet 9 inches to 3½ feet and have top rails that will break if struck with force.

The race card at Howard County includes timber races and a flat race, sponsored by the Amateur Riders Club of America. Other races listed are for ponies and for foxhunters.

Admission: Front row parking for patrons costs $100, $50 on the second row. General admission is $15. While the number of horses entered in the race is growing, crowds are small compared to Virginia point-to-points and later races in Maryland.

 ## ELKRIDGE-HARFORD HUNT POINT-TO-POINT RACES
Atlanta Hall Farm
Monkton, MD

When: Generally the first Saturday in April

Time: First race at 1:30 P.M.

Contact: Kate Bell
16460 Marco Road
Monkton, MD 21111

Phone: 410-472-9279

Directions: From I-495, north on I-95 to I-695 west toward Towson, MD. Exit 27B on Route 146. Travel north 13 miles to Pocock Road, turn left. Course is one mile on left. Driving time from the Washington Beltway is about one hour and 15 minutes.

Elkridge-Harford is a good example of an old-style, informal point-to-point, according to Joe Gillet, its chairman. The crowds do not equal those at the Virginia point-to-points, though the atmosphere of the race does approximate that of the Piedmont Point-to-Point in Upperville. Contestants at both go out into the countryside and run around a bit, instead of traveling the oval courses, like formal steeplechases, that many point-to-points feature. Crowds can be good if the weather is balmy, but the decision to go or not to go can generally be made the day of the meet without fear of being shut out at the gate by a sell-out.

If spectators aren't elbow to elbow, the bounty of horses is large. As many as 100 horses have been entered, resulting in up to 10 races. The race program features timber races and flat races, along with races for junior riders and foxhunters. The jumps are straight up and down post and rails and plank fences, and the course tracks through rolling countryside. Gillet, who has had success as a trainer and rider in the Maryland timber classics, says that timber horses ran every weekend in April in the old days. Now, most trainers pick two or three out of four in quest of the Maryland Hunt Cup. Elkridge-Harford is a good starting point for a first year horse aimed at the Hunt Cup, according to Gillet. That is because the jumps are smaller than those found at later Maryland races, and also because horses get a week off before facing the Grand National. Because its jumps are sequentially higher, yet not on par with the Maryland Hunt Cup, the Grand National cannot be missed. A horse with seasoning, however, might possibly go straight to the Grand National by way of My Lady's Manor, the week after Elkridge-Harford. My Lady's Manor, also in the Elkridge-Harford hunt country, offers significant money prizes. Elkridge-Harford, in point-to-point tradition, does not.

Admission: General admission is $15, with top of the line parking going for $100. The $100 ticket includes reserved spaces within view of the finish line, four passes to the races and admission to the party at the hunt club afterwards. The party includes live music, tapes of the races, open bar and food.

 MARLBOROUGH HUNT RACES
Roedown Farm
Davidsonville, MD

When: Generally first Sunday in April

Time: First race 12:30 P.M.

Contact: Edward L. Coffren
P.O. Box 277
Upper Marlboro, MD 20773

Phone: 301-627-3614

Directions: From I-495, exit 50 east to Route 424, Davidsonville Road. Turn right at second traffic light onto Route 214, Central Avenue. Travel one mile, turn left at the fork onto Queen Ann Bridge Road. Travel 1½ miles to Roedown Farm, on right side of road. Drive time from D.C. is about 20 minutes. Those coming from Virginia can exit from the Beltway onto Route 214.

In crowd size, quality of the entries and general set-up, Marlborough closely resembles a sanctioned steeplechase. The race committee has considered the idea of asking for NSHA approval, and may some day make the move. On the other hand, the all-volunteer crew, led by Marlborough Master of Foxhounds Ed Coffren, pretty much feels it has its hands full with the point-to-point. Prime parking spaces sell out, and general admission parking overflows to lots pressed into service across the road. The course is entirely visible from the hillside viewing area. Backdrop for the course is Roedown, a Georgian brick house built before 1750. The house draws its name from a 2,000-acre colonial grant made in 1668 to George Yates by Lord Baltimore.

Patrons of the race come from Baltimore, Annapolis and Virginia, as well as Washington. The success of the race has drawn in corporate sponsors who put up significant purses, a perk for horsemen usually not offered at point-to-points. Through the years the race has attracted jumping horses of the highest ilk, including NSHA champions Von Csadek and Joe's O.K. The nation's best trainers are always represented, drawn down from Pennsylvania and Virginia and Maryland itself. One hundred twenty six horses were entered at Marlborough in a recent year. Not every horse started, but a lot of horses race there each year.

The course covers flat pasture land with one significant slope, and is basically oval shaped with a long straight both on the backside and down to the finish line. Timber jumps are medium size and feature a slight pitch and ground lines. Both these features make the jumps easier for the horses to gauge. They encourage both veterans on their first outing of the season as well as newcomers that have had few starts over timber. The Camden-style brush jump is used for hurdle races. These were developed in, where else? Camden, SC. They are perhaps a little less challenging than the standard National fences, and certainly less daunting to construct. They vary from the National fences in that broom straw is used to add the element of brush instead of simulated birch. The birch used in the National fences is both hard to manufacture and hard to find.

Admission: General admission is $5 per person, with subscriber parking starting at $30 and ranging to $150. The top dollar ticket includes reserved front row parking, four race passes and invitations to the party afterwards, which goes on and on and features live music, according to those who know, or should we say, go.

MY LADY'S MANOR RACE MEET
Elkridge-Harford Hunt Club
Monkton, MD

When: Two Saturdays before the Maryland Hunt Cup, which is the last Saturday in April

Time: First race at 3:30 P.M.

Contact: Ladew Topiary Gardens
3535 Jarrettsville Pike
Monkton, MD 21111

Phone: 410-752-8727

Directions: Take I-695 around Baltimore in the direction of Towson. Exit 27B, travel 13.8 miles north on MD Route 146. The course is located at the corner of Route 146 and Pocock Road.

My Lady's Manor began, as did many of the oldest jump races, among foxhunters. Tradition has it that five friends first put their favorite hunters to the test to prove which ran fastest and was also the best jumper. The race took its name from the site of the original course, which was located right in the center of My Lady's Manor, the colonial tract deeded to the Carroll family. In 1909, My Lady's Manor became the junior member of Maryland's triple crown of jump races, which includes the Grand National, founded in 1902, and the Maryland Hunt Cup, which dates from 1896. In the '30s and '40s, My Lady's Manor included hurdles races and was more like standard steeplechase meets. When development began encroaching on the race course, current race chairman Turney McKnight led a drive to move it away. In 1978, it was moved three miles to its current location on the grounds of the Elkridge-Harford Hunt Club. Like the other Maryland meets, the new course does not cross the same jump more than once. It courses up hill and down dale in a contest reminiscent of the very earliest steeplechase races across the English and Irish countrysides.

It must be noted that this unique element of the race demands fitness and fast-footedness on the part of the spectator. Anyone intent on seeing as many as possible of the 16 unique and attractive jumps should start downhill towards fence No. 7, then move on to jump No. 10 in time to see the field go by there, and finally hightail it across the course to the top of the hill to view the horses making a figure eight over the final seven jumps. First-timers intent on seeing as much as possible might do as the tweedy set does and wear "trainers" (English slang for Reeboks and other brands of running shoes). The less hardy may opt for standing on the hay wagons on top of the hill. Those in the catbird seat are corporate guests at parties in tents on top of the hill; here the race can be followed on telecasts from cameras set up on the course.

The corporate sponsors are attracted by the race's association with Ladew Topiary Gardens, located just down the road. Ladew is the site of the post-race party for top dollar subscribers and race sponsors. Until Ladew Topiary Gardens became the beneficiary of the race, modest purses were drawn from the pockets of the race chairmen. Now the two races feature $15,000 purses, putting My Lady's Manor in the upper echelon of timber races.

Current race chairman Turney McKnight notes with pride the strong correlation between winners of the Maryland Hunt Cup and My Lady's Manor, and also the high calibre of horse that has participated through the years such as Jay Trump, Jacko and Von Csadek. Jay Trump was the first American bred, trained and ridden horse to win the English Grand National. Most Hunt Cup horses have already had one run over the big course before entering My Lady's Manor. McKnight, who has won the Hunt Cup, as has his wife Elizabeth, says that first-time starters cannot afford to miss the Grand National Point-to-Point, because the fences there are bigger. Once having proved the point, the trainer may elect to run seasoned charges thereafter at My Lady's Manor, followed by a week off before the Hunt Cup. This is the route chosen by the handlers of the great Von Csadek, winner of the Hunt Cup in 1992. Von Csadek demolished the field at the Hunt Cup, though he had settled for third at the Manor in a year that saw records fall in both of the day's races.

McKnight, who has won the feature race four times, believes that those riding the hilly course for the first time make the mistake of holding their horses back in the early stages. Actually, the course, a short three miles, rides fast. Climbs on the course are short and sharp, and horses seem to handle them well. Crowds at the Manor appear horsey and knowledgeable. Comments around the paddock indicate that they know the difference between a forelock and fetlock. McKnight describes them as dedicated. They have to be dedicated to tolerate some of the mid-April weather. Though well attended, the races do not attract the mobs often seen at area races.

Admission: General admission is $25 a car, with the upper end ticket being the subscriber's packages for $150.

GRAND NATIONAL STEEPLECHASE
Butler, MD

When: The next to last Saturday in April

Time: First race 3:15 P.M.

Contact: Charles Fenwick, Jr.
P.O. Box 1
Butler, MD 21023

Phone: 410-666-7777

Directions: Take I-695 toward Towson to MD Route 25 north to Butler. Turn left (west) on MD Route 128 one mile to the course which is on both sides of the road.

The Grand National Steeplechase, founded in 1902, is the youngest of a triumvirate of jump races sharing the same name. The most famous of these—in fact, the most famous steeplechase in the world—was founded in 1840 and is run in Aintree, England. The third similarly named race, begun in 1899, is run in Far Hills, NJ.

The Maryland Grand National, which, with My Lady's Manor and the Maryland Hunt Cup, is the third of the trio of elite Maryland timber races, is like an old style point-to-point. Riders dash out into the countryside, around surrounding barns and outbuildings, then back into view for the finish. About two-thirds of the course is visible from either of two points, and since there are two races, it's fun to watch a different one from each vantage point. Spot #1 is on the driveway between fences three and four. From there, the start of the race can be viewed, along with most of the jumps; but it lacks a view of the opposite corner of the course and the finish line. From Spot #2 on top of the hill above the finish, one can see neither corner of the course, but can get a good shot at the finish. The competitors are in view long enough so that one can gauge the progress and strategy of the race. Spectators generally picnic at their cars, or perhaps on blankets on the hillside, and move to one of the two points described to watch the race.

Horsemen intent on winning the Maryland Hunt Cup, this country's most daunting steeplechase race, consider the Grand National a must do. This is because the jumps are substantial— up to 4'4" in height, and straight up and down without ground lines, a la the Maryland Hunt Cup. Charles Fenwick, Jr., who has more wins in the Grand National than any other rider and also serves as the race's chairman, describes the course as demanding. Its distance of three miles suggests that speed would be a major requirement, but the height and difficulty of the fences keeps the horses rocked back on their hocks and jumping up. The jumps are even higher at the Hunt Cup.

It's interesting to note that the winner of the Grand National does not necessarily win at the Hunt Cup, perhaps owing to the difference in distances. The Hunt Cup winner, though, is pretty surely going to have started here at Butler, and will possibly even place before facing the ultimate test the following week. In the early years of the race, when horses started week after week in the Maryland series, nearly 30 accounted for double wins. Freeman's Hill, winner at the Grand National in 1984, was the most recent. His victory at the Hunt Cup didn't come until 1988.

As the jumps become more difficult over the weeks, the crowds build. Five to ten thousand turn out for the Grand National, partly attracted by the first-rate parking and ticket availability. (At the Hunt Cup a week later the best spaces have been reserved for years, passed down from generation to generation.)

Admission: General admission parking at the Grand National, which may be purchased the day of the race, costs $30 per car. Paddock parking, which must be purchased in advance, costs upward of $100.

MARYLAND HUNT CUP
Worthington Farm
Glyndon, MD

When: The last Saturday in April

Time: Post time 4:00 P.M.

Contact: Maryland Hunt Cup Association
Glyndon, MD 21071

Phone: 410-666-7777

Directions: From I-695, travel north on I-83. Exit west on Shawan Road four miles to the course, which is on both sides of the road.

The Maryland Hunt Cup represents the ultimate in tradition for the Maryland horseman. Racing secretary Charles Fenwick, Sr. has lived his whole life in view of the course, which was moved to its present location by his father in 1915. From its founding in 1896 until 1915, the race was run at first from one spot, then another. The jumps were line fences that kept in cattle and farm horses. The race was initially held closer to Baltimore, but was moved when development encroached.

For Charles Fenwick, Jr., son of the current secretary, what makes Maryland Hunt Cup the one to win is this long heritage of staying in one spot, unchanged. Also, the course is as long as, and has fences higher than, any other race in America.

"There is no other race comes close," Fenwick, Jr. says flatly. He has won the Hunt Cup five times. He has won every other timber race in Maryland many times, most of the timber races in Virginia, and is one of only three American riders to win the English Grand National. The fact that the first three finishers in the Hunt Cup automatically qualify for the Grand National in England reveals something of the prestige of the race around the world. (Horses racing in England must have won a

93

certain number of races and a certain amount of money before they are permitted to start in the Grand National).

Fenwick, Sr. admits that seeing his sons, Charles, Jr. and Bruce, ride in the race gives him undeniable pleasure. But he magnanimously chooses as the most memorable race of all the races one in which neither of his sons rode. That was the race in 1966 when Mountain Dew and Jay Trump squared off. Both had two previous wins in the race, and Jay Trump had won the English Grand National in the meantime. Because of their stature and the difficulty of the course, only one other opponent took on the two titans. Jay Trump won, and Mountain Dew got his third victory the following year. If this was the best of times, it was also the worst of times for the race committee.

Only three starters such as there were in the 1966 race, made too slim an entry. After much soul searching and many suggestions that included making the course easier or opening the all-amateur event to professional riders, the committee finally agreed to put up a money purse. It now totals $25,000. The other elements, including the amateur restriction and high rails, were left in place and remain as they were in 1896 when hot blood chased around to prove whose hunter was most worthy.

Another big decision faced by the same committee after 1966 was whether to permit women to ride. The gender gap was breached by Kathy Kusner, who had made her mark in the world of hunters, show jumpers and race horses, and was eminently qualified. Still, this was a time when women were thought to be too frail for that sort of challenge and the committee was concerned over crowd reaction if Kusner fell. Kusner did finish but did not win. Since that time in the mid-60s three women have won, two twice: Joy Slater and Sanna Neilson (Sanna's father Paddy has won three times); and Elizabeth McKnight (her husband Turney has also won).

The Maryland Hunt Cup is unique in almost every way, including the fact it is the only race run on its course that day. At the English Grand National and at the Kentucky Derby the big race is only part of a full card of races. To fully enjoy the event, and to avoid traffic that snarls on the narrow road accessing the course, Fenwick, Sr. suggests arriving no later than 3:00 P.M., an hour ahead of time. Most Baltimoreans who make the race a family tradition come early in the afternoon, and have a picnic and enjoy the setting in the Green Spring Valley.

Admission: All parking must be purchased in advance, and the best spots in the paddock area just don't come up for sale, as noted. General admission parking is available for $30 and is a good half mile from the hillside from which most spectators view the course. A call several months in advance can assure you of very good parking in the field adjoining the course for $60. The field is a short walk from the paddock and the hillside, from which almost all the course can be viewed. Any true aficionado will want to attend the race more than once because, to be appreciated, it must be viewed from the hillside once to get the big picture of the horses moving across the course and a second time from the famous and aptly numbered 13th fence, the first of five rigorous fences to top five feet. From the 13th fence, on the far side of the course, one can also view the challenging 16th, which is at the three-mile point, and the 19th. Having gone twice, a spectator may realize what attracts thousands of devoted fans year after year. Like the Olympics, the course produces heroic performances that can be remembered when a point of inspiration is needed, especially in today's world.

POTOMAC HUNT RACES
Bittersweet Field
Seneca, MD

When: Generally second Sunday in May

Time: First race 12:30 P.M.

Contact: Potomac Hunt
21315 Peachtree Road
Dickerson, MD 20842

Phone: 301-972-7621

Directions: From I-495, exit River Road. Proceed west 12 miles to the course, located on the corner of River Road and Partnership Road.

Potomac is a short drive from D.C., and another of those mega point-to-points that is big and slick enough to be an NSHA sanctioned meet. Large crowds in attendance are drawn from northwest Washington, suburban Maryland and northern Virginia, just a short drive away via the picturesque White's Ferry. The meet offers well-filled, professionally-run races, plus generous purses, thanks to sponsorships from friends of the races and companies wanting to be associated with a good thing.

The course is gently rolling with a long straight. This brings decisive action in close for the spectators. The flat and brush courses are entirely visible to spectators, and the timber course is too, except for one dip behind a hill. After the seemingly endless number of spring point-to-points and steeplechases, Potomac somehow manages to draw a large number of entries—119 in a recent year, with so many in the open timber race that two divisions were run. The favorite does not always win, but good quality horses are always there trying. Potomac Master of Foxhounds, Irvin Crawford, figures competitors like the course and the purses. Immediately following the races, prizes for the Maryland Governor's Cup series, based on the most points won in Maryland jump races, are awarded. (See Chapter II for more detail.)

Admission: General admission parking costs $20 per car, and reserved railside spaces go for $150, which includes admission for four. Front row railside in the vicinity of the finish line sells out in fairly short order. To accommodate ever-increasing crowds, infield parking has been added.

LAUREL, PIMLICO AND FAIR HILL

Please see Chapter VI for details on steeplechases at these tracks. Laurel and Pimlico, Maryland's biggest parimutuel tracks, have added a few steeplechases to spice up their race cards. Fair Hill, an all-steeplechase parimutuel course near Wilmington, DE, holds meets on Memorial Day and Labor Day.

VI

FLAT RACING AND PARIMUTUEL

How to Lose Money Legitimately

Jump racing abounds in the spring and fall, but fans in the D.C. area can catch a flat race at parimutuel tracks in Maryland and West Virginia almost any day of the year. Steeplechases and point-to-points are held in open fields, but parimutuel racing is almost always staged at large, modern facilities that include paved parking lots, multiple choices in seating and eating, and many betting stations in between.

Steeplechases and point-to-points are sponsored by hunts or non-profit organizations, with profits going back to the community in one way or the other. Major tracks, on the other hand, are big, for-profit businesses. Money does actually flow into the community from these in the form of taxes, and more importantly through the state's take of parimutuel handles, as the betting pool is called. When racing was the only form of legalized gambling in town, tracks earned hefty revenues and chalked up large handles. The worm has now turned, and the gambling dollars siphoned off by lotteries, bingo and other forms of legalized betting have hurt race tracks.

Maryland (where horses race at Pimlico, Laurel, Timonium, Fair Hill and Marlborough), feels the pinch but has perhaps done better than many other states (where tracks have closed). With its long tradition of racing—dating back to 1743—and well-structured system of breeder's incentives for horsemen, Maryland

They're off and running at Pimlico, home of the Preakness, the second leg of racing's Triple Crown.
Credit: © The Washington Post. *Reprinted by permission of the D.C. Public Library.*

still enjoys a very high level of competition. Horses, racing, and related business activities comprise the state's third largest industry, after agriculture and the Port of Baltimore.

Recent hard times temporarily reduced the number of live performances at Pimlico and Laurel from 10 races to nine, but that has since come back to ten. The number of horses racing is down, too, as the economic crunch is felt by horse owners as well as the rest of the population. Charles Town in West Virginia shows the pinch by having reduced racing to four days a week.

Still, the Maryland Jockey Club, which owns and manages Laurel and Pimlico, offered 258 days of racing in recent years. Attendance per day averaged 10,470, a 4½ percent decrease from previous years. While the two tracks remain healthy in today's climate of declining attendance at horse tracks, it must be noted that they are the last of their breed in Maryland. Bowie, once on a par with Laurel and Pimlico, was absorbed by the other two. No longer used for live racing, Bowie now serves as a year-round training facility. Havre de Grace, once considered a major track, closed back in 1950. Havre de Grace is still remembered by old-timers as the track where 1948 Triple Crown winner Citation made his debut and the great Man O'War raced. Timonium, held in conjunction with the Maryland State Fair, is the last of what was once a vital circuit of five half-mile tracks in the state.

It would be a great loss to thoroughbred racing as well as to the region should the remaining tracks not continue to flourish. Horse-related industry employs 20,000 in the state of Maryland, and the high quality racing and large purses offered by the Maryland Jockey Club assure that breeders, owners and trainers in the state will have the financial justification to continue in the business. State rolls list 4,000 racehorse trainers and owners. Maryland thoroughbreds number 28,000, compared with 32,000 in the most famous racing state of all, Kentucky. The Maryland Department of Economic Development estimates that racing amounts to a three billion dollar industry. The modern racing plants represent huge capital investments and have been consistently modernized and upgraded since they were built. Finally, the state has a long history and tradition of flat racing.

By 1743, racing became formalized with the founding of the Maryland Jockey Club in Annapolis. The Jockey Club offered the Annapolis Subscription Plate, the second oldest known racing trophy in America, on May 4, 1743. (The Annapolis Plate is now on display at the Baltimore Museum of Art.) Meetings during a portion of the next decade were a bit irregular due to the pressing business of the French and Indian War, but Maryland Jockey Club racing was still going strong and almost 20 years old when General George Washington attended races sponsored by the club in 1762. The general returned as a frequent visitor until the racing schedule, by then well established, was disrupted by the Revolutionary War.

As Baltimore grew, it usurped the track from Annapolis. The Maryland Jockey Club's new charter, which resides in the Library of Congress, was issued in 1830, and President Andrew Jackson, himself an avid racehorse owner and breeder in Tennessee, became a member of the club in 1831.

Pimlico, which held its first race meet in 1870, is the second oldest race track still in operation. The track and stands at Timonium were opened in 1879, but races have been held on the same site since 1820. The Preakness Stakes, held at Pimlico, is the second leg of racing's Triple Crown, and also the second oldest in the series. Founded in 1873, the Preakness pre-dates its famous cohort the Kentucky Derby by two years, but is six years younger than the Belmont Stakes.

The Preakness represents Maryland's biggest day of racing. Other special days on the racing calendar include Laurel's Washington D.C. International Mile, which in 1952 was the first race to pit top quality foreign competition against America's best. The Pimlico Special Handicap, like the Preakness and Washington International, carries a Grade I stakes rating, horse racing's highest designation. Other big days include the Maryland Million, begun in 1985, which is the highlight of Pimlico's fall racing schedule, and the Frank DeFrancis Memorial Dash, a top quality sprint. The Dash is named in honor of the late DeFrancis, who served as president of both Laurel and Pimlico. His son, Joseph A. DeFrancis, now occupies those positions.

These big racing days require advance planning on the part of spectators, as do weekends, to a lesser extent. Weekdays are easier for those who go to the track on the spur of the moment and want a trackside table in the dining room and good seating in the clubhouse. Any day of the week, no matter what the racing card, racing fans can certainly expect a pleasant day with plenty of opportunities to bet and to see fine horses run. Specifics will follow, but a couple of suggestions for those going to the flat track for the first time hold true at any venue. First, unless you are a woman who routinely wears high heels and plans never to venture far from the seat, wear comfortable flats or low heels. Considerable walking is involved in taking in all the sights and excitement at a race track.

Visiting the paddock is fun, seeing the horses up close and assessing their readiness for the race. At this critical time while they are being saddled, you'll also see jockeys and trainers conferring over strategies and owners trying to look nonchalant, as if their stomachs weren't already in knots. You should try watching at least one race standing right on the rail, especially one of the races that starts right by the stands. Before the start you can watch horses being loaded into the starting gate. Here's where you really feel the electricity crack through man and beast when the bell sounds, the gate flies open, the jockeys yell and the hooves pound.

The day's physical activities may include trips to the betting window, though betting is not an essential part of a visit to a flat track. One fact that anti-gamblers overlook about pari-mutuel racing is that racing provides a pleasant day's activity at a relatively small cost. One can enjoy seeing beautiful thoroughbreds up close in the paddock and on the track. Races can be watched from tables in the dining rooms, box seats, grandstand seats, benches in front of the clubhouse, or standing right at the rail, close enough to hear the powerful hooves drum by. Races can be seen on the numerous television monitors, and replays of the day's racing are shown over and over again on a bank of TV screens.

BETTING

Betting can add to the fervor with which you cheer on your favorite horse. Where to bet, for those who choose to, will be readily apparent. There are many betting windows at any track—a full 750 set up to handle the crowds at Preakness Day. Should one line look unusually short compared with its fellows, it might be wise to check to see if it is the line designated for bets of a $50 minimum. With this one exception, all other windows will accommodate the $2 bettor along with big spenders betting say, $6. Betting is definitely an important part of the racing structure, it provides purses for the horses, a portion for the track, the state and also the Breeder's Fund, while giving back 83% to those holding winning tickets.

To place a bet, walk up to a window and give the teller the amount of the bet, the number of the race, the number of the horse, and the type of bet. More than one horse can be bet in a race. Horses can be bet to win, to place (come in second), or to show (come in third). Horses can be played to finish in any combination of these two, or played across the board. Betting across the board means that ticket holders collect if the horse finishes first, second or third. Should a horse whose ticket you hold across the board win, money is picked up as if it finishes first, second and third. Should the horse come in third, then the across the board ticket pays bettors the third place payoff only. Tracks offer various exotic bets, too, as wagering on multiple races or combinations within races. Explanations of these options are listed in the program.

A few cardinal rules for bettors: never, but never walk away from a window without checking your ticket. Should it not be for the horse you wanted to bet, this is your only chance to change it. Never bet more than you can afford to lose, and remember, there's no such thing as a sure thing. Hold all tickets until the race is final. The track puts thousands back in its pocket each year in the form of "breakage" fees, the designation for unclaimed winning tickets. Remember that wagering closes before the horses enter the starting gate. Watching the horses come onto the track or the changing odds may help solidify your selections, but if you don't get to place the bet because you waited too long, it hardly matters.

The tote board in the infield and on the television monitors shows an ever-changing pattern of the betting on the upcoming race. Bettors themselves set the odds for the race and determine the amount paid back to those holding a winning ticket. A horse can be picked on its appearance in the paddock, its name, which may strike a special chord, or a particular affinity to the colors worn by its jockey. If one does wish to be a bit more scientific before making an actual wager, there is plenty of information to help pick a winner. *The Washington Post* carries lists of entries and racing charts from the previous day's races, plus good day-to-day news written by Vinnie Perrone, along with occasional commentary by the Post's own outstanding racing columnist, Andrew Beyer. The race program, inexpensive tips #sheets and the *Daily Racing Form* provide still more information.

Race programs at the Maryland tracks show the number of the horse, owner, trainer, rider, weight the horse must carry, color, sex, age and breeding of the horse, colors to be worn by the rider, monies won in the current year and previous year, number of times in the money (first, second or third), and probable starting odds. Further, the conditions of the race, amount of the purse, and distance for the race precedes the list of entries. The list of entries is followed by detailed information on recent races in which those horses have run. Picks are made by the track handicapper under the heading "program selections" and by the *Daily Racing Form,* along with comments on the probable favorites by the *Racing Form's* "Trackman".

Those who want a more complete scoop can buy a *Racing Form,* a worthwhile investment of $2.50. With it, one can while away hours at the luncheon table or on a sunny bench, handicapping the races. To the information found in the program, it adds the name of the breeder, state bred, name of the dam's sire (sort of like the horse's mother's maiden name), lifetime record of monies won per year, times to finish in the top three or "in the money", and times the horse has scored on the turf as well as on wet tracks. Recent records, sometime going back several years, are shown for each race the horse has started in, complete with date, track, track conditions, race conditions, fractions or times recorded at designated intervals, and the place in the field the horse had achieved at that point of the race. The winners of that race are listed, as well as a terse account of how the horse performed that day. From this information, each amateur handicapper can determine if his choice runs from behind, favors a particular track, distance, or track condition—muddy or firm, for example. Often horses in the same class of competition have tilted before that day, and the results listed in past performances will in some cases indicate how competitors have fared in previous tilts. Another lead to picking a winner that horse players look for is a horse being dropped in class—an also ran for $25,000 could be a winner in a $10,000 claimer—or the return of a horse after a long lay off. The question in the latter case is did the horse suffer an injury and will it run fresh and sharp its first time back. To save its readers the tedium of rifling through the records to collect these and other facts, the *Racing Form* now features a section headed "Top Contenders at a Glance." Under this heading, one finds horses singled out that have the fastest speed last race at the distance, that ran into trouble last time out, that are making their first start after a layoff of 30 or more days, that are dropping in class, that are moving up in class, that were beaten favorites in their last race, and that have proven off-track (muddy, sloppy) ability.

Pimlico and Laurel both offer bettor's seminars on Saturdays during the race season. These are free, held in the grandstand area, usually at 11:30 A.M. Speakers for these handicapping extravaganzas are leading trainers, riders and touts.

For the really serious bettors, Pimlico and Laurel have created Sports Palaces, located within their clubhouses. The Sports Palaces charge an additional admission fee and have a dress code barring short shorts, cut off levis, obscene slogans on T-shirts, etc. These take on a decided Las Vegas atmosphere, plush, glittery, and dark. One can view the races on big-screen color monitors while being served food and beverages in plush, lounge-style seats. Some seating offers a direct view of the track. Plentiful ticket windows are located in the Sports Palace confines. More important, here one can access by computer and VCR mind-boggling amounts of information.

On the computers, one can key up a complete record for a particular trainer, jockey, or horse on that track. Cost for use of the computers, indeed all such bells and whistles, are included in the price of admission to the Sports Palace ($5 weekdays, $7 weekends). The computers are simple enough for the novice to operate, and no doubt great repositories of knowledge for those more experienced in posing questions in computer language. What's more, actual films of a horse's previous races can be viewed on one of the Sports Palace's multiple VCRs.

Those who like to bet and don't care about going to the paddock or seeing the horses live can wager at Laurel when Pimilico is running, and visa versa. Further, the really big races of $100,000 plus that are being run in New York, California, Arlington and Kentucky are simulcast at the two Maryland locations so that local bettors can place some money on the big ones. Charles Town now carries daily simulcasts from Santa

Anita, and Gulfstream Park, along with simulcasts of the Kentucky Derby, Preakness, and Breeder's Cup.

TYPES OF RACING

The bulk of races at parimutuel tracks are held "on the dirt," the mix of sand and other substances each track's management feels produces a surface that is the most consistent, weather-resistant and kind to the horses. Like European and English courses and the cream of America's parimutuel tracks, Pimlico and Laurel also offer a full complement of turf races. Horses look beautiful racing on the turf. Many horsemen feel grass is easier on horses' legs and, as if to confirm, some horses have no stomach for the dirt, possibly in reaction to having clots of mud or stinging particles of sand being kicked into their faces. Charles Town, Timonium and Marlborough have only dirt tracks. Fair Hill, a steeplechase course, has only a grass track.

Facilities vary from modern heated and air-conditioned grandstands loaded with creature comforts at Laurel, Pimlico, and Charles Town, to a fairground grandstand at Timonium to open stands at Fair Hill, to temporary seating at Marlborough.

 PIMLICO RACE COURSE
Baltimore, MD

When: The last weekend in March through the first of July, and for a month starting the second week in September, every day except Mondays and Wednesdays

Time: First race 1:00 P.M.

Contact: Pimlico Race Course
Hayward and Winner Avenues
Baltimore, MD 21215

Phone: 410-542-9400 general information; 410-542-9127 for dining reservations

Directions: From D.C., take I-95 north to I-695, the Baltimore Beltway, in the direction of Towson. Take Exit 26, Liberty Road, right for four miles to Northern Parkway, then 2½ miles to Park Heights Avenue. Turn left on Hayward Avenue, ¼ mile to the track. Small, brown Pimlico signs dot the route to direct and reassure the traveler.

PREAKNESS

Every year millions see Pimlico on television the third Saturday in May when the nation's top three-year-olds compete in the second leg of the Triple Crown, the Preakness. In recent years, close to 90,000 have seen the race live.

In assessing the importance of the race, think of it this way: every Triple Crown winner has raced in and won the Preakness. More than a dozen Kentucky Derby winners have also triumphed in the Preakness, but failed in the Belmont. Slightly fewer have won both the Preakness and the Belmont, the shortest and longest of the series, but not the Derby. Triple Crown winners are immediately given their place in history. Among the best in this category according to Joe Kelly, racing journalist and racing official for more than 50 years, were Secretariat and Citation, neither of which was particularly tested at the Preakness. Both seemed to tower over their peers. The list of those falling short of this prize but who won the Preakness adds more names that live on in horse racing history, either by subsequent racing victories or success in the breeding shed. These include the most famous of all, Man O'War, and the most influential stallion of modern times, Northern Dancer. Northern Dancer, who chalked up a good racing record, fathered a high percentage of champion runners and a number of his sons are in turn siring champions. After his racing career, Northern Dancer, now deceased, was retired to stud at Windfields Farm in Maryland. Now here's a question: why didn't Big Red win the Triple Crown? Because he did not start in the Kentucky Derby.

The Preakness was named for Preakness, the horse that won Pimlico's first stakes in 1870. That first stakes, the Dinner Party, was the reason Pimlico was built. Maryland Governor Oden Bowie was at a dinner party at Saratoga when the idea of the new stakes was conceived. Bowie guaranteed to build a new track near Baltimore if the stakes would be awarded to Maryland. It was and he did. Its name was changed to the Dixie Stakes in 1872, and the race continues to this day as a turf race which, with brother races at Churchill Downs and Belmont, is part of a $1 million series.

But we digress. Preakness, the winner of that first stakes, was described by his admirers as tall and massive. By some, he was derided as a cart horse, because of his big, ungainly appearance. However, he followed up his victory in the Dinner Plate Stakes, as that first stake was named, with a distinguished racing career, concluding with a victory in the Brighton Stakes in England where he was retired to stud.

The Woodlawn Vase, given to the winner of the Preakness, is considered the most valuable trophy in racing. The sterling silver trophy was created by Tiffany in 1860 for the now defunct Woodlawn Racing Association in Louisville, KY. Capt. T.G. Moore, who won the trophy that year, preserved it during the Civil War by burying it with other family plate, lest it be discovered and melted down. After the war, it was passed from one track to the other until it was won by a member of the Maryland Jockey Club, who handed the prize over to the Club, which added it to the booty for the 1917 Preakness. The Vase is now kept in Maryland, and a replica is given each year to the owner of the winning horse.

Famous Preakness traditions include presenting a wreath of Black-eyed Susans to the winner, playing "My Maryland" during the parade to the post, and painting the colors of the winner on the weather vane over the grandstand's cupola immediately following the race. The Black-eyed Susans are painted; they are actually yellow daisies in disguise, because Maryland's state flower does not bloom until fall.

Advanced planning is required for getting tables or seats for the Preakness. Tickets for the Preakness go on sale at Thanksgiving and plans are best made before Christmas. Those who are on Pimlico's mailing list are sent information. Otherwise, one can call 410-837-3030 for details. As the big race approaches, the city of Baltimore begins a build up featuring everything from a balloon race to a parade. Check out details in Chapter XII.

PIMLICO SPECIAL HANDICAP

The Preakness, on the third Saturday in May, unquestionably brings the best three-year-olds in the nation to Pimlico. The Pimlico Special brings the best older horses there the second Saturday in May, kicking off a week of hoopla and especially good racing leading up to the big day. The Pimlico Special, like the Preakness, is designated a Grade I Stakes. First held in 1937, it lapsed from 1958 until 1988, but when it came back, it came back with vengeance. Not only does it carry a hefty purse, $600,000 in 1990 compared with $445,900 to the winner of the Preakness that same year, but it has also produced some interesting re-matches of previous Preakness winners. The race is open to horses four years and up carrying handicap weights (weights assigned by the racing secretary to hypothetically bring horses of varying ability over the finish at the same time) over a distance of 1 3/16 miles.

MARYLAND MILLION DAY

Maryland Million Day highlights Pimlico's fall season. The races, brainchild of sportscaster Jim McKay, are written to showcase Maryland stallions and breeders. The races are open to horses sired by stallions that stand in Maryland, and which have been nominated to the series. Purses total more than $1 million. McKay, who owns a Maryland horse farm, has bred the winner of one of the races and owned a winner of another. Along with a full complement of flat races, both on the dirt and on the turf, Pimlico's only steeplechases are held that day.

A week of horse-related events are held to further spotlight the Maryland horse breeding industry. The state is home to an estimated 500 thoroughbred farms. You'll find further details of the week in the final chapter of this book.

In order to be assured of getting a table or box seating for Maryland Million Day, one should make reservations a month in advance. Call 410-252-2102 for details.

THE REST OF THE YEAR

The good news for those who are turned off by the mammoth crowds at the Preakness is that Pimlico is open a hundred or so other days of the year. Things are pleasantly bustling on Maryland Million Day, the track's second busiest, with 20,000 or so in a facility with seating for 13,786. Throwing those two big days into the pot of statistics makes the track's average attendance 11,314. The crowds are not exactly thick weekdays, but action picks up on weekends. For tables on the weekend, the maitre d' in the Turf Club suggests calling a day ahead. Some horse players call ahead to make certain that their lucky number table will be held for them. A tip for those who fail to book in advance on a fairly busy day: check with the maitre d' after the first race. This is when he starts giving away tables held for no-shows.

DINING FACILITIES

The dining and seating options are myriad at a normal track, and Pimlico is no exception. For the important stuff first, here is a rundown on eating options. The Triple Crown Room, as the clubhouse dining room is called, is entered from the upper level of the clubhouse and accessed by elevator. Tables may be used for the day. The view of the track, especially from the front row tables, on what is called the terrace level, is very good. TV monitors, on which the entirety of the race is televised live, are in view of all the tables, and betting windows and restrooms are nearby, too. There is a cover charge for tables only on busy days.

The food and prices are the same in the Triple Crown Room, the Member's Club and the Sports Palace. Good, fairly priced specials are listed each day, in addition to the standards such as crab cakes for $14.75, crab cake sandwiches at $8.95 and tuna sandwiches with slaw for $9. Tempting desserts are available, as well as full bar service. The Triple Crown Room is comfortable and attractive and affords a very good view.

The view is not as uniformly good in the Member's Club, but the decor is plush. This area is open only to members of the Maryland Jockey Club and their guests. Those who receive an invitation to sit in the Member's are advised that the dress code there requires gentlemen to wear a coat and tie; women must wear suitable garb as well. Suitable would generally be considered a dress or dressy pants outfit. No shorts, jeans, or abbreviated fashions are allowed.

The Sports Palace, which has the atmosphere of a casino, has a dress code, too. Though coat and tie are not required, the list of thou-shalt-nots includes short shorts, cut-off jeans, and T-shirts with offensive slogans.

There are several bars throughout the clubhouse and grandstand. Some have seating and television monitors, and some are walkups. Beer is available from a number of venues. Seating is also available in some of the fast food spots. No table service restaurants are located in the grandstand area, but there are ample reasonably priced eating options there. Menus at order stands include franks, sandwiches, chicken, soup and salad, soft pretzels, ice cream and yogurt. If the food stand you frequent doesn't have seating, there are places to perch throughout the stands, and pleasant trackside benches out front.

Admission: Grandstand tickets cost $3, the clubhouse, $5, and the Sports Palace, $5 on weekdays, $7 weekends. The Sports Palace is located in the clubhouse, as are the deluxe table service restaurants and comfortable indoor reserved seating. Preakness Day, the clubhouse costs $15, the infield $15, and general admission $12. Other days, outdoor boxes cost $2 per seat, indoor boxes cost $2.50 per seat. There is plenty of free seating everywhere. The free seating tends to be higher up than the box seats, which come at an additional charge, but the view is very good from most spots. Should you wish to purchase reserved seating, ask about it when you pay the admission fee. They'll fix you up. Reserved seating for special days requires advanced planning. Allow one month for the Maryland Million; for the Preakness call before Christmas.

There are some limits to each area, and some advantages. Outdoor seating in the old grandstand, for instance, is covered and cooled by gentle breezes. When the weather is seasonable, it feels good to sit there, and it has sort of a nice, old-fashioned feel to it. The stands were renovated in 1987. They are located a good hike from the paddock, to mention the down side; the outdoor boxes block the view from lower seats, and it is hard outside to see the TV monitors.

The new grandstand, which is heated and air-conditioned, offers plenty of free seating in any kind of weather. The view of the backside of the track from the outdoor boxes in front of the new grandstand is blocked by the tote board. Those sitting on the right side of the new grandstand have the advantage of having the finish line right under their noses. The view from the free seats is excellent. The indoor boxes are plush, with two comfortable seats, a table for drinks and race cards and TV monitors in each box.

There are also free benches in front of the new grandstand, and free chairs in front of the clubhouse. The paddock is inside, between the new grandstand and the clubhouse.

112

Non-smoking Areas: Areas are offered during simulcasts at Pimlico in designated areas within the Sports Palace, the clubhouse reserved seating sections numbers 3 and 5, in a special area outside the dining room and on the first floor of the grandstand at the end of Main-line number 2.

Parking: Untouched by inflation, general admission parking costs $1, the same parking price the Maryland Jockey Club charged for four-wheel carriages at its now defunct Central Course in 1831. At Pimlico, general admission parking is handy to the grandstand. Preferred parking, closer to the clubhouse, costs $2, and valet parking, a nice feature in bad weather, costs $3. Signs guide you to the desired parking area.

 LAUREL RACE COURSE
Laurel, MD

When: In recent years, live races have been held at Laurel from January 1 to the final weekend in March, and from the first weekend in July through the final weekend in August, and the first weekend in October through December 31. The track is dark, or closed, on Mondays and Wednesdays. It is open for all holidays except Christmas and Easter. International Day, the track's biggest day of racing, is generally mid-October.

Time: 1:00 P.M., when daylight savings time ends: 12:30 P.M. weekdays, NOON on weekends and holidays.

Contact: Laurel Racing Association Inc.
P.O. Box 130
Laurel, MD 20725

Phone: 301-725-0400 (general information), 301-725-0770 (dining reservations)

Directions: From D.C., travel north on either I-95 or the Baltimore-Washington Parkway to Route 198. The exit from I-95 is 33A, and the way to the track, three traffic lights away, is marked. The track is about one mile west of the Baltimore-Washington Parkway.

WASHINGTON D.C. INTERNATIONAL MILE

Long before thoroughbreds were being jetted across the Atlantic to race in the Breeder's Cup or Kentucky Derby, Laurel was hosting an international competition. The Washington D.C. International Mile was first run in 1952. Through the years, 25 countries have been represented. In a world where equine jet lag can play havoc with the odds of success, the record stands U.S. 20—foreign challengers 20. The most foreign winners, 16, have come from France, with England claiming two victories, and Venezuela, Ireland, Australia and Germany racking up one each. When asked to pick a favorite among the previous winners, veteran newsman Joe Kelly, who now does special promotions for Maryland racing, named the American horse Kelso, winner of the International once and runner-up three times, and Eclipse Horse of the Year. The day, which has generated real excitement among the racing fraternity for its quality of entries, has also captured the imagination of the public, with over 40,000 in attendance in the record year of 1958. More recently, 25,000 attended, still more than a houseful at Laurel, which seats a little over 10,000.

INTERNATIONAL TURF FESTIVAL

For racing fans, the draw of an international turf race may be plenty good enough. However, to further glorify the event management created the International Turf Festival, of which the International itself is the crown jewel. Since 1987, additional stakes races have been added to the big fall racing weekend, with the International and two other stakes on Saturday and two additional stakes on Sunday. These include stakes for fillies and mares, 3 and up, for 2-year-old fillies and colts and for sprinters, 3 and up. Total purses for these stakes in a recent year was $1,350,000.

The extra races, like the International, are all on the turf, racing's classic surface. The difference between dirt, standard at all parimutuel race courses in America and turf, until recently the only racing surface found in other racing countries of the world, is similar to the difference between Astroturf and real grass in other athletic fields. Turf produces fewer injuries and besides, thoroughbred horses look beautiful racing on a well-tended grass course. Both big Maryland tracks have always had turf courses, it may be noted, unlike Kentucky's tracks which have only recently added turf.

When dirt tracks were used for the first time in England in 1989, it caused a great stir in the press and racing community. How could the Jockey Club allow horses to compete on such an unnatural surface? The answer is simple really, and the explanation for why dirt tracks have predominated in America. Turf tracks must be used sparingly, and races on turf may have to switch to dirt tracks in inclement weather. Because the survival of American racing depends on extended race seasons, dirt tracks prevail. In Great Britain hundreds of small racing venues open only for two to four days several times a year. Still, some horses do not like to run on dirt; seeing horses race on turf, as they do for these stakes at Laurel, is an opportunity for fans to see racing at its classic best.

Admission: The grandstand tickets cost $3, the clubhouse $5 and to the Sports Palace $5 on weekdays, $7 on weekends and holidays. On Tuesdays and Thursdays, senior citizens are admitted to the track for $1.50. Grandstand boxes cost $2 per seat any day. Clubhouse boxes cost $2.50 per seat, cinema theater seats, $2. The theater seats located on the second floor have no outside view but feature comfortable seats and big screens on which "punters," as the Brits describe race goers, can watch the races.

Seating in the clubhouse as compared with the grandstand is separate but equal. Ample free seating is available in each area. Plushy reserved seating is located in the clubhouse. As at Pimlico, the deluxe, sit-down restaurant and Sports Palace are in the clubhouse area. At Laurel, the paddock is on the clubhouse side of the track. The finish line and winner's circle are equally accessible to both areas.

Laurel's grandstand, first opened in 1911, now bears little resemblance to its former self. The entire stand is now modern, glass-enclosed and climate-controlled. The only outside seating is on free benches, spotted around the area in front of the stands. The paddock imparts the last of the old-fashioned flavor. Set outside the main grandstand on the clubhouse end, the round shaped, high-ceilinged, open-ended paddock is a magnet for soothing summer breezes.

Dining: Laurel shares caterer Harry M. Stevens Inc. with Pimlico. The two have more in common than that, actually. The staff in most cases is the same. Joseph A. DeFrancis serves as president of both tracks and also heads the Maryland Jockey Club, which owns both tracks.

The main dining room at Laurel, the Brass Horse, is especially handy to the paddock. This feature makes a table, claimed for the day, especially desirable. The area around the entrance has lounging tables, betting windows and the "ladies" and "gents." Like Pimlico, there is also a private dining room for members of the Maryland Jockey Club. Of its bars, the one near the paddock end first floor is very handy, being in a high traffic area that makes meeting up with friends going and coming to the paddock easy. Also in this area, not far from the clubhouse entrance, one finds TV monitors which simultaneously play and replay the day's races, so that you can see your horse win or lose multiple times.

Non-smoking Areas: At Laurel Race Course, non-smoking areas are in designated sections of the Sports Palace, in the grandstand outside the Sports Palace and in the Mezzanine Theater.

Parking: General parking costs $1 and is a pretty good walk. Preferred parking, $2, is handy to the clubhouse, and valet parking, $3. Laurel also offers a VIP valet for $5 and Park and Lock for $3.

 TIMONIUM RACE TRACK
Maryland State Fair Grounds
Timonium, MD

When: Ten days of racing to end Labor Day and to coincide with the Maryland State Fair.

Time: First race 1:00 P.M.

Contact: Timonium Race Track
P.O. Box 188
Timonium, MD 21094

116

Phone: 410-252-0200 general information, 410-252-4210 dining reservations

Directions: From D.C., take I-95 north to I-695, the Baltimore Beltway, toward Towson. Take Exit 24 onto I-83N (the Harrisburg Expressway). Take Exit 17, Padonia Rd. Bear right off exit. Turn right on York Rd. The Fairgrounds is ½ mile up York Rd. on the right.

Timonium races are a part of the Maryland State Fair. The grandstands were built in 1878, making Timonium one of the oldest tracks in the country. The fair celebrated its 100th birthday in 1981, the same year the races were declared 126 years old. Even earlier, all the way back to 1820, Fair scholars figure races were held on the site. How the grounds got their name is a story in itself. The land now incorporated in the state fairground was owned by Sarah Buchanan, a daughter of the second governor of Maryland, back in the 1700s. She changed its name from Bellefield to Timonium, which means sorrow (according to a 1879 newspaper account, not to a modern day *Webster's*) following the death of her best friend, Mrs. Cassandra van Pradelles, "whom pirates forced to walk the plank off the coast of North Carolina."

Early accounts of the state fair contain descriptions of the races, comprised of both flats and trots. Many of the trotters, it was observed in newspaper accounts, were not "professional high fliers," like those that came to the races back in the 1830s, but animals whose chief duty in life was to pull the family's wagon to the store, market and church. Race results were flown to Baltimore and Alexandria, VA, by carrier pigeons, according to the *Maryland Journal*, September 4, 1880. Alas, this age of innocence was being overtaken by automobiles and other modern conveniences. An article from 1920 decried that "Horse races are not like they were when everyone knew the horses, and Cousin Asas come up from the flats with his old stallion, father to half the colts in the county. The horses are brought in by railcar, and the young people don't seem to care—their minds having been corrupted by the telephone, the moving picture and now the radio."

In spite of changes, racing remains part of the fair tradition. However, the track, which once offered 45 days of racing, now limits its season to the run of the fair. Once upon a time, Timonium was part of a circuit of five half-mile tracks which operated during the summer. Long since gone are the tracks at Cumberland, Bel Air and Hagerstown. Marlborough still runs an odd day of racing now and again but Timonium is the only survivor of the old half-mile circuit still going strong. The additional racing days it once controlled have been given to Laurel and Pimlico. Like most racing states, Maryland allows only one parimutuel track to operate at a time. Having made that definitive statement it must be admitted that Fair Hill, Timonium's neighbor to the north, has held races on Labor Day of late. Fair Hill, which features steeplechases on the turf, asked Timonium, a dirt track, if they would object and Timonium, which offers only flat races, said no, go ahead. And while we're clearing up possible points of confusion, the track at Timonium has been lengthened to five-eighths of a mile.

Horses for the short meet are drawn from the Maryland tracks, and from nearby Charles Town in West Virginia, and Penn National in Pennsylvania. Most of the riders come from Maryland, but some of the state's best take a vacation during Timonium. To compare racing there with other Maryland tracks, purses in a recent year have averaged around $55,000 per day. Day in and day out Pimlico and Laurel hand out over $100,000 in purses, with lucrative stakes races on one or both days each weekend along with holidays and even some weekdays. Winning jockeys take home, in addition to a straight rider's fee, a portion of the winning purse. You can see how the top ten riders, booting home winners of over a million dollars each year, may take a break from the grind of dieting and risking their necks.

Like the jockeys, some staff members who troop from Laurel to Pimlico as the season changes take their vacation during Timonium. Others wouldn't miss it, and say it is their favorite time of the year.

Admission: In fact, there's a lot to like. A $3 admission for adults, (children under 12 free), grants entry to not only the track, but also to the state fair. True horse fans can divide up their time between the track and the horse show, which features different breeds daily. Kick in the entire midway and agricultural show and it's a big entertainment value. Like the State Fair in

Virginia, Maryland State Fair is not state operated. It is a privately owned non-profit corporation formed to promote the state's agricultural products.

Seating: Free bleacher seating for approximately 3,000 is available, on a first come, first serve, basis. It is interesting to note that an account of the grandstand when it was brand new back in 1878 described it as an eye-catching facility with seating for 1,400. The place hasn't completely lost its sense of intimacy through the years. Now there are about 300 reserved seats, and 50 or so boxes. Some of the boxes are purchased by the same families or stables year after year, but reserved seating is almost always available on any day.

Dining: The midway has the food one associates with a fair, and the track grandstand has the food one associates with Maryland tracks, because it is served by Harry M. Stevens, the caterer to Maryland tracks since 1936. The dining room, which is not trackside, seats 400. Tables are usually available, but to make certain on a weekend, reservations may be made. Informal dining is available in the Timonium lounge along with beer and liquor.

Parking: Alas, not the best part of the story about this race meet. One parking lot with about 2,500 spaces serves the total needs of the track and the state fair and the horse show. Among the complaints lodged against the fair back in 1906 were scarcity of shade, sparse number of water closets, no beer or wine, and too few hitching posts. Some of shortages have been corrected.

 FAIR HILL RACE COURSE
Fair Hill, MD

When: Memorial Day and Labor Day. The Breeder's Cup Steeplechase, at $250,000 the most lucrative of its kind in America, was held at Fair Hill for four of its six years.

Time: First race 1:00 P.M.

Contact: Cecil County Breeders Fair, Inc.
P.O. Box 2334
Elkton, MD 21922

Phone: 410-398-6565

Directions: Take I-95 north of Baltimore to Exit 100, left on Route 272, toward Rising Sun. At intersection of Route 272 and 273, turn right toward Newark, DE. The track is a one hour drive north of Baltimore, 25 minutes from Wilmington, DE.

Fair Hill Race Course is located on the estate of the late William duPont. The 5,600 acre track is now owned by the state of Maryland, which operates it as an equestrian and wildlife sanctuary. The state prefers to allow separate non-profit associations manage the various events held at Fair Hill for a usage fee or a percent of the income.

The races are managed by the Cecil County Breeders Fair, which duPont organized before his death in the mid '60s. The fair board is composed of local civic leaders who see to the details of the race, and coordinate with the Cecil County Hospital, beneficiary of the races.

Like the other races described here, Fair Hill comes under the auspices of the Maryland Racing Commission, and offers parimutuel wagering. Fair Hill Races, however, are organized as not-for-profit, with extra dollars going to the local charity. Also, Fair Hill does not have a dirt track, only turf; and its emphasis is on steeplechasing, though it supplements the jump races with a few flat races. On a rainy Labor Day, crowd estimates topped 11,000, better than most Maryland tracks on an average day. But handles (the take from dollars bet) were around $250,000, half of the take at Timonium and one fourth of Laurel's and Pimlico's. The fact is that those who attend Fair Hill probably don't attend another parimutuel meet during the year; they come for the racing, not the betting, and are not very sophisticated about the wagering. That's not to say the betting set up is any different from other Maryland tracks. Highly regulated races are held under the watchful eyes of Maryland racing officials; a photo finish camera confirms the placings of the races, and state-approved tote boards and ticket takers issue betting tickets and make payouts following each race.

Please see the listing for Fair Hill in Chapter VII.

OTHER EVENTS

Besides the steeplechases, Fair Hill offers a wide range of equestrian events, from trail rides to Olympic level three-day events. Call Dennis Clocum at 215-347-2024 for more information, and see Chapter XI for specifics on driving, eventing and dressage at Fair Hill.

MARLBOROUGH RACE TRACK AT PRINCE GEORGE'S EQUESTRIAN CENTER
Upper Marlboro, MD

When: The third and fourth Wednesdays in October

Time: First race 12:30 P.M.

Contact: Marlborough Race Track at Prince George's Equestrian Center
14900 Pennsylvania Ave.
Upper Marlboro, MD 20772

Phone: 301-952-7990

Directions: From D.C., take I-495 to Exit 11A. Take Pennsylvania Avenue (Route 4) seven miles from the Beltway. From Virginia travel south on I-495 to Exit 11A, the Upper Marlboro exit.

Races were held at Upper Marlboro from 1745 until the track fell victim to a Maryland political scandal in 1972. However, it cannot be said that racing was not without other gaps through that 250 or years. Anti-British sentiment closed things down in the days before the Revolutionary War and once again following the War of 1812. Racing got going again in the mid-1800s, only to be stopped by the Civil War. A new grandstand was built in 1914, and that bright new era ended in 1972. The plant then sat empty until bought in 1980 by Prince George's County.

Racing was reinstated by an act of the legislature in 1988. The races are now part of a promotion of the ambitious Prince George's Equestrian Center, a 100-acre tract being developed by the Maryland-National Capital Park and Planning Commission. About 12,000 turn out for Marlborough's two days of racing. Fans come predominately from northern Virginia and Maryland, especially the counties along the Baltimore-Washington Parkway. Many come from Prince George's County, and for those who live within a five- to ten-mile radius of the track, a visit to the track can represent a sentimental journey, back to see the old place they last visited in 1972.

To aid fans who have not been to the track in 20 years, or perhaps ever, Marlborough offers an especially good handicapping segment over the TV monitors and loudspeakers before each race. One commentator makes his picks (two of three consistently hit the boards - finish in the top three - every race), and another commentator gives tips on using previous forms to make betting selections. One year a fan outguessed the excellent commentators and claimed the biggest win of the day: a new Lexus, won as part of a special promotional contest entered before the races began on the day of the $40,000 Nationwide Infiniti Marlborough Cup.

At $40,000, the track can be reasonably sure that its feature for three-year-olds and up is the richest race in the country on that particular day. Its other headline race is the $15,000 Marlborough Nursery for two-year-olds. Those who come to watch apparently come to bet (higher than a total of $400,000 recently wagered at the two-day meet). Besides benefiting the state in the form of its cut of the handle and horsemen in purses, the meet also benefits Prince George's therapeutic riding program.

The track itself is a 5/8-mile oval. The racing complex includes 200 stalls, and is used as a year-round thoroughbred training facility. The majority of the horses racing at Marlborough are based in Maryland, but may be competing at Delaware Park, Charles Town, and Penn National. Most of the jockeys are regulars at the Maryland tracks.

Admission: General admission costs $3. The general admission section includes two large heated tents with betting windows, TV monitors and very limited seating. Basically, it consists of a tent pitched on an asphalt parking lot. Limited bleacher seating is available outside. Knowledgeable Marlborough fans show up with their own picnics and chairs, which they place right along the rail. A limited number of picnic tables along the rail are also available. The Marlborough Club, which costs $8, offers indoor seating in a heated, carpeted, fully enclosed tent, along with a special sponsors' area, betting windows and TV monitors.

Dining: Bars and food service are located in both the general admission and reserved areas. As at other Maryland tracks,

Harry M. Stevens is the caterer. Menus are very limited, but prices are reasonable. Big, juicy, real hamburgers (as opposed to the machine-made kind that taste like plastic) are sold for $3.25 each.

Parking: General admission parking costs $1, preferred (next to the track) $2.00. Those who desire preferred parking, which is limited, should get into the right lane as they approach the track. General admission parking is on the other side of Pennsylvania Avenue on grass lots.

OTHER EVENTS

See Appendix A for a breakdown of other horse events at Prince George's Equestrian Center. Prince George's has a 40,000-square-foot indoor ring.

CHARLES TOWN RACES
Charles Town, WV

When: Racing January 1–December 29; no racing on Super Bowl Sunday, Easter or December 6–25

Time: 1:00 P.M. on Sundays, Wednesdays, Thursdays and major holidays. 7:00 P.M. on Friday and Saturday. Santa Anita simulcasts daily, Wednesday–Sunday 3:30 P.M.

Contact: Charles Town Races
P.O. Box 551
Charles Town, WV 25414

Phone: 304-725-7001, 800-795-7001

Directions: Travel west on I-270 to Frederick, MD. Take the Charles Town exit onto Route 70, then one exit later turn onto Route 340 west almost to Charles Town. The track is located on the right just after Route 340 picks up Route 51 west.

From D.C., Charles Town is a pretty substantial drive. Moreover, the races end late on Fridays and Saturdays. Charles Town certainly provides a laid-back atmosphere and plenty of competitive racing. The purses are much smaller than Maryland's and the horses are a noticeable step down in class. The funny thing, though, is that two of steeplechasing's greatest stars raced at Charles Town. In fact, they couldn't win at Charles Town. The legendary Jay Trump, who won England's Grand National Steeplechase and the Maryland Hunt Cup, came from Charles Town. So did the equally awesome Von Csadek, winner of both the Virginia Gold Cup numerous times and the Maryland Hunt Cup. In an effort to equal Jay Trump's record, Von Csadek was sent to England and won several races, but suffered a training injury which knocked him out of the Grand National. This is all to sound a cautionary note about the use of "Charles Town horse" as a put down. Plenty of horses from Charles Town have turned into swans in the hands of the right horsemen. Many top horsemen spend lots of time studying horses there to find the next great steeplechaser, show horse or field hunter.

Marylanders running for lucrative purses may sneer, but Charles Town with its $2,500 claimers and $1,800 in prize money nevertheless fills the fields, something other tracks don't always do. The races do not feature Secretariat, of course, but the fields are competitive which makes handicapping and betting fun.

Local historians trace racing in Charles Town back to 1786, and the first Charles Town Jockey Club was founded in 1806. Remember, West Virginia was part of its horsey cousin Virginia until peeled off in retribution for the Civil War. Racing closed down after the war, and for a long time, residents had to content themselves with horse shows and exhibitions. Then, in 1933, the Charles Town Horse Show sold its property to the Shenandoah Valley Jockey Club. Huge crowds, literally shoulder to shoulder, were pictured at the track through the '50s. Things were so good, in fact, that a rival track, Shenandoah Downs, was built nearby. Unlike Maryland and most other racing states, West Virginia permitted both tracks to be open at the same time, so the two slugged it out for bettors and for entries. The two eventually joined forces, swapping racing dates, until for economic reasons Shenandoah was converted to a training center and the racing staff and equipment stayed on the Charles Town side of the road.

WEST VIRGINIA BREEDER'S CLASSIC

Charles Town does have its annual moment in the national sun during the West Virginia Breeder's Classic, the brainchild of Sam Huff, Football Hall of Famer, and his racing partner Carol

Holden. The stands are packed and fans are hanging off the rafters for this annual event, generally held on a Friday night in late September. Huff, born and raised in West Virginia, saw the night as an opportunity to give something substantial back to his home state, and also to his new found interest in horse breeding and racing.

The hoopla begins with a star studded black tie gala the Thursday before. At the races, ordinarily casual fans spiff up for the occasion, and those with seats in the dining room and especially those presenting trophies are downright fancy.

Highlight of the evening is the $200,000 Ronrico Breeder's Classic, a mile and an eighth tilt for West Virginia breds. The race is aired on ESPN's Racing Across America series. The rest of the card, also featuring West Virginia breds, carries well-funded purses, sponsored for the most part by West Virginia businesses. Total purses for the night are $380,000.

Tickets can be bought the night of the Classic, but don't expect to find a place to sit, or to get a seat in the dining room unless arrangements have been made in advance. The dining room is totally booked months ahead, with priority given to the many race sponsors, owners and officials.

Admission: The grandstand costs $2, the clubhouse, $4. Reserved seats cost $.50 extra. Box seats in the grandstand cost $1.25 and in the clubhouse, $1.50. Special rates are given to groups of 25 or more; dinner packages are offered to groups. The grandstand has a capacity of 4,000 seats, the clubhouse 600 seats and the dining room 1,000.

Parking: General, $1; preferred, $1.50 extra; valet, $2 extra.

VII

FALL STEEPLECHASES

Where Jack Kent Cooke Goes When He's Not With the Redskins

Compared with spring events, fall races tend to be low key, but still high quality. Fall Virginia meets like Foxfield in Charlottesville and the Gold Cup in The Plains, produce a less crowded version of each of their spring extravaganzas. That's not altogether bad because the crowds at the spring races can be shoulder to shoulder. Fall offers better seating at lower prices, and an opportunity to enjoy the beautiful setting at the Gold Cup with fewer race fans afoot. Morven Park in Leesburg is not noticeably crowded in either spring or fall. Middleburg, while always maintaining a genteel atmosphere that provides race goers plenty of space, draws fewer people in the fall and provides, if possible, even more natural beauty then. Fairfax, near Leesburg, draws a pleasant bustle both spring and fall. Montpelier, in Orange, has only fall races, and they are a delight. Filling the infield in front of the house of the late President James Monroe (more recently owned by the late Marion duPont Scott), the fans prove they love it. Shenandoah in Mt. Jackson drew hefty crowds to its inaugural running in 1992 and has plenty of space for growth.

Mounted officials gather in front of Montpelier for the annual fall steeplechase. Race horse owner and breeder Marion duPont Scott gave Montpelier, the home of President James Madison, to the National Trust.
Credit: Matthew Gentry, **The Daily Progress**

Maryland does not have any fall steeplechases, other than the jump races at Pimlico on Maryland Million Day, and racing at the steeplechase course at Fair Hill on Labor Day.

The horses running in fall can be quite good. Many are either survivors of the big time August steeplechases at Saratoga—high quality horses with enough run left to try a few more races before settling down for a long winter's rest—or they are three-year-olds that will be the stars of the following spring season. Three-year-olds, that can be nearing the end of their careers on the flat, are just coming onto the steeplechase courses in the fall for a sniff and a look around. Steeplechasers remain competitive much longer on average than their flat racing counterparts, in part by having been given the time to finish maturing before really being put to the rigors of racing.

FAIR HILL RACES
Fair Hill Race Course
Elkton, MD

When: Labor Day

Time: First Race 1:00 P.M.

Contact: Cecil County Breeders Fair, Inc.
P.O. Box 2334
Elkton, MD 21922

Phone: 410-398-6565

Steeplechases are held at Fair Hill on Memorial Day and on Labor Day. Fair Hill is a goodly trek from Washington. However, it is do-able in a day.

Admission: For more race details and ticket prices, please refer to Chapter VI.

SHENANDOAH RACES
Mt. Jackson, VA

When: Second Saturday in September and fourth Sunday in October

Time: First race 1:00 P.M.

Contact: Shenandoah Races
P.O. Box 60
New Market, VA 22844

Phone: 703-740-8666

Directions: From D.C., travel west on I-66 to I-81 south. Take Exit 273 (Mt.Jackson-Basye) to Route 11 south. Turn left through Mt. Jackson, across the north fork of the Shenandoah River over a steel truss bridge. Turn left onto the race course. From Warrenton, travel south on Route 211 to New Market. At Route 11, turn north to the course, about six miles on the right.

For an added treat, visit one of the state's few remaining covered bridges, located a short distance from the course. To see the covered bridge, turn south on Route 11 for ⅓ mile to Route 720. Turn right (west) and travel ½ mile to the bridge.

In 1992, its inaugural year, the Shenandoah Races got good support from area residents. Fans also came from horsey Middleburg and Warrenton, and as far away as D.C. and MD. Mt. Jackson is a three-hour drive for those from D.C. However, as one delighted race fan put it, where else could you shop for antiques and "junque" and buy cider and local apples on your way to the races? The drive from D.C. on I-81 is faster than taking Route 211. Route 211 is shorter, though possibly slower, but adds to the beauty of the drive, cutting over both the Blue Ridge and Massanutten mountains.

The Shenandoah Races will surely be remembered as one of the best first efforts in the history of steeplechasing. Freemont Day, the landowner, had never even seen a steeplechase before close to 5,000 folks showed up in his front field to watch 11 well filled races. Day obviously knows about farming, and gave credit to the flat, fertile land for the results of his toils: newly planted but lush, smooth and level turf on a ⅞-mile oval. Race organizer Jay Hirsch further insured the success of the new event calling on steeplechasing's coolest hands, announcers Will O'Keefe and Mike Hughs, racing secretaries Virginia Beach and Cindy Tucker and a supporting cast of other capable horse people who have put their shoulders behind many another Virginia race.

The September race gained charm and no doubt wide local support from involvement by the New Market and Mt. Jackson Chambers of Commerce. Local pride beamed in the pre-race color brochure hyping Shenandoah County. Delighted volunteers reported selling out of all race concessions—ball caps, tee shirts and what-nots with the attractive race logo. Who could blame area residents from being proud? The delightful flat, fertile valley is accentuated by the backdrop of the Massanutten Mountains. Scenery at the course is made even more striking by the Massanutten shelf, a dramatic escarpment that towers over Mt. Airy plantation, which traces its history back to 1772.

The September race had an extra attraction in the Stonewall Brigade, a group of Civil War buffs dedicated to preserving the battlefields of the Shenandoah Valley. Their prominently placed tent was bedecked with maps tracing the routes of the battles and filled with knowledgeable members who brought to life the tales of Civil War skirmishes and major encounters. The race program itself was filled with snippets of history about the farm and the surrounding area.

The maiden hurdle race, Turner Ashby's Flight, memorializes a most enchanting tale about a Civil War skirmish that took place on the Days' farm. It seems Stonewall Jackson was especially fond of camping on Rude's Hill, the rise south of the race course. Jackson did not want to stage a major engagement on these grounds, however. When he received word that a large Union force was headed his way, he retreated. Artillery placements, along with a cavalry unit under Turner Ashby, were left on Rude's Hill to slow down the Union approach. Ashby's men stung and twisted and beddeviled the approaching force. It is said that through field glasses, the Union forces appeared to be led by an officer on a magnificent white charger. The Confederates stationed on Rude's Hill recognized him as their General Ashby, with hostile troops in close pursuit. Ashby had sent his men ahead over the bridge across the Shenandoah. The plan was for Ashby to set fire to tinder left on the bridge, slowing the approach of heavy artillery and the main force. Unfortunately, Ashby did not accomplish his mission. A shot intended for him went through his boot and struck his horse. Ashby fled for his life across the meadow on his wounded steed, which made the climb up Rude's Hill, then fell dead. The distance of this valiant run was 1⅞ miles, the same distance of steeplechases now held at Shenandoah. Ashby's flight crossed the very meadow used for the current race course.

131

Shenandoah's first race meet was so good it is difficult to pick the high point of the day. In addition to the grass and setting, credit must be given to Katie Couric of the "Today Show," who brought a star quality to the event and was as fetching off screen as on. In the same breath mention must be made of some particularly adorable pony jockeys, and some memorable mules. So hard fought was the Shenandoah Mule Race, that a match race had to be scheduled between the top two finishers.

The October races had a star quality of their own, brought by actor Robert Duval, who not only graciously presented trophies but also requested a spin in one of the racing chariots. Besides a standard card of flat races and a couple of jump races, a unique Arabian chariot race was added. Four chariots drawn by teams of Arabians raced around a figure eight course, providing a death-defying remake of *Ben Hur*.

Admission: General admission is $7 in advance, $10 at the gate and includes parking and a free race program. Front row reserved parking, which admits one vehicle and two occupants, costs $50 in advance, $60 the week of the race.

FAIRFAX STEEPLECHASE RACES
Belmont Plantation
Leesburg, VA

When: September, third Saturday after Labor Day

Time: First race 2:00 P.M.

Contact: Randolph D. Rouse
6407 Wilson Blvd.
Arlington, VA 22205

Phone: 703-787-6673

Directions: From D.C., travel west on Route 7 toward Leesburg to Belmont Plantation, which is on the left approximately 15 miles from I-495.

In fall, Fairfax Hunt sponsors a real steeplechase, though the crowds who attend their spring race probably feel that it is the real race (see Chapter III for details). The difference lies not in the size of the crowd, which is about the same at both, but in the fact that the fall race is recognized by the National Steeplechase and Hunt Association. For horsemen, this recognition causes certain things to occur: purses are offered and points count toward year-end championships. Successful out-of-state trainers, owners, horses and riders participate in ever-increasing numbers. As at the spring point-to-points, Virginia horsemen heavily support the meet. Race chairman Randy Rouse believes that champion steeplechase trainers like Jonathan Sheppard and Janet Elliot have added Fairfax to their fall schedule due in part to the flat races on the card. Most steeplechases have only races over jumps, but trainers sometimes like to find a spot on the flat to tune their charges, especially good older horses, for the big moneyed races that follow in the fall.

Running even two races a year at Belmont Plantation is tricky, according to Rouse. The soil is clay based, which means if the course is wet for the races, hoof prints are permanently indented into the turf. To undo such damage, the course must be rolled after each race meet so that the turf can heal.

Admission: Prime spaces in fall are more pricey than in spring. Patron parking, on the front row at the top of the hill near the finish line, costs $180. Sponsor parking, also trackside, costs $100. Each of these options includes admission for two, and the opportunity to purchase additional tickets for $5 each. For a nominal fee, patrons and sponsors can purchase tickets to a catered luncheon on the grounds before the race, and a cocktail reception after, both with live jazz. General admission tickets cost $5 a person purchased in advance, or $10 at the gate.

FOXFIELD FALL RACES
Foxfield Race Course
Charlottesville, VA

When: September, Sunday following Fairfax

Time: First race 1:00 P.M.

Contact: Foxfield Racing Association
             P.O. Box 5187
             Charlottesville, VA 22905

Phone: 804-293-9501

Directions: See Foxfield Spring Races in Chapter IV.

Like other fall races that have spring counterparts, Foxfield Fall is smaller than Foxfield Spring. Nonetheless, Foxfield Fall is very large. Though both meets are undeniably popular with students from the University of Virginia and most other Virginia universities, a spring break atmosphere prevails in spring. In fall, students seem more intent on striking a pose and showing off their favorite new back-to-school togs.

Those who cast their eyes to the race track will see an interesting variety of thoroughbreds passing by. Fall timber stars like Lenape Way regularly add their names to trophies at Foxfield. Steeplechase fans got their first look at Hodges Bay, winner of more than $1 million on the flat before starting his new career as a jumper. Foxfield's flat race and to a lesser degree the allowance hurdle are virtual showcases for the fall champion races, the Colonial Cup and the Novice Chase. These equine champions come to Foxfield because of its race date and an established and well-maintained course. Purses are a bit smaller in the fall, but the races still draw a variety of horses from Virginia and points north.

Admission: Though the fall crowds of spectators are large, one still has a better chance of getting a good reserved parking space than in the spring, a virtual sell-out. One has a very good chance of getting tickets for either the orange or green sections of the infield. Tickets for either cost $65; be advised the orange section is the designated student section. Rail spots on the outside of the course are harder to come by, but if that's what you want, send in your check early and something might turn up. A racing membership which includes parking near the finish line costs $125. For a $200 sponsorship, one not only receives railside parking, but also four tickets to a catered luncheon beforehand. General admission tickets cost $12 per person in advance, $15 at the gate, with $5 charged for parking. A big push is made to sell tickets in advance. One could easily miss the first three races waiting in line to buy a ticket. When planning what time to arrive, it's not a bad idea to come early and carry a picnic.

134

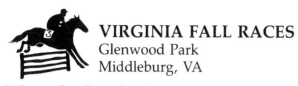

VIRGINIA FALL RACES
Glenwood Park
Middleburg, VA

When: October, first Saturday and Sunday

Time: First race 1:30 P.M.

Contact: Virginia Beach
P.O. Box 2
Middleburg, VA 22117

Phone: 703-687-5662

Directions: From D.C., take I-66 west to Route 50 west. At Middleburg's only traffic light, turn right. Course will be about two miles on the right.

Like the Virginia Spring Races (see Chapter IV), the Virginia Fall Races are simply stunning. The course is a glory, and the backdrop of the Blue Ridge Mountains, a wonder. The crowds, while not overwhelming in the spring, are smaller in the fall.

Races are held on both Saturday and Sunday. Race enthusiasts can get a price break by buying reserved tickets for both days. The Saturday race card is less high power than its spring counterpart. The Sunday races, not recognized by the NSHA, are definitely laid back. The races are not written for big stars, but the riders and trainers represented are certainly of the best. On Saturday, the three-year-old hurdle race gives a preview of future stars.

Sunday's special feature, besides a card of three flat races and two jump races, is the North American Hunter Championship. Finals for the Hunter Championship are held at noon Sunday before the afternoon races. The horses that make it to the finals have been selected after being assessed in the hunt field for four days. The championships are well-filled with magnificent field hunters and riders out to capture the trophy for their hunt. The competition also provides an excuse to spend four days riding with local hunts, which are eager to please the large fields of visitors by treating them not just to good sport, but also to an assortment of parties and hunt teas. In the finals, selected horses gallop across the race course behind hounds that are following a drag line. From that lot, judges ask a dozen or so to perform special individual tests, such as taking a course of jumps and opening gates.

Admission: Ticket prices are $200 for front row parking one day, $280 for both days; second row parking $125 for one day, $200 for both days. Rail parking costs $50 for one day, $75 for both days. Boxes on the lower level cost $100 for one day, $150 for both; on the upper level, $60 for one day, $90 for both.

 MORVEN PARK RACES
Morven Park
Leesburg, VA

When: October, second Saturday

Time: First race 12:30 P.M.

Contact: Morven Park Steeplechase
  Route 3, Box 50
  Leesburg, VA 22075

Phone: 703-777-2414

Directions: From D.C., take Route 7 west. At Leesburg, take the Route 15 by-pass north. The course is on the left, one mile from the conjunction of the by-pass and Route 15.

The Morven Park Races, which were founded in 1979, share their race course with the Georgetown Races, first run in 1990. The course was developed by Race Director Joe Rogers, himself a successful owner, trainer and, at one time, a leading amateur rider. The course looks simple, just jumps spotted around a field of magnificent grass. Actually, achieving this effect required good racing design, drain work, irrigation, and dirt moving to produce a course with such a classic sweep. The lush grass and slight gradients hold back the blinding speed which can produce hard spills. The gradual arc of the final turn and the long straight regularly produce close finishes. So that the spectators get a good view of the races, Rogers has built a small mountain in the midst of an otherwise flat field.

Races are full and hotly contested. Like at Virginia Fall, three-year-olds are sent out in profusion for a start before they

136

face a full campaign in the spring of the following year. The Samuel H. Rogers Memorial Timber Race, named for the chairman's father, also draws a full field. The timber race is run under handicap conditions, with weights assigned by the NSHA racing secretary. The idea of a handicap is to equalize the competition using weight. This worked well at this race in 1993, with the first three horses finishing within a neck of one another. Full fields came for the maiden and allowance races over brush, too. This shows how much horsemen value the meet, because it annually faces competition for entries from two or three other meets that day.

Admission: Tickets cost $5 per person for general admission plus $5 per car. Parking is on the Route 15 side of the course and a five-minute walk from the ample viewing areas. The $25 reserve parking, which permits a carload to park in an area that is not so long a walk away. The reserved parking areas cost $80 for arena parking, $150 for patron parking, which is on the rail, and $160 for terrace parking, which is located higher up in what is considered the prime viewing area. Both the patron and terrace parking provide not one but two parking spots, so guests of space holders can drive right in behind their hosts.

INTERNATIONAL GOLD CUP
Great Meadow
The Plains, VA

When: October, generally the third Saturday

Time: First race 1:30 P.M.

Contact: Virginia Gold Cup Association
P.O. Box 840
Warrenton, VA 22186

Phone: 703-347-2612

Directions: From D.C., take I-66 west. For north side parking, exit at The Plains, travel south on Route 245 to the course, which will be on the left. For south side parking, exit at Marshall. Turn south on U.S. 17. Turn left on Route 245. Traffic can be heavy, so it is advisable to plan to arrive no later than 12:30 P.M.

The splendor of the Great Meadow course is heightened even more in fall by the foliage colors, which generally peak in time for the race.

The International Gold Cup is not as large as its brother race, the Virginia Gold Cup in the spring (see Chapter IV for details), nor the Foxfield Spring Race which is second. No one denies that the Gold Cup is the biggest, and really fills up Great Meadow. But the International Gold Cup crowds are now pushing 30,000, and prime spots sell out. A newcomer is more apt to get into the most desirable parking areas in fall, however, than in spring. Patrons of the fall race do not, alas, get first dibs on the same space at the Virginia Gold Cup.

The International Gold Cup came to Great Meadow by way of Gallatin, TN, and Ligonier, PA. First staged in 1930, the race was created by wealthy New Yorkers who formed Grasslands Hunt Club in Gallatin. The club and course, built on the thick, rolling sod of Tennessee, were established by Joe Thomas of Middleburg, VA. Those who have driven past Huntlands, the grand estate Thomas built in Middleburg in the early part of the century, will not be surprised that his idea of a race course was to duplicate the English Grand National. The prize for the International race, which drew the best steeplechasers in the United States, was a magnificent gold trophy donated by Alfonso XIII, King of Spain. General R.K. Mellon of Pittsburg, PA, won the King of Spain trophy in 1931.

Even such a wealthy club as Grasslands was not Depression-proof, and the club closed. With the King of Spain trophy collecting dust in his case, General Mellon started the Rolling Rock Steeplechase six years later in Ligonier, PA in 1937. The King of Spain Gold Cup was given to the winner of the International Gold Cup, a race that drew its name from the name of the trophy and the fact that, like the Maryland Hunt Cup, the winner automatically qualified for the English Grand National. The highly successful Pennsylvania race was discontinued in 1983, following the death of Alfred Hunt.

Meanwhile, down in The Plains, VA, newspaper owner Arthur "Nick" Arundel was well along with plans to develop Great Meadow, a charitable trust which would preserve the open space needed for staging a major steeplechase for generations to come. A quick-witted man, Arundel negotiated to move the magnificent trophy to Virginia, where it was first presented in 1984. Unlike the previous International Gold Cup races, this version was held over Great Meadow's Championship timber course. In an interesting and fitting aside, like General Mellon, Arundel's great champion Sugar Bee had claimed the King of Spain trophy in its previous venue (in this case Ligonier). The race there was held over brush, but Sugar Bee showed his worth by winning the magnificent gold trophy a second time in Virginia, this time over timber. Sugar Bee also won for his owner the Virginia Gold Cup and the Maryland Hunt Cup, and now carries Arundel hunting. He also carries the microphone-carrying anchor of the live telecast of the Virginia Gold Cup.

Like Sugar Bee, the majority of horses whose names have been added to the King of Spain Gold Cup since the move to Great Meadow in 1984, have also gone on to win the Virginia Gold Cup, which is a half mile longer. So far, two of the first 10 winners have also won the Maryland Hunt Cup.

Co-featured with the timber tilt is the Future Champions Cup, a steeplechase for three-year-olds. A victory in the Future Champions generally prophesies who will become the three-year-old champion for the season.

Admission: Tickets to the prime Boardview box area aren't even offered for sale; these are simply passed down from generation to generation, and can be an object of contention in case of divorce. Those who send their money in as soon as invitations are mailed will at least have an outside chance of getting a Steward's Stand parking space, which is first or second row parking on Member's Hill, plus admission to Member's Hill for four; or an Oakwood box, which also costs $350, and includes seating for four at the top of Member's Hill. Parking is a short walk away. Member's Hill is an exclusive fenced-in viewing area where the swells hang out and the corporate party tents are located. The paddock and finish line are in this area, and the trophy presentations are made here.

Rail parking is not on Member's Hill, but includes four passes to the area, so one can mosey over and check it out. Prompt response when invitations are mailed should get a space on Rail 1, or a good space on Rail 2. Previous space holders get first dibs by virtue of an earlier mailing, but spaces not claimed by opening day, four or five weeks before the race, go up for grabs on a first come, first serve basis. Rail 1 costs $250, Rail 2, $175, and Rail 3, $75. For $160, one can purchase a Rail 4 space; these are extra large spaces and can be used for an over-size vehicle or tent. Spaces north of the finish line have a good view of the final turn; those on the south side of the finish line are closer to the actual finish and paddock.

General admission parking, which admits up to six, costs $40 in advance, $45 on race day. General admission parking is far from the course. There are special parking areas that offer a good view from the cars, which in recent years cost $70. Individual tickets to Member's Hill cost $30 in advance, $35 at the gate.

Any number of party options are available, and invitees accept eagerly. Corporations, clubs, and associations have long recognized the entertainment value of the race. Political bigwigs are predictably present, adding incentive for lobbyist types to make the trip to Great Meadow.

MONTPELIER HUNT RACES
Montpelier Station, VA

When: November, first Saturday

Time: First race 12:30 P.M.

Contact: Montpelier Steeplechase
P.O. Box 67
Montpelier Station, VA 22957

Phone: 703-672-2728

Directions: From D.C., take I-66 west. Take the Warrenton exit, traveling south on Route 29. At Culpeper, turn south on Route 15. At Orange, follow the signs to the course via Route 20. Montpelier is a half hour trip from the Washington Beltway. The first race starts at 12:30 P.M. and traffic into the course via the one-lane road is ferocious, so allow plenty of time.

The drive to Montpelier is a reward in itself. With luck, the tail end of autumn colors are still clinging to the countryside. Route 29 from Warrenton is a good four-lane, lightly traveled road, so even the driver can enjoy the trip. Orange, the county seat and once General Robert E. Lee's winter headquarters, is a bustling market town going about its Saturday routine. However, down the road at sleepy Montpelier Station, which consists of a railroad siding and a general store, one enters a time warp which the mansion itself and surrounding countryside do nothing to jar.

Montpelier was the home of President James Madison and later of the duPont family. Following the death of Marion duPont Scott, the house and surrounding grounds, including the race course and stables, were given to the National Trust for Historic Preservation. The land came into Madison's family via a colonial grant made to President Madison's grandfather in 1723. When the future president married Dolley, the couple expanded the small brick house with the help of William Thornton, one of the architects for the Capitol in Washington. Following his term in office, distinguished visitors descended on the place like locusts. By the time of Madison's death, part of the original 10,000 acre tract had been sold, because it did not produce enough income to feed the hordes. Both President and Mrs. Madison are buried in a small graveyard overlooking farm fields at Montpelier.

William duPont, a principal in the family business, E.I.duPont de Nemours and Co., bought Montpelier in 1900. His daughter, Marion duPont Scott, reported in her memoirs that her father came to the area in search of a healthful environment in which to raise his children, Marion and Willie, away from the damp climate of the Delaware River. The house was greatly enlarged in a typical adaptation of the Georgian style. The gardens remain generally unchanged from the Madisons' time, as does the icehouse, which is shaped like a small, classic temple, similar to other garden follies of the time. The house is little changed from William duPont's day, though Marion added horse stables, the race course and a training track. Unlike the imposing mansion, the barns are no-nonsense, perfectly adequate structures ordered from Sears and Roebuck.

Mrs. Scott's love affair with horses began even before she moved to Montpelier. She was proficient riding side-saddle, the style of the day, but learned to ride astride, figuring it was the only way to beat men riders. In 1915, she became the first woman to win a blue ribbon at the National Horse Show at Madison

Square Garden in New York. Marion and Willie were also great foxhunters, and their skill led them to steeplechasing. Following the death of her parents in 1928, Marion built the steeplechase course and held the first race there the same year. She bred many champions at Montpelier. The homebred Battleship, son of Man Of War, became the first American horse to win the English Grand National Steeplechase. Her love of steeplechasing lasted to the end of her life. Besides Montpelier, Mrs. Scott developed the Springdale Training Center in Camden, SC, which is the home of the Carolina Cup and Colonial Cup Steeplechases.

The jumps at both Montpelier and Camden are not today's standard "National" fences, but rather big, natural brush favored by Mrs. Scott. This shakes things up a bit, as not every horse used to hopping over National fences can leap the large living hedges at Montpelier. After one of her favorite horses was critically injured in a timber race, Mrs. Scott never again owned a timber horse.

After Mrs. Scott died, a substantial timber course was added at Montpelier. To add interest to the race, it has become the final leg of a Virginia Fall Timber Series. The series winner collects a $7,500 bonus for earning the most points at Foxfield, the International Gold Cup and Montpelier, with the proviso that the winner must start in each of these races. This series assures that the best timber horses out in the fall will be at Montpelier the first Saturday in November as opposed to being at, say, the Pennsylvania Hunt Cup the same day.

Before the steeplechases begin, two flat races are held on the dirt training track in the center of the steeplechase course. The flat course is in full view of those who stand along the rail, but the view of jump courses is not good. Spectators are corralled on a slight rise in the center of the course. Tents and trees at times block the view of the horses. The course also drops behind the flat track, so should the other impediments be removed, there would always be that. To top it all off, the horses finish down the center of the course, the stretch being lined by a press of humans, blocking the view of those who have wandered onto the brow of the hill to watch the jumps. All of this sounds discouraging, but the course is beautiful and the race well worth the effort. The backdrop of the house adds to the magnificence of the natural hedges and lush turf. One wonders if the steps of the house wouldn't provide the best view of all. The people who can answer that question are the members of Congress and the state legislature who are special guests of the race as a thank-you for state and federal funding since Mrs. Scott's death.

Since the drive back will be in the dark, one might as well make reservations for dinner at one of the charming inns in the Orange or Sperryville-Little Washington-Flint Hill area, taking an alternate route home via Rt. 522 and Rt. 211 to Warrenton. Enjoying an admirable dinner at one of these spots that would otherwise be a "fur" piece from D.C. maximizes the whole day in the country. Or one can make a weekend of it by booking at a local inn or B&B. Be advised that accommodations are very limited and require advanced reservations. If this is your choice and you want to do it up right, make plans in advance to attend the gala the night before the race, an "elegant black-tie dinner dance" that costs $150 per person.

Admission: Parking options range from a paddock-side tent for $2,000 and up, to general parking for $5, general admission tickets $4 per person purchased in advance, $5 race day. Finish line parking may be the best option for access to the paddock, view of the finish and view of the flat track, costs $125; it includes admission for four. Infield parking in a non-reserved section costs $50, and RV parking is available for $200. Tickets to a pre-race luncheon cost $25 each (cash bar), and to an informal after-the-races party, $15. General admission and infield parking is infinite, but all three areas of reserved parking often sell out.

VIII

POLO

The True Significance of Those Little Men on Ralph Lauren Shirts

Polo is an ancient sport that looks very handsome when played in the modern world. The sport really is glamorous. One look at old polo photos makes you want to be a blond heiress or a handsome square-jawed fellow in swanky boots and camel's hair coat. Today, the blond heiress may be on the field, too, rather than gracefully slouching on the sideline. No wonder Ralph Lauren chose the polo emblem as his trademark. (Lauren, by the way, is an annual sponsor of the Washington, D.C., Capital Polo Club.)

Polo was probably first played in Persia about 600 B.C., shortly after the eureka! moment when man first attached stirrups to his saddle, thus providing the stability needed to swing the mallet. Polo was picked up in India by British officers stationed there. The first modern polo club was founded in Calcutta in 1862. Polo came to the U.S. by way of England. The Westchester Cup, an international match between the two countries, began in 1886, the year the U.S. Polo Association was founded. (It took another decade before the first U.S.P.A. club in Washington was recognized.) Although the Westchester Cup was discontinued in the '30s, it now has a counterpart in the National Capital Polo Association's annual match with the British Combined Services team, which is played biennially on Lincoln Mall Polo Field, located in West Potomac Park.

Opposing polo teams face off at West Potomac Park, across the street from the Lincoln Memorial.
Credit: © **The Washington Post.** *Reprinted by permission of the* **D.C. Public Library.**

Polo came to Virginia in 1921, when the Fauquier/Loudoun Club, which has since evolved into Middleburg Polo, was sanctioned. Back in the 1920s, polo was a way of life for some. In the '30s, wealthy polo players provided one of the few means of support for many in the depression-stricken Middleburg-Warrenton area of Virginia. They were playing polo at the Greenbrier in White Sulphur Springs in the '30s. The Army Polo Association, founded in 1902, changed its address to Washington in 1935. Polo exited when World War II erupted, but returned in 1968 when the field near Lincoln Mall was opened. The Maryland Polo Club, which now plays in Monkton, MD, was begun in the Baltimore area in 1926. Potomac Polo traces its roots to 1957, when Washington players started getting back in the swing of things in the wake of the war.

FIELDS

Middleburg's Kent Field is the oldest in the area, planned and planted by M.G. Phipps in the '30s. Its special attribute is Goose Creek, which waters it through summer droughts and helps fertilize it with spring floods. The large deciduous trees clinging to the creek's banks provide shade for spectators on the patrons' side of the field. The sand base of the field makes a comfortable cushion for the ponies.

Potomac boasts nine excellent playing fields. Their Number One Field, used for Sunday matches, is set for crowds, with a members' bar and enclosure at center field. Patrons' boxes, covered with gay striped awnings, top the enclosure. The adjoining corporate hospitality area, located next to the "Members", sports tables and chairs shaded by bright umbrellas. With ample bleacher space near the corporate area, general admission has not been forgotten.

Polo at the Mall features a beautiful, tree-lined field in sight of the Lincoln Memorial, Tidal Basin and Washington Monument. Players say that temperatures on the field are moderated through the playing season by gentle breezes off the nearby Potomac. The field has a sand base for good cushion, and grass there as elsewhere on the Mall is kept short and neat assuring a smooth playing surface.

Standard polo fields are 160 yards by 300 yards long, covering approximately 10 acres, which is the size of 10 football fields. Indoor and arena polo fields are smaller. Arena polo is played at the University of Virginia. Potomac has an indoor arena in addition to its numerous outdoors fields. Construction on an arena polo ring at Great Meadow, site of the Virginia Gold Cup Steeplechase, was completed in 1993.

Players say that a putting green, if dead level, would make an ideal field. The smoother and more regular the playing surface of a polo field, the better. Goals are 24 feet wide and at least 10 feet tall. Goal posts are padded for the protection of horse and rider. They are constructed to collapse on impact. Teams change ends of the field following each goal. Side boards are a maximum of 11 inches high. Ponies seem to have the ability to daintily skip from one side of the boards to the other without even breaking stride. The ends never have boards but are marked with end lines.

PONIES

Polo ponies are not actually ponies, a term usually applied to equines that measure no more than 52 inches at the shoulder (that's 14.2 hands in horse lingo, each hand being four inches). The term pony is assumed to be a carry-back to the days when small, hardy local beasts were used in India and across Asia for polo and polo-like games. Polo ponies may be any size and any breed, but high quality ponies are small thoroughbreds (about 15 hands). They may be registered, like their counterparts at the race track, or merely of the thoroughbred type. Players agree that the thoroughbred blood is needed for the speed of the local games. A player has to be able to hit the ball, but to do that, he has to get to it—that is the pony's job.

Prices for acceptably-trained ponies start at $5,000. Top ponies for high-goal polo can cost 10 times that. Owen Rhinehart, a Virginian and America's only current native-born, 10-goal player (polo's highest rating) owns 25 ponies. Rhinehart, like other top pros, is sponsored in his endeavors. Most of the players in the Washington area must do other work to support their polo habit. They need to own six to eight ponies to keep up with the fast-moving game played here.

Col. Robert O'Brien, who played through his service years and has seen action on polo fields both at Middleburg and on the Mall, says the main attribute he looks for in judging a prospective polo pony, aside from speed, is a willingness to make body contact with other ponies while galloping down the field. Most ponies can be trained to accept mallets whizzing around their heads, according to O'Brien, but not all will cope with the physical side of the sport, or accept full bridles and other polo rigs used to provide rapid braking power. The game is fast and confusing, so a pony must be absolutely obedient to his rider's commands, and nimble enough to spin and pirouette while following the constantly changing course of the game.

Stamina is another precious quality in good ponies. Because the game is so fast, ponies are seldom if ever asked to play more than one seven-minute period or chukker. When tournaments featuring out-of-town players are drawn up, scheduling is constructed to give the ponies a day or so between games to rest, when possible. Visiting foreign players and teams, like the British Combined Service that comes biennially to the Mall, are provided ponies by the host club.

STICKS AND BALLS

Mallets feature willow shafts and hardwood heads. They weigh about 18 ounces and are approximately 50 inches long, depending on the size of the player and height of the pony. Some players favor a particular length mallet, regardless, but most have a variety of sticks which are cued to the height of the pony. Balls, made of plastic or hollow wood, are 3½ to 4½ inches in diameter and weigh 4¼ ounces.

PLAYERS

Players come in all sizes and ages, but Joe Muldoon, Sr., patriarch of the Potomac polo monarchy, says that playing early and often really helps. Many players don't come to the game until middle age, when they have earned the wherewithal to afford it. A number of players in this area, particularly those who play at Middleburg, have had the leg up of exposure in the University of Virginia's fine intercollegiate polo. UVA trains both men's and women's teams.

The proximity of UVA at Charlottesville to D.C. and the number of graduates who settle near D.C. has added to the pool of very good players in the area. Started in the early '50s as an extra-curricular activity, the program now has 40 to 60 students participating at a given time. It is generously supported by alumni who feel they benefited from their playing days at UVA.

UVA offers the public a summer polo school, which has two-, four- and six-day clinics with a visiting pro. A prerequisite is riding ability, not playing skill. With reasonable dorm housing and fair prices, this gives a range of riders an opportunity to try out the game.

Muldoon, Sr. warns that polo can be a form of addiction and that the sky is the limit for the amount a player can spend to feed his habit. The Potomac Polo School, founded by Muldoon in 1981 and one of the oldest of its kind, does its part to keep polo strong in Maryland. The Potomac Polo School gives those who have not grown up in a polo-playing clan or come up through the ranks of play at a prep school or university a chance to take lessons prior to investing in horse trailers, backyard barns, multiple horses and other accoutrements of the game.

In Argentina, little tykes on the large haciendas are given small scaled sticks and ponies early on, and this helps more than anything to build that country's large store of high rated players, Muldoon claims. This theory is backed by the fact that the highest rated players in the D.C. area are products of polo playing families, including Muldoon's own sons Joe, III and Charlie, a five-goaler. Ten-goaler Owen Rhinehart grew up in the Charlottesville area playing with his kin. His father and brother grace the fields at Middleburg when their Ivy team plays there.

Women may play if and where they can, and it is not unusual for one or two of the players on a given Sunday to be women. Polo requires riding ability, which women can more than master. In addition, carrying and repeatedly swinging polo mallets for the rapid moving 42 to 45 minutes of regulation play requires a certain amount of upper body strength, though seasoned players can cite examples of slightly (or unathletically) built players who mastered the game by employing smooth, effortless swings and follow-throughs akin to those of top golfers. Polo also requires hand-eye coordination. One player likened it most to shooting skeet, which requires the same lightning fast reaction to a rapidly moving object.

DRESS—PLAYERS' AND SPECTATORS'

Players' typical kits include white breeches and brown leather boots, a T- or polo shirt in the team colors, a regulation protective helmet, knee protectors, whip, and a mallet scaled to the player's size and the height of his pony. Some wear blunt spurs and a face guard as well.

A review of old volumes of the U.S. Polo Association's annual yearbook shows players back then wore T-shirts. It was not until the early '50s that knit shirts with collars, now known as polo shirts, made their appearance, at first on California teams. Ralph Lauren cleverly put little polo players on his version of this sports classic and called it the Polo (with a capital P) shirt. His entire line of clothing became known as the Polo brand.

The crowds watching matches can be pretty swank, too, depending on the location and circumstances. At Potomac on a hot summer afternoon, attire ranges from neat Bermuda shorts to slacks or jeans accented by very casually draped Hermes scarves. Tournaments and the accompanying cocktail parties inspire a dressier look at Potomac. The attire of the everyday crowd at Middleburg ranges from neat, conservative sportswear devoid of any flashy displays of designer labels, to handsome and correct coaching attire for those who drive horses, not cars, to the match. Some regulars turn out in big straw hats and Sunday-go-to-meeting dresses, with men in boaters and snappy summer wear. On the other hand, the large crowds who show up for Capital Polo look pretty much like run-of-the-mill D.C. tourists.

HANDICAP

The U.S. Polo Association annually assesses and rates all registered players, assigning handicaps ranging from -2 to a top of 10. The handicap system permits teams of individuals of uneven ability to play a competitive match. Often the term "goal" follows the number assigned, but the rating is not to suggest the number of actual goals the player is expected to score on a given day. Rather it represents a subjective rating of his ability against other players. For example, if the sum of handicaps of one team is five, and that of their opponents is eight, the team with the lesser tally starts the match with an automatic score of three to zero.

Polo in the Capital area is pretty good polo—in the five- to 12-goal category. The higher the goal polo being played, the faster the game.

Most of the players on area teams carry ratings of one to three. More of a range is seen at Potomac, where neophytes from the polo school may be rated minus one or zero. This is offset by a mingling of pros and local lights like Charlie Muldoon who carries a rating of five plus. Matches in the five- to eight-goal range are common in the area, with matches of 12 or better held throughout the season, especially at Potomac.

Not on a par with polo centers in California and Palm Beach, Washington nevertheless has long been a polo mecca, and offers about the highest level play non-pros can hope to achieve. To earn a rating of six and above, one must play high-goal polo—over 12 goals. To do that, one must either be an extraordinary player or be able to bankroll his own team of Argentinean pros.

THE GAME

The game begins when the umpire throws the ball in between opposing players, as in basketball. Goals are earned when players or their ponies put the ball through the opponents' goal. When a goal is scored, the teams swap ends of the field and play begins again from mid-field with a toss-in by the ump. The toss-in is also used when a ball goes out on the sideline. If a ball goes out the end, the opposing team shoots it back in.

The game is divided into six seven-minute chukkers, divided by a ten-minute half time. A whistle is blown at the end of a chukker, but if the ball is still in play, the chukker extends to 7½ minutes. If the score is tied or nil, play is resumed following the final chukker and continues until one team scores. A brief pause, a maximum of five minutes, occurs between chukkers so that players can dash back to their trailers to exchange their hot horses for fresh and waiting mounts. Do not stand daydreaming on the path between the trailers and field while this maneuver occurs. And be prepared for the venerable polo tradition of stomping down divots during the half to level off the spots where the ponies' hooves have marred the turf.

OFFICIALS

Two mounted umpires officiate, backed up by a referee in the stands who arbitrates if the umpires disagree or need advice on a technical point of the game. In lieu of a mallet, umpires carry a pickup stick, which is fitted with a special cup for scooping up the ball in case of a toss-in or a foul. A goal judge stands behind each goal, signaling when a goal has been scored. A timekeeper keeps the clock. Local teams have knowledgeable announcers who do play-by-plays during the game. The umpire blows his whistle to stop the clock in case of a foul, safety, serious injury, broken tack or broken ball. Time is not stopped for a broken mallet, or for a fall, unless the rider is injured or the loose horse interferes with the game.

TEAMS

Teams are made up of four players each. In games of four or fewer goals, unlimited substitution is permitted. In higher-goal games, substitutions are permitted if a player is unable to finish a game.

Players wear numbers 1 through 4. Each number fulfills a different function. Numbers 1 and 2 push forward the offensive game, moving the ball towards the opponents' goal. Logically, Number 1 pushes forward in advance of Number 2, taking the shot or peeling off for his Number 2. Number 2 passes the ball forward to Number 1 from Number 3, or takes the goal shot set up for him. Number 3 is generally the team captain and the best and most versatile player. Number 3 often calls the shots, carries the offense for Number 2 if need be, or helps Number 4 (the back) defend the goal. The back provides goal line defense and is to turn back the other team's Number 1. All is lost for the offensive team if their Number 1 loses the ball to their foes' Number 4. In theory, the opposing Number 4 covers Number 1, Number 3 covers 2, 2 covers 3, and 1 covers 4. As play continues downfield a skillful team rolls off, continually changing positions to carry the ball forward. Players are intent not only on carrying the ball forward toward their own goal, or taking it from opponents and reversing the direction of play, but also with keeping the men they are covering away from the ball.

FOULS

Polo is like a very fast sailboat race in that rules are strict in regards to right of way based on an imaginary line. The line in sailing is reckoned by the direction of the wind. In polo the line of the ball counts. When a player has established his right of way on the line of the ball, the line may not be crossed by an opposing player in such a way as to raise the risk of collision. Otherwise, body contact between opposing players is permitted. A player can push his opponent off the ball, using his own body, but not his elbow. Body contact is also permitted between the ponies, unlike the rules at the race track where pushing, shoving or even making intimidating moves are not tolerated. This body contact, similar to blocking in football, heightens the rough and ready aspect of polo.

A player may also hook an opponent's mallet to spoil a shot, provided the mallet is not raised above shoulder height, or between the pony's legs. Fouls are called for illegal stick work, dangerous riding, or delay of game.

Timeout is called when the umpire blows his whistle to signal a foul. Team captains may discuss penalties with the umpire, but other players may be sent off the field for jawing at officials. Penalties for fouls range from a toss-in, like that in basketball, to free shot. Unlike basketball, where the man fouled takes the shot, the team designates the player for a free shot.

Now, here are the details on area polo venues:

 MIDDLEBURG POLO
Kent Field
Middleburg, VA

When: Sundays, May through September, field conditions permitting. Most years, play begins in mid-May.

Time: Match begins at 1:30 P.M.

Contact: Middleburg Polo
P.O. Box 908
Leesburg, VA 22075

Phone: Game schedule and cancellations 703-777-0775

Directions: From D.C., exit west from I-66 onto Route 50. Proceed through Middleburg approximately five miles to Crenshaw Road, Route 624. Turn left and proceed to field, about one mile on the right just after crossing Goose Creek. There is a sign on Route 50.

Middleburg plays on a field in a bend of the omnipresent Goose Creek, which courses picturesquely through the prime hunt country and pasture land of northern Fauquier and southern Loudoun counties. Kent Field, against the verdant backdrop of Goose Creek is as pretty a setting as you will find. It is one of the oldest fields in the area, dating from the days when the Phipps and other racing families filled their summers with polo and winters with foxhunting. The field is privately owned by Redskins owner Jack Kent Cooke. Formerly the field was owned by art patron Paul Mellon, then by Senator John Warner. The club maintains the field with members' dues and support from subscribers.

Organized games have been held in the area since 1921, when the Fauquier-Loudoun (later, changed to Middleburg) Polo Club was recognized by the U.S. Polo Association. Nowadays, other than the regular patrons (pronounced pat-ROONS, in the Spanish manner), who turn out to cheer on the home team, few spectators find their way back to Kent Field. R.C. Riemenschneider, a Middleburg player who serves as executive vice president of the U.S. Polo Association, says that the team enjoys spectators, but turns its limited resources towards field maintenance, not publicity and advertising. Annual subscribers receive reserved parking on the creek side of the field. They come weekly, often by Benz or by four-in-hand carriage.

The whole scene at Kent Field is unassuming and quaint. Even without previous experience watching polo, spectators can sense that at Middleburg players are participating for the sheer joy of the game, without the glory of big crowds or high profile tournaments. Medium goal polo, in the five- to eight-goal range, is played at Middleburg. Teams are drawn from the Virginia Polo League, a loose confederation that keeps tabs on the U.S.P.A. clubs in the area and on the players' handicaps for the purpose of scheduling matches and keeping track of wins. In July, playoffs are held between the most successful teams in the league.

Players for Middleburg carry ratings of from one to three goals. They are drawn from UVA alumni and local horsemen who cross over from racing and hunting. Former Middleburg players who still come around to help with announcing and officiating include retired foreign service and military officers. The Rappahannock team, which plays regularly at Middleburg as well as on their home field in Laurel Mills, VA, survived regional play-offs and bested 46 teams to win the President's Cup, the U.S. Polo Association's national eight goal tournament. The play-offs for the President's Cup are held in conjunction with the U.S. Open Polo Tournament.

Admission: The annual subscription of $160 includes prime reserved parking and season passes for four. General admission costs $5 per person. General admission parking is on the road side of the course. Those who desire to have their picnics by the creek may enquire as to the availability of a one-day subscription.

No matter where you park, do at least walk over for a better view of the creek and a closer look at the often-present carriages. At the trailer area you can view the preparation that goes into getting each mount ready for action. Be sure to stand well out of harm's way, particularly when players charge in after each chukker to switch mounts. The scene reveals the scale of commitment on the part of the players. Each comes with a trailer full of ponies that stand picketed waiting their turn during the match. Each player also brings a pickup truck full of bridles, mallets, martingales and bandages, and all have at least one hardworking groom. Occasionally family members are recruited as well to keep the wheels humming backstage.

 POTOMAC POLO CLUB
River Road
Potomac, MD

When: Matches are held from the second Sunday in May through mid-October

Time: Games start at 3:00 P.M.

Contact: Potomac Polo
5101 Wisconsin Ave., Suite 508
Washington, D.C. 20016

Phone: Game schedule and cancellations 301-972-7757

Directions: From D.C., exit the Beltway onto Route 190, River Road. Follow River Road north for 12 miles. Turn left at the stop sign by the Brentwood Golf Course and follow the continuation of River Road to the fields. From northern Virginia, there's an alternate, scenic, perhaps shorter, though not necessarily faster, route. Take White's Ferry, which is located off Route 15 north of Leesburg to Poolesville, MD. One mile beyond Poolesville, turn right on Budd Road to Hughs Road. Turn left and continue several miles to the field, which is at the corner of Hughs and River roads.

Potomac Polo Club boasts nine primo playing fields. Fed by the Potomac Polo School, scrimmages and actual matches are held throughout the weekend. The feature event is held at 3:00 P.M. Sundays on the main playing field. Though attendance at the games has been off recently, the place is set up for crowds and the public is both welcomed and made to feel comfortable. It is not lack of quality of play that has caused a decline in numbers of viewers, but lack of promotion. The club has no problem finding sponsors for its tournaments. Sponsors generally host catered luncheons in a special area adjoining the members' enclosure. On the grounds directly behind the members' enclosure is a large indoor riding hall, used for lessons and competition in the winter and opened for large company picnics and special polo functions at other times. This area is leased to concessionaires who provide catering, hayrides, staging for bluegrass bands and other trappings that go along with special events. Those scheduled for Sundays, of course, include polo.

Potomac has players in the four- and five-goal range. The club can field 12-goal matches from its own numbers. For higher-goal matches, firepower is added from the ranks of foreign pros. Potomac sponsors polo on the Mall in Washington and often sends teams to play there. Special tournaments include several 12-goal tilts, an eight-goal tournament, the Embassy of Chile match and a game against the popular British Combined Services Team. Further, club members travel to Palm Beach, Mexico and other venues to gain high-goal playing experience.

Admission: General admission is $5 per person. Grandstands, located at mid-field right next to the corporate area, are provided for the general public. Railside spaces, available almost always, may be purchased for the day for $15, and this is a good alternative if one wants to plan an event and take along pals. Full social membership costs $300 initially with a price break for renewals and under the age of 30. Social membership includes access to the Members' enclosure, plus invitations to all social events. One must be a social or playing member in order to purchase box seats or season railside parking. Covered boxes cost $200 for the season and are located on the upper level of the members' enclosure. Railside parking costs $150 and $100, depending on location, for the season.

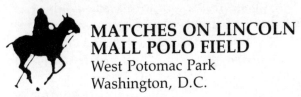

MATCHES ON LINCOLN MALL POLO FIELD
West Potomac Park
Washington, D.C.

When: Matches are played on Sundays at 3:00 P.M., May through October. Occasionally, the match times will vary—signs on Ohio Drive indicate playing times. The field is closed in August. If you find yourself there an hour early due to a last-minute change, you can take a walk to the Lincoln Memorial. If the game is canceled, you can take in one of the museums on the Mall.

Phone: The National Park Service, 202-426-6841

Directions: The field is located between Independence and Ohio Drive just west of the Tidal Basin and across the street from the Lincoln Memorial. Street-side parking can be found on Ohio Drive.

The U.S. Polo Association, as noted earlier, recognized the Washington Polo Club in 1896. Unlike other clubs listed in the U.S.P.A. yearbook, the Washington club did not list players and their handicaps. Perhaps the club organized matches between teams of players temporarily stationed to Washington. Whatever its modus operandi, the charter of the Washington club was dropped way back when. The U.S. Army changed the address of its chartered team to Washington in 1938. Officers stationed in the nation's capital long played polo on a field across Ohio Drive from the current field. Until the war, polo had been a

158

major preoccupation both at cavalry and at artillery posts. Back in the '30s, then Major George Patton wrote that polo, along with steeplechasing and football, best approximated the constant and real physical hazards of battle. If a man had faced no more risk than dodging autos while crossing a street, he said, the "insinuating whisper of bullets about his sacred person will have a more disquieting influence than would be the case had this same person received frequent cuts and broken bones on the polo field."

Those who were around at the time remember the sight of Patton and other Army players coming across Memorial Bridge, riding one horse, leading four more, for Sunday matches. Be-

General George S. Patton, Jr., at the head of the column, and other officers played polo while stationed at Fort Myer in 1940. Patton was a colonel at the time this photo was taken.
Credit: Courtesy of the Old Guard Museum at Fort Myer

sides Patton, Generals Devers, Wainwright, Truscott and Waters played on Ohio Drive regularly until 1941.

Patton's philosophy must have been viewed as sound through numerous branches of the service. In 1938, the U.S.P.A. Southeastern Circuit Championship was played at Potomac Park. Represented were eight military teams, of which only one, Quantico Marines, was drawn from the naval services. The third U.S. Cavalry triumphed over the War Department in that tournament, by the way. In 1941, two of the best teams in the nation, Texas and Meadow Brook, played in an all-star match at Potomac Park in a benefit dubbed "Bundles for Britain." The biggest crowd of the year for a polo match turned out to see 10-goaler Cecil Smith, aided by Michael Phipps, Winston Guest and J.P. Grace, ride to victory for the Texas team. Polo ground to a halt in the war years that followed, and afterwards first re-emerged in Maryland.

John J. Sted, who played polo as an undergraduate at Kenyon College pre-WWII, saw polo moving further and further away from the nation's capital. To reverse the trend, he founded the National Capital Polo Association. With the National Park Service and the non-profit West Potomac Park Beautification Foundation, Sted headed the move to claim an area for the field once covered by makeshift buildings used by the military. The factory-like buildings, erected during WWI and WWII, were torn down during the Johnson administration. Tons and tons of soil were moved in to cover curbs, manholes and the foundations of the buildings. Though more soil is added each year, players claim to this day they can feel the remnants of those buildings as they gallop down the field. The Franklin D. Roosevelt Memorial was penciled in for this area, but has never been built. The current field is right across Ohio Drive from the polo field long used by military leaders. Play on the field began in 1968.

U.S.P.A. recognizes the National Capital Polo Association, but the group who form the home team is better known as the Lincoln Mall Polo Club. Today, major support for the field is received from the Potomac Polo Club. Three Potomac players currently draw up the schedule of play, and tend to week-to-week details of the games. The Park Service maintenance of the area is further enhanced by the West Potomac Park Beautification Foundation, which provides grass seed, hedges, labor and materials over and above the Park Service budget. The Park Service provides grass seeding and regular maintenance accorded other open spaces and playing fields on the Mall. The Foundation won tax-free status in 1979. At that point the largest donor, coming in with $1,000, was Michael Butler, the promoter of the hit musical, "Hair." Today, the Foundation beefs up donations with an annual formal party at the British Embassy.

Players love the Ohio Drive field because, some say, large crowds gather to cheer them on. Certainly there are enough people wandering around the Mall on a seasonable Sunday to swell the ranks of spectators to several thousand. The temperate influence of the Potomac permits play earlier in May and later in the fall than at other area fields. Breezes off the Potomac and the large old oaks that shade the sides of the field provide relief to spectators and to players and ponies between periods. Again, this is a good spot from which to view the behind-the-scenes activity associated with polo. Trailers are parked on the grass on the Lincoln Memorial side of the field. Ponies and crowds are separated by rope fences, and their path onto the playing field is similarly delineated. One can stand very close, though. Watching players slouch back in director chairs planning their campaign, one is again struck by the stylish good looks long associated with the sport.

Two U.S.P.A tournaments that have been held at the Lincoln Mall field are the Eastern finals for the six-goal Governor's Cup and the ten-goal Centennial tournament. Other tournaments and charity benefits are held throughout the season. International matches are staged when possible; Barbados, the British Combined Services team, Tidworth (England), and Pakistan are among the opponents local Virginia and Maryland teams have faced on the West Potomac Park field. The international flavor adds a nice bit of dash. One veteran of the early days of Lincoln Mall Polo recalls staging a match in which locals were used liberally to bolster the British Service Team. The surprised British ambassador, who presented the trophy, asked one of the American stand-ins what regiment he was a member of and was given instead the number of a U.S.Army Division. The British Combined Service tournament, with a full complement of British officers, has lived on to become a mainstay of Capital Polo events. In even years, the British team plays on the Mall, generally the Sunday after Labor Day. Alternate years Capital polo players travel to England for a match. The host team provides ponies, transportation, housing and hospitality for the visiting team.

Admission: General admission to the matches is free. Parking along Ohio Drive is free on weekends. Chairs are even available in the area near the announcer. Spectators may also pitch blankets or set their own folding chairs almost any old place along the rail. Be advised that shade is not available right along the rail, so wear sunscreen and a hat. For a fee of $125, patrons receive railside parking passes for the year.

MARYLAND POLO CLUB
Ladew Topiary Gardens
Monkton, MD 21111

When: Sundays, mid-May to September

Time: 3:00 P.M.

Contact: Maryland Polo Club
P.O. Box 214
Monkton, MD 21111

Phone: 410-557-6448 (number activated annually May 1)

Directions: From D.C., take I-95 north to I-695 toward Towson, MD. Exit on 27B on MD Route 146 north for 14 miles to Ladew Topiary Gardens, which are on the right.

Monkton, MD, is a bit of a hike from D.C. On the other hand, good quality polo and an opportunity to see beauteous Ladew Topiary Gardens where the Sunday playing fields are located justify the trip. Ladew has topiary to delight all comers; riders will especially admire the boxwood fox and hounds that gallop through the garden. The polo club leases a portion of land from Ladew and the two exist separately.

The club of 30 to 40 members plays other days, too, on three fields located on various members' farms. In the off-season, arena polo is played at Garrison Forest. Polo, long a tradition in the horsey Glyndon-Monkton-Elkridge area of Maryland, lay dormant for almost a half century, until revived in 1986 by members of the local foxhunting and steeplechasing community. As in Virginia, a number of the founding players are graduates of the successful University of Virginia program.

Admission: Admission to Ladew Gardens costs $5 for a self-guided tour, or $7 for a guided tour of the house and gardens. The fee for polo is $10 per car.

PACK THE COOLER, BUT . . .

The Washington Post carries polo schedules in its Friday "Weekend" section, as do local papers in the Potomac and Middleburg areas. It is always best to call before setting out, however. The decision to play or not to play can be made as late as Sunday morning after careful examination of the field. The fields are only used if the footing is near perfect. Playing on a wet field can render it unplayable for weeks to come. Slippery conditions must be avoided at all cost, because it would be too dangerous to attempt the quick stops and sharp turns on anything but ideal footing. Matches may be canceled on a bluebird sunny day due to rain earlier in the week.

Since crowds are usually small, reservations are not needed. Weather cancellation can lead to disappointment, especially in the case of a tournament. Once when the annual Arthritis Benefit match at Middleburg was called off because of a wet field, organizers, who had sold tickets and planned a big whoop-de-do, served the wine and had the party anyway, sans a game. They called it the phantom match and had a good time anyway.

From the standpoint of watching the crowd or a top live athletic performance, Sunday afternoon polo matches provide a good alternative to watching the telly. The setting is aesthetically pleasing and the required physical activity is minimal. The quintessential couch potato will not be pressed beyond reaching into the picnic basket for another peeled grape or cucumber sandwich.

IX

HORSE SHOWS

The Oldest and the Best

As much racing as there is in Maryland and Virginia, there is even more horse showing. Upperville, the nation's oldest horse show, and the Washington International, one of the top four indoor shows in North America, are interesting spectator events. Some of the others are riveting if your 12-year-old granddaughter is competing, but less compelling for the rest of us. Shows in Maryland or Virginia, from big American Horse Shows Association A-rated affairs to small country shows, attract beautiful horses and top riders and are entertaining in small doses. To help the newcomer understand the jargon of horse showing, class and breed specifications follow in this chapter.

Most horse shows start early and end late: in between, there is a lot of sameness. Like CNN Headline News, they can be watched until the same stories start coming up for the second time. Horse shows are held every weekend of the year, and many weekdays through the temperate months. Very few shows charge an admission fee and spectators are welcome. In addition to Washington International and Upperville, details on Warrenton and Washington Bridle Trails shows, along with state and county fair shows, follow. More information about the numerous shows held weekly or monthly at training stables and horse show complexes may be found in Appendix A.

Both Virginia and Maryland have highly organized horse show associations, which schedule sophisticated circuits. Large

Upperville, the nation's oldest horse show, features
venerable oaks and very good show hunters.
Credit: © **The Washington Post.** *Reprinted by permission
of the D.C. Public Library.*

boarding and teaching barns schedule their own show circuits, with competitions once or twice a month. Finally, there are several multi-million dollar horse show complexes that schedule a variety of horse events throughout the year.

Suburban newspapers usually list area shows, and local tack shops have the scoop on anything about horses. Upperville and Washington International are two must-sees to note on your calendar. Most other shows can be incorporated as a few hours' entertainment on a day devoted to enjoying the countryside.

UPPERVILLE COLT AND HORSE SHOW
Grafton Farm
Upperville, VA

When: June, first weekend. Show runs Tuesday through Sunday.

Time: Classes start at 8:00 A.M. daily and last until dark. The $50,000 Michelob-Upperville Jumper Classic begins at 2:30 P.M. Sunday and is generally over by 5:00 P.M.

Contact: Upperville Colt and Horse Show
             P.O. Box 1288
             Warrenton, VA 22186

Phone: 703-347-2612

Directions: From D.C., take I-66 west to Route 50 west. Travel through Middleburg toward Upperville. The show grounds are located on both sides of Route 50 just east of Upperville. Hunters and young horses are shown at Grafton Farm on the south side of the road, jumpers on the Salem Farm or on the north side of the road.

Upperville is where horse showing began in 1853, and continues each June. The show is still held under the same venerable oaks, and it may be the most beautiful setting for a horse show to be found. The show continues along in the tradition of that original show, featuring classes for beautiful young colts and fillies raised, for the most part, on area farms. Through the years, a variety of performance classes have been added. These, along with the divine setting, diverse shops set up around the arena and quality of performances, equal a day hard to beat.

The nation's oldest show was founded for the purpose of encouraging production of top breeding stock, with a class for colts and one for fillies. A magazine report of the 1857 show listed classes added for riding stock and draft horses, along with an extended program for young horses—one-, two- and three-year-olds. Such was the interest in the show that the Upperville Union was formed to encourage breed improvements. In a public spirited act, the founder of the show, Richard Henry Dulany, bought champion stallions and made them available for mating with local mares. Dulany purchased a Morgan, a descendant of Justin Morgan and the prize-winner at the Vermont State Fair, and Scrivington, a Cleveland Bay, winner of the Royal Agricultural Show in England. In later years, Scrivington escaped Yankee annexation during the Civil War by being sent to Pennsylvania with Dulany's black groom. After the war, the faithful servant and stallion returned to Virginia.

The show was temporarily discontinued during the Civil War, springing to life again in June 1869. The show has been held on its original show date and show grounds ever since. Records are sketchy for some of the years, but an official program indicates that by 1902, the show had been expanded to two days. Pony and driving classes, as well as classes for saddle horses and hunters had been added. That year, thoroughbred divisions were included along with draft breeds.

Through time, the feature class became the High Jump. In 1958 the High Jump was won by a local 18-year-old, Kathy Kusner, who set a world's record for women by clearing 7'2½" riding an old, gray mare named Freckles.

The High Jump class has been supplanted by the Michelob-Upperville Jumper Classic, featuring not one jump of ever-increasing size, but an entire afternoon of Olympic-level riders tackling a difficult course of jumps that start at four to five feet, with spreads up to six feet and a water jump ten feet wide. The course is technically difficult and draws about 50 entries.

More than 5,000 pay to see the Jumper Classic. The competition is easy to follow, even for the uninitiated, because the name of the game is to complete the course without knocking down or avoiding any jump, either by balking or running out.

Faults are given for falls of rider and/or horse. Horses that exceed a pre-determined time limit are also given penalties. Should two or more horses jump the course without a fault, a timed jump-off is held over a shortened, but even more difficult, course.

Holding the big jumping class on the Salem Farm side of the road gives the course designer a larger span of grass and slightly rolling terrain to put up a long and challenging course. Unfortunately, it lacks the beautiful oak trees of the Upperville ring, placing spectators, box seat holders and general admission alike, in the middle of a field. In June, that means it can be hot. Spectators should slather themselves with sunscreen, even if the day is overcast, and wear a hat.

Those who journey to Upperville to the Jumper Classic should arrive before noon, if possible, in order to enjoy classes for young horses and the up-scale booths on the Grafton Farm side of the show. The classes for young thoroughbreds and non-thoroughbreds are shown "on the line"—led by their reins, rather than ridden—under the magnificent oak trees. Rather than being judged on jumping ability, horses are compared for conformation and potential. Since they are, for the most part, too young to ride, entries in the breeding classes are led around the ring. Judges first eye their movement and overall body shapes, then have them line up so they can carefully assess their builds. Finally, horses are lined up head-to-tail in the order of the judges' preferences and given a final going over. Meanwhile, some of Virginia's best horsemen mill around the center of the ring, making their own mental notes about the comparative worth of the entries.

Classes are divided into thoroughbreds and non-thorough-breds, fillies and colts, and by age groups. Fuzzy-tailed foals, with moms comforting them close by their sides, parade around the ring, as do large, beautifully formed yearlings. The sights and sounds of the strange new world can rile some young horses. The two- and three-year-olds, for the most part, are old hands at striking a pose for the judges. The broodmares, the grand dames of the show, stand at the in-gate watching their beautiful babies. Virginia horsemen have selectively bred horses for hunting since before Upperville was founded. The quality of the horses shown will be apparent even to the novice. It is simply an opportunity not to be missed for those who love horses!

Outside the ring, merchants hawk hand-knit sweaters in horsey motifs, antique jewelry with equestrian twists, fanciful hats, and such utilitarian things as tractor-trailer loads of tack and riding supplies. The blacksmith sets up a booth under the spreading oak tree. Horses and riders can be seen preening and warming up in the nearby practice ring.

Very good hunters and jumpers are shown Tuesday, Wednesday, Thursday and Friday. Though the classifications vary, formats are similar.

Saturday offers more variety. That day, classes in Ring Number One, as the main ring in front of the stands is designated, include a pony breeding division along with performance classes for ponies and junior riders (under 18). The variety comes with the leadline classes, 30 or so children six and under, some so young they are strapped on the back of fat, dog-sized ponies in English wicker baskets. Then comes the walk-trot class, for children just old enough to show on their own, followed by the hotly contested family class, with several generations, often on perfectly matched horses, riding together against other family units. The ladies sidesaddle division follows, with elegant horses and riders showing over fences as well as on the flat. The local hunter division is as hotly contested as any classes anywhere during the year. As one sage pointed out, within the 60-mile "local" radius of Upperville, one finds a majority of the national champions in the hunter division. You can bet these folks like to win at their big local show.

Food is pretty good at Upperville and the prices are reasonable. The Ladies' Auxiliary of the Upperville Volunteer Fire Department, beneficiaries of the show, dish out mean bacon and egg sandwiches in the morning, grilled burgers for lunch, and homemade desserts. A frozen yogurt stand provides welcomed treats should the weather be warm. At the Jumper Classic, picnics from home prevail, and impressive spreads are also spotted at reserved parking spaces around Ring One on the hunter side of the road.

Admission: Reserved parking spaces that line the Grafton Farm side of the road cost $125. Those around Ring One sell out. Front row boxes at Ring One cost $100, second row $75. Those who wish seating or parking in either of these areas should call at least a month in advance. Box seats that line the course for the Jumper Classic cost $125. This area fills up, too, but those who call ahead can be accommodated. General admission during the run of the show for those without reserved parking or seats costs $5 per person. General admission parking is on the Salem Farm side of the road. The meadow slopes up from the Jumper Ring, providing good seats for everyone for the Jumper Classic. No seating is provided for general admission, so bring a blanket or chairs.

Several words of warning: first, spectators on the Salem side should protect themselves from the sun. Second, it can rain during Upperville, and when that happens the world turns to mud. Tractors stand by to promptly pull out hapless motorists without charge. At day's end, traffic does not move promptly in either wet or dry conditions, since everybody leaves at the same time.

 ## WASHINGTON INTERNATIONAL HORSE SHOW
USAir Arena (formerly known as the Capital Centre)
Washington, D.C.

When: October, begins and ends on a Sunday. Dates vary, due to the need for coordinating with the New York National and Toronto Royal Winter Agricultural Fair. Special classes: Hunt Night, the first Sunday of the show; Handy Working Hunter, Monday night; international jumping, Tuesday night through the final Sunday night.

Time: Classes start at 2:30 P.M. and 7:00 P.M. the first Sunday, and at 8:00 A.M. and 7:30 P.M. Monday through Friday. The final weekend classes start at 7:00 A.M. and 7:00 P.M.

Contact: Washington International Horse Show
9079 Shady Grove Court
Gaithersburg, MD 20877

Phone: 301-840-0281

Directions: From D.C., travel east on Pennsylvania Avenue. From northern Virginia, take I-66 to the Beltway; take Exit 15A.

Each night has special features, including terrier races, dressage (in which horses gracefully perform movements to music), draft horse hitches, champion cutting horses working cattle, classes for ladies riding sidesaddle and celebrity appearances.

The Washington International Horse Show is one of the few shows in the area that strives to create entertainment for the spectators, both through exhibits and its class schedule. At most shows, competitors are happy enough to have good judges and ring conditions, forget about cheering fans. In fact, daytime classes at the International are standard hunter and horsemanship stuff. Few spectators come in the daytime. By limiting the number of entries, the show avoids the complete monotony sometimes seen at horse shows. Participants have qualified for the opportunity by winning the most points and prize money at other shows. In fact, some riders show their horses all year in hopes of qualifying for Washington, the New York National (now actually held in New Jersey at the Meadowlands Sports Complex), and the Pennsylvania National in Harrisburg, PA.

Qualification standards assure good quality entries, and the board and staff of the show work hard to make certain the entertainment factor is there for paying customers. They offer a variety of horse acts and exhibitions in addition to the international jumper division. Each year, three or more teams are invited to compete against representatives of the United States Equestrian Team (USET) at Washington and then again at the New York National and Toronto's Royal Winter Fair. Classes are held each night culminating in the $50,000 International Open Jumper President's Cup Grand Prix on the final Sunday.

Nightly international jumping classes offer interesting variety. A favorite is the $10,000 Crown Royal Gambler's Choice Stakes. Competitors are given a time limit to complete as many jumps as they can in whatever order they choose. Each jump is posted with a numerical value—the more difficult are given higher ratings. Riders chalk up the highest number of points possible for clearing jumps in the allowed time. The pair relay is a variation on the same theme, with two riders trying to earn the highest total points over a set course.

Thursday night is always Diplomats' Night, when invited members of Washington's diplomatic community come to cheer for their nation's team versus the USET. Members of the horse

U.S. Equestrian team member Katie Monahan makes a good effort in the Puissance Class at the Washington International Horse Show.
Credit: © **The Washington Post.** *Reprinted by permission of the D.C. Public Library.*

show board and their invited guests wear evening gowns and black tie or hunting scarlet on Diplomats Night, Hunt Night and on the final night of the show.

The puissance class, or test of power, is featured on Saturday night. In this class, the course of jumps is short, but the jumps are of the greatest height. USET member Anthony d'Ambrosio set the show's record at 7'7½" in 1983. One year petite Margie Goldstein, riding with her leg in a cast from a previous mishap, came within a hair of clearing 7'8½." Her big white horse Daydream barely scraped a hind hoof over the mammoth wall, but flipped his slight rider off on the landing side when he made a final magnanimous effort to get his hind feet over the jump.

The show program carries the criteria for the jumper classes and they are easy to follow. The big souvenir program carries lots of other information and plenty of color. Published well in advance, the $7 program is not the final authority on entries, or dead accurate about scheduling. For this, nightly lists of the jumping lineup are handed out.

In recent years the show has added dressage exhibitions. The final weekend classes are held on Saturday, and on Sunday, when the U.S. League Final for the Volvo Dressage World Cup opens the evening performance. The four Americans who qualify for the class by earning the highest scores through the year compete with the winner, qualifying for the World Dressage Cup in Sweden. The 1992 U.S. finals were a bang-up success, won by Carol Lavell on Gifted, who had been the unexpected bronze medalist in the Olympics at Barcelona and spearhead of the most successful U.S. Dressage Team since 1980. Each exhibition is performed in a darkened ring under a spotlight, with the horse and rider performing a graceful ballet, choreographed to music.

On Hunt Night, the first Sunday, members of the many area hunt clubs pour into USAir Arena to cheer on members of their club. In the finale, the hunt team class, three members in full hunting regalia take a course single file Indian style, in theory coming abreast over the final jump. Jumps and courses for Hunt Night are made to simulate obstacles encountered in the hunt field, as opposed to the brightly painted and decorated jumps used in the jumper classes or in the classes for show hunters. Bear in mind that field hunters that have spent their lives in fields are not accustomed to the buzzing, brightly-lit USAir Arena. This can lead to some erratic behavior. When done right, as the Rappahanock team from Sperryville, VA, winners in 1991 and 1992 did it, teams fan out on the final turn and take the final jumps abreast. When hit spot on, the effect looks sharp.

The Jack Russell Terrier Races, long a feature of the show, are very popular. The spunky little Jack Russells are a favorite of the hunt and jump crowd. Perhaps this affinity is in part explained by the fact that terriers are traditional companions of foxhounds, either taking short cuts through the countryside to keep up or riding in special terrier baskets aboard horses. The Jack Russell's job is to bolt the fox, should he go to ground in a hole, pipe, or thick brush pile. The Jack Russells wade in tooth and claw against foxes, rats, groundhogs, skunks, or whatever other varmint cross their paths. At the International, Jack Russells race over a series of pup-sized jumps, in hot pursuit of a fox tail. In the final strides of the race, the terriers dive boldly through a small hole formed by straw bales, which simulate the fox den. Judges score the winners while handlers retrieve their wrought-up charges. Highlights are replayed on the telescreen above the arena. So popular is the feature, that the crew from the International were invited for an all-expense-paid plushy holiday in New York for a guest performance on David Letterman's show.

The big telescreens replay not only key moments of the terrier races, but give information throughout the show, flash scores, and rerun efforts by the equine jumpers, good and bad.

The trappings of the show are fairly pricey. Parking costs $5, and food in the cafeteria is expensive. One man seen in a cafeteria line holding a glass of tap water turned ashen when the cashier asked him for $2—for the paper cup, she explained. Once one has paid the piper, it's best to sink down into one of the comfortable seats and enjoy the show.

Dining: Options include the cafeteria and the really swish tables for eight in the Crown Royal ringside cafe. Three tiers of tables glitter and twinkle on the end of the ring facing the in-gate. The view is good, and the effect is too glamorous for words. Tables cost $200 to $350 per night or $1,500 for the run of the show. The buffet dinner costs $35 per person, and there is a cash bar. The Capital Club is open for table service most nights of the show. For reservations and questions about the food service, call (301)840-0281.

Admission: Tickets cost $36 for box seats week nights and Sundays, including Hunt Night, $16 for reserved seats. The final weekend, tickets go up $5 each. Friday and Saturday the crowd is large, though a sell-out in the 17,000-seat USAir Arena is not going to occur. To reach the USAir Arena, call 202-432-7328.

175

WARRENTON HORSE SHOW
Warrenton Horse Show Grounds
Warrenton, VA

When: Labor Day weekend, show runs Tuesday through Sunday

Time: Show starts at 8:00 A.M. daily, with evening sessions starting at 7:00 P.M. Saturday and 4:00 P.M. Sunday.

Contact: Warrenton Horse Show Association
P.O. Box 535
Warrenton, VA 22186

Phone: 703-347-2612

Directions: From D.C., take I-66 west to the Warrenton exit, Route 29 (this is the second Route 29 exit, but the only Warrenton exit). Exit Route 29 on Business 29 (marked "To Warrenton, Route 211, and Route 17"). The show grounds are located approximately 3 miles on the right.

The Warrenton Show was a trend setter when it was founded in 1899, and continues to be a popular show with the local folk, who flock there to see and be seen. The other thing that attracts spectators is the fact that locals are by and large knowledgeable horsemen and the competition is very good. Like Upperville, young horses, too young for the riding classes, are led in for a kind of beautiful baby contest. On Sunday night, the hunt members come out to cheer on representatives of their hunt who are warming up for competition at the Washington International Show.

The atmosphere is friendly and familiar, like it was in the '30s, before the major portion of the grandstands burned down. Unlike most big modern hunter shows which keep three or more rings of competition going at all times, Warrenton adheres to a one-ring tradition that makes it an anomaly in today's world. There are special classes held on Saturday by the Virginia Horse Show Association (VHSA) Futurity, for yearling colts and fillies, followed by a complete program of classes on the line for young horses, starting at noon or after. On Sunday, about mid-day, the VHSA Pony Hunter Medal Finals and the VHSA Hunter Seat Medal Finals take place at 4:00 P.M.—Hunt Night.

Admission: Tickets cost $3 per person. Reserved parking for the run of the show costs $125 for a front row space, $100 for the second row. A front row grandstand box costs $50 for the run of the show. Seats in the grandstand cost $1 each, well worth the price in case of rain or scorching heat.

WARRENTON PONY SHOW

Other shows held at the Warrenton Show Grounds include Summer's End, the final weekend in August, and the Warrenton Pony Show in late June, booked as the "oldest pony show in the United States." No admission is charged at either. The pony show will delight any child who loves horses. It is long on classes for ponies and riders 18 and under and draws the very best in the nation. Ponies jump round after round in absolute perfection. It's a wonder judges can select the winner. For details on Summer's End, call 703-349-0086; for the Warrenton Pony Show, call 703-347-1744. For information about schooling shows held at Warrenton Show Grounds call 703-788-3603.

WASHINGTON BRIDLE TRAILS HORSE SHOWS
Meadowbrook Show Ring
Chevy Chase, MD

When: Shows held in May, July, and September, over a Saturday and Sunday

Time: Classes begin at 8:00 A.M.

Contact: Washington Bridle Trails Association
9412 Holbrook Lane
Potomac, MD 20854

Phone: 301-587-9762

Directions: From D.C., exit the Beltway south on Connecticut Avenue. Turn left on Route 410, East-West Highway. Go to the second traffic light and turn right onto Meadowbrook Lane. Show rings are located behind Meadowbrook Stable.

Perhaps the only horse showing left within the beltway, Meadowbrook gives a glimpse backward to the days when senators kept their fine saddle horses in the handsome Victorian barn, and bridle trails reached all the way to Hains Point. The level of competition itself does not warrant a special trip to Meadowbrook, but the location is handy and one can see very good performances by professional riders from the area. Spectators, besides exhibitors' families, include neighborhood folks, bicyclers from Rock Creek Park and other Washingtonians enjoying sunshine on a sleepy Sunday.

Two or three rings are kept in motion all day. Classes for children are featured on Saturday; adult classes are featured on Sunday. Classes for amateur riders, riding students and less experienced horses prevail.

Meadowbrook Stable is a magnificent old barn, open for riding lessons and to boarders with private horses. It is now managed under the auspices of the Maryland/National Capital Park and Planning Commission. Meadowbrook adjoins the northern-most reaches of Rock Creek Park. The first horse shows at Meadowbrook were held in 1940 to promote the beautiful bridle trails through Rock Creek Park. At that time, the show featured classes for bridle path hacks, stable hacks, as well as hunters and jumpers, which predominate at today's shows. Members of the Washington Bridle Trail Association are the main users of the trails, which still course through the park. Some of them remember the days when the eight-mile-per-hour speed limit on trails was rigorously maintained by mounted police.

A number of private schools in the area, along with the University of Maryland, offer riding classes through Meadowbrook. Please see the final chapter in the book for more information on riding opportunities in Rock Creek Park.

Admission: Free

FAIR HORSE SHOWS AND EXHIBITIONS

Both Maryland and Virginia stage horse shows in conjunction with state fairs. A number of county fairs do too. Some of the fair horse shows are returning to an earlier tradition of offering classes for draft horses and mules. These feature both classes on the line in which the form and shape of the animals are judged, and performance classes in which these predecessors of the tractor are shown pulling or driving.

VIRGINIA HORSE SHOW OF ATLANTIC RURAL EXPOSITION, INC.
Strawberry Hill
Richmond, VA

When: Starts late September, lasts 11 days

Contact: Atlantic Rural Exposition, Inc.
P.O. Box 26805
Richmond, VA 23261

Phone: 804-228-3238

Directions: From D.C., take I-95 south to Richmond. Take Exit 82, Chamberlayne Avenue to Laburnum Avenue. This route puts you on the proper side of the fairgrounds for access to the horse show, via Gate 4.

This horse show is a many-day, multi-faceted event. It is best described as a series of mini-shows under the guise of a state fair. One competition is for 4-H members. Others are for Arabian horses and llamas, for Shetland ponies and miniature horses, for draft horses and for quarter horses. Special events include a draft horse pull and a mule pull, in which teams are hitched to sleds piled with ever increasing weight. It is like a tractor pull with one or two horse power. These shows are each two-day affairs, during the run of the fair. The horse show complex at the fair has three arenas with plenty of spectator seating. One of them is under cover.

The draft horse show is the unique part of the state fair. If you stand near these gentle giants as they prepare to enter the show ring, you get a feel for their size and majesty. It is easy enough to envision one of these monsters carrying a knight in full battle armor, or dragging a plow to break up new ground. The draft horse and mule pulls leave nothing to the imagination about the power of these animals.

A series of horse shows are held at the Strawberry Hill Equestrian Center, site of the horse show, throughout the year. A schedule of these events is included later in this section.

Admission: The fair costs $10 per person, $12 at the door, all events along with the horse show included.

HORSE SHOWS DURING THE MARYLAND STATE FAIR

Maryland State Fair Grounds
Timonium, MD

When: Nine days; ends on Labor Day

Contact: Maryland State Fair
P.O. Box 188
Timonium, MD 21094

Phone: 410-252-0200, x 223

Directions: From D.C., take I-95 north to I-695, the Baltimore Beltway, toward Catonsville. Take Exit 24, the Harrisburg Expressway (I-83) to Exit 16E, Timonium Road. Follow the signs to the fair grounds.

Along with its usual fair activities, the Maryland State Fair also offers a horse show, along with ten days of thoroughbred racing. The Timonium races and other activities, with the bonus of daily horse shows, make the Maryland State Fair a low-cost entertainment bonanza.

Ponies are judged the first Saturday of the fair, with horses taking center stage the second weekend. Classes for horses include classes for thoroughbreds, non-thoroughbreds and Arabians. Classes for ponies include Shetlands, Welsh, crossbred and hunter ponies and Ponies of the Americas, which are little appaloosas. Like classes for cows and other domestic animals shown at the fair, many classes for horses are "on the line."

Horse classes focus on conformation, or shape of the animal, soundness, and way of going or movement across the ground. Like classes for other animals, horses are being viewed as potential or actual brood stock. Besides classes for foals, yearlings, two- and three-year olds, classes are held for "get of sire" (youngsters fathered by the same stallion), "produce of dam" and for broodmares. In the production classes, the worth of the stallion is judged by considering three of his foals. In the "produce of dam," or mother, two of her offspring are judged.

Although lead-in classes may not be as exciting as good performance classes, they are in keeping with the long tradition of fairs to recognize the best breeders and producers in the state.

In some of the Arabian classes, horses are shown under saddle, and a number of performance classes for youngsters and 4-H members are scheduled as well. There are driving classes for ponies, and also for draft horses and mules. The latter two divisions juice up the program and add to the flavor of an old-timey fair. Conformation classes for draft horses feature Belgians, Clydesdales, Percherons and Shires. Mules and draft horses are also shown in hitch classes and pulling contests.

During the rest of the year, the Maryland State Fair complex is used for a variety of events, many of which are not horsey. However, a dozen horse auctions take place here. The Maryland Horse and Pony Show, an "A" rated hunter show, is held the weekend after the State Fair. The Maryland Horse Shows Association Futurity is held on Sunday during the show. Like Warrenton and the Washington International, the Futurity show includes classes for bona fide field hunters on Saturday. For details on this show, call 410-472-2782.

Admission: $3, includes entry to Timonium races and fair

ROCKBRIDGE REGIONAL FAIR
Virginia Horse Center
Lexington, VA

When: Mid-July

Contact: Virginia Horse Center
P.O. Box 1051
Lexington, VA 24450

Phone: 703-463-7060

Directions: From D.C., take I-66 west to I-81 south. Turn west at Exit 191 (I-64) to Exit 55, Route 11 north. Turn left on Route 39 west, just ¹⁄₁₀ mile from I-64. The Horse Center is one mile on the left.

The Rockbridge County Fair was resurrected in 1992 after many years absence. The fair was held in the convenient and entirely satisfactory grounds of the 400-acre Virginia Horse Center complex. Beside normal fair attractions, a Morgan horse show and a hunter and jumper show are held.

Admission: $5 per carload

THE GREAT FREDERICK FAIR
County Fair Grounds
Frederick, MD

When: September, starts third weekend and lasts Saturday through Saturday.

Contact: Maryland Draft Horse & Mule Association
3301 Urbanan Pike
Ijamsville, MD 21754

Phone: 301-663-5895. Questions specifically about the horse show to 301-874-2167.

Directions: From D.C., travel west on I-270 to the first Frederick exit. Head south on Market Street, then follow signs to the fair.

There's a lot to like at the Great Frederick Fair for someone interested in horses and old-timey fair atmosphere. Draft horses, mules and, as an extra bonus, harness racing are featured.

The draft show has attracted over 100 horses, along with 30-plus mules. These animals were shown in halter and under hitch. Sufficient draft horse entries warrant dividing classes by breeds. A wide variety of driving classes are offered, including one for antique farm implements other than wagons, and for six-horse hitches, just like the Budweiser Clydesdales except without the beer. The draft and mule show is held the first weekend of the fair. Harness races are held Tuesday through Friday of the fair. Races begin at 1:00 P.M. daily, and may be viewed from bleacher seating, which is partially covered. No betting is offered on the racing, which showcases the standard-bred horses that train year-round at the Frederick fairgrounds.

Admission: Call for prices. The horse and mule shows and the harness races are included with admission to the fair.

HOWARD COUNTY FAIR
County Fair Grounds
West Friendship, MD

When: Mid-August

Contact: Howard County Fair
15021 Frederick Road
Woodbine, MD 21797

Phone: 410-442-2641

Directions: From D.C., exit the Capital Beltway onto Georgia Avenue, Route 97. Turn right on Route 144 to the fairgrounds.

Howard County Fair offers a full range of horse classes. A different breed is featured every day. At a recent fair the popular draft horses and mules were shown the first day—on a Sunday. Other breeds displayed include Arabians, hunter ponies, Welsh and Shetland ponies, miniature horses, paints, plantation walking horses and quarter horses. Classes for young thoroughbreds and sports horses are featured. The final day of the fair offers a horse pulling contest and a full range of hunter classes.

Admission: Call for prices. Admission to the fair includes the horse show.

FOR MORE INFORMATION:

On horse shows, or any type of horse event, the best source of information can be the local tack shop. Every burg in the Capital area has its own. It can be expected to be a hot spot for information and gossip, as well as needed saddlery, riding apparel and horsey gifts. Check their bulletin boards.

Local newspapers such as the *Fauquier Times-Democrat, Loudoun Times* and *Rappahannock News,* all owned by Arthur "Nick" Arundel, chairman of the Virginia Gold Cup Steeplechase, list shows and other horse events each week. *The Washington Post* lists a number of horse events in its "Weekend" section each Friday.

Another source for information about horse shows is the Virginia Horse Show Association. This association annually lists around 60 shows, including the largest hunter-jumper shows in the area along with some activities for saddle and walking horses. For a complete listing, contact VHSA, 703-349-0910. The Maryland Horse Show Association lists about the same number of shows. Their phone number is 410-337-0681.

Please see Appendix A for more information about training stables that sponsor series of shows, and horse show complexes that offer shows and other events on a weekly basis.

CLASS SPECIFICATIONS DECODED

Hunter: Classes at horse shows for hunters were once off-season diversion for fox hunters and their one all-purpose horse. Over the past 30 years, hunters that now win have evolved into show animals that would probably be quite shocked by the sight of foxhounds. The exceptions are those shown in genuine hunter classes at the Washington International and at Warrenton.

Horses are judged on style of jumping, way of moving and manners. These three elements are weighted differently for different classifications of competition. Obviously, manners are first among equals in classes for children and amateurs. The other categories of hunter classes at "A" rated shows are: green hunters, in their first or second year of recognized competition; open working hunters, seasoned show ring veterans that jump a full four feet; and conformation hunters, judged on sheer physical beauty as well as performance. There are other categories as well. In addition, most shows have a dizzying variety of unrecognized divisions. Participation in these does not affect a horse's permanent show record.

As good as the horses and riders are in this area, it is a foregone conclusion that winners will have eight perfectly measured jumps, generally taken from a graceful flowing stride. Considering that most go around in an almost mechanical fashion (precluding any lapse of manners), one wonders how judges do select winners.

Jumper: Jumpers quickly become favorites of spectators. First-time watchers quickly get the hang of the rules and can make judgments themselves. Basically, the winner is the horse that clears the course in the time allowed. In case two or more horses clear the course within the time limit, a jump off is held over raised jumps.

Most shows, including small schooling shows, have classes for jumpers. Only at the Washington International and Upperville do jumps reach dizzying heights, starting at an imposing 4'6", and going up to five feet in height and five to six feet in width. No matter what the size of the jumps, the competition can be fun and exciting if a jump off is involved.

Here is the schedule of jumping faults:

- knockdown of obstacle - 4 faults
- foot in water jump - 4 faults
- first refusal to jump on course - 3 faults
- second refusal or run-out - 6 faults
- third refusal - elimination
- fall of horse or rider - elimination

Elimination is also dealt out for some technical faults, such as jumping a fence that has been knocked down in the course of a refusal before it has been reset.

Equitation: These classes are judged on the form of the rider. Most are for riders under 18 and often are further sub-divided by age. These are the especially prestigious medal classes:

- VHSA medal with a final competition held for all class winners at the Warrenton Show in September
- AHSA Medal with finals at the New York National
- ASPCA which has finals at the Pennsylvania National
- Washington International Horse Show class, with finals at the show of the same name
- US Equestrian Team Medal class, with finals in three locations chosen annually, one in each broad geographic region of the country.

Thoroughbreds: Classes for thoroughbreds, along with complementary classes for non-thoroughbreds, are held at a number of shows, notably Upperville, Warrenton, and the Maryland Horse and Pony Show, along with a number of fairs. Horses in the thoroughbred classes must be registered with the American Jockey Club or one of its equivalents in a foreign country. These horses share the same registration with race horses and steeplechasers. What makes Virginia and Maryland horse shows interesting is that breeders have worked hard to produce horses with substance and grace, just as horses have been bred in the past for race track speed. To the true horseman, the results are gratifying and most enjoyable to behold.

Crusty old horsemen and younger folks bent on learning may be seen peering at handsome youngsters being scrutinized by show judges. These classes are shown "in hand" (led, rather than ridden). Competing horses first parade around the ring as a group. Then they are stood up, or put in a flattering pose so that judges can carefully inspect them, one at a time. The judges line up the horses head to tail in order selected, to make sure the sequence can be justified in their own minds. The shrewd observer can look from the first to the last to second guess the qualities the judge is rewarding.

Futurities: These are showcases for state-bred yearlings, nominated at birth by their breeders.

Quarter Horses: One of the breeds America made, they represent the largest horse registry in the country. Only in Virginia and Maryland do other types of horses approach quarter horses in prevalence. Most of the big show centers and fairs do have shows and/or classes for quarter horses. Developed as the sound, sensible and extremely nimble companions of American cowboys, quarter horses are generally shown under western tack with riders dressed in western-style hats and boots. To show the versatility of the breed, big quarter horse shows offer English and jumping classes as well, along with games such as pole bending and (where facilities permit), roping classes with live cattle. Performance classes may require horses to demonstrate skills used when working cows, such as figure eights which show a horse's ability to turn smoothly and obediently in both directions.

Arabians: One of the world's oldest improved breeds of horse, this famous breed is considered purebred by reason of the harsh desert environment in which they came to be. On the desert, prized Arabians were literally members of the family, kept in select small groups. Breed characteristics include a very fine coat and finely chiseled head with large, expressive eyes. They display natural animation that comes through in the various saddle classes. One of the more colorful classes to watch is the mounted native costume class, in which horses wear desert regalia and riders dress in the native Bedouin style.

Morgans: Justin Morgan had a horse, it is said, and descendants of that horse and that style of sturdy, versatile animal still may be found. True, one is more likely to come across a Morgan in its native New England, but some shows and fairs in the Capital area do offer classes and shows for Morgans. Morgans looks like

Arabians on steroids. The Morgan has a slightly dished face and a neck set like an Arabian, but is a bit stockier and more heavily muscled. Classes for Morgans are much like classes for Arabians, with hunter and western classes along with a predominance of park-type pleasure classes. Morgans also excel in driving classes.

American Saddle Horses: Though not common in this area, this breeds attracts a following when they do go on display. Managers at the Virginia State Show and at the Virginia Horse Center report that shows featuring saddle horses, especially on a mixed venue with other breeds, enjoy a good draw. Unlike the Tennessee Walking Horse, originally used in the fields and to pull wagons, American Saddle Horses are a refined breed developed in Kentucky for strutting their stuff on the roads. Had the Saddle Horse been developed in England rather than America, it would have been the pick for taking a turn around Hyde Park to impress passers-by. Bred to have fine coats and natural animation, Saddle Horses are high steppers. Depending on their training and natural inclination, they may be shown pulling fine harness carriages driven by ladies in evening dresses and long earrings. They may be ridden at a walk, trot and canter in three-gaited classes, or at those three natural gaits as well as at the slow gait and rack, two man-made gaits, in five-gaited classes. Before shows specialized in just one breed or type of horse, five-gaited classes went on just before closing, and the crowd always stayed around to whoop and cheer when the command "rack on" was given and entries erupted into the fast, showy gait.

Tennessee Walking Horses: This breed evolved from sturdy, useful family horses, known for their gentleness and sturdiness. Unlike almost every other breed, they do not naturally trot but have a smooth ground covering gait known as a running walk. Through the years, by training and mechanical devices, this gait has been engineered into an extremely high-stepping gait that is favored at walking horse shows in Tennessee. In its natural state, the walking horse is a very comfortable horse to ride. Because of its nature, it's a good one for adults who start riding late in life. There are not many area shows for walking horses. Walkers shown here are plantation horses or pleasure horses that are shod naturally and lack the high-stepping artificial flash of an open class.

Draft Breed: Once the staple of fairs, draft breeds had all but disappeared until recently. Maryland now is especially blessed to have these gentle giants featured at a number of its fairs. They are displayed in such numbers that they can be subdivided and judged by breed, and are also shown in harness and in pulling contests, such as truck pulls limited to one or two-horse power.

The huge horses were originally developed to carry knights in hundreds of pounds of armor into battle. It is said that Henry VIII, very large even without armor, decreed that any stallions under 15 hands that were not ponies should be put to death. This accounted for a proliferation of horses 18 or 19 hands in height (four inches to the hand) during his day. With the development of gun powder, the fast-moving horses from the desert became the desired mode of transportation. The huge draft breed switched over to use in harness, pulling heavy loads.

Percherons: This breed originated in Normandy. The horses' heads are smaller in relation to their bodies than in other draft breeds. They are claimed to be quicker and more agile than other heavy horses. One of their dominant colors is dapple grey, making for a handsome large horse. In America, Percherons have been mixed with thoroughbreds or other light breeds to produce large hunters for large men.

Belgians: Known as the great horses of the medieval day, Belgians stand at 17 to 18 hands and weigh up to 2200 pounds. They are known to be docile and tractable, as well as powerful. The predominant color is a light chestnut. This breed has made its mark on the world of mules. A Belgian stallion bred to a jenny (female donkey) produces a consistently large, handsome mule of the same color of the sire.

Clydesdales: These stately animals were first bred near the River Clyde in Scotland. The Clydesdale has become one of the best known draft breeds through its association with Budweiser products. Usually brown and white with curly white feathers of hair adorning its lower legs, the Clydesdale makes a striking heavy harness horse for pulling large wagons like those used by old-time breweries. There are three teams of Clydesdales that tour the country as Budweiser's goodwill ambassadors. One should not miss an opportunity to see them. Standing or performing, they are natural wonders.

Shires: Shires have thick, straight hair on their lower legs, adding to the overall impression of power. They are the tallest of the draft breeds and can reach up to 20 hands (80 inches) to the withers, the highest permanent point on the back. In the hunting Shires area of England, this breed has been used to produce horses to carry large men in the hunt field.

X

FOXHUNTING

"Yoicks!", the Fox

Foxhunting, along with racing, fostered the intense selective breeding that has produced the excellent horses found in Virginia and Maryland. Like their English brethren, colonists had a keen appreciation of the trinity of horse, hound and fox. They cheered hounds forward after the fox with a hearty "yoicks!" (a cheer used to urge hounds forward after their quarry).

The first American fox hunt probably occurred in Queen Anne County, MD, in 1650. From ships' records it is known that Robert Brooke, Esq., who was deeded 2,000 acres of Lord Baltimore's grant, brought along a pack of hounds with his family. To put this event in historical perspective, the first formal fox hunts occurred in England in the late 1680s.

Robert Brooke was reportedly a man of wealth and property, though not on a par with the English lords who kept packs exclusively for foxhunting. Brooke, most historians surmise, hunted foxes with his imported hounds, though they were perhaps used for other game as well. His descendants continued for generations to breed and hunt foxhounds from that first stock. The ancestral tract is currently hunted by the De La Brooke Foxhounds W, which drew their name from Brooke. Lord Baltimore encouraged hunting in the New World by insisting that any settler on his land bring with him at least one dog.

Some of the settlers had developed a taste for the new sport of foxhunting before emigrating. The wealthy settlers who came

The Warrenton Hounds move out from The Grove. Virginia has more recognized fox hunting clubs than any other state, and Maryland runs a close third.
Credit: Douglas Lees

to Maryland and Virginia started foxhunting as quickly as land could be cleared. Excerpts from diaries and early published works collected by J. Blan Van Urk for his fine and definitive book, *The Story of American Foxhunting*, put it this way: "Men in Virginia and Maryland have always placed fighting, foxhunting and making love above all other pursuits, and depending on circumstances, foxhunting was usually no worse than number two. Settlers sensed hounds and horses were made for one another, and the fox melded to make things all the better."

Why foxes? As Joe Rogers, long-time master of the Loudoun Hunt, puts it, there wasn't anything much to talk about in the country except hunting. Tales of hunting foxes were more interesting than stories about hunting opossums and squirrels, neither of which put up much of a chase. This relatively benign pastime had become a preoccupation by the time wolves had been hunted to extinction and sports like bear-baiting and bull-fighting had fallen from favor.

Unlike the wolf and other large predators that were purposely exterminated, the red fox has always been welcomed—so much so that it was imported in large numbers to improve the sport. Manifests showed that red fox were first brought here by wealthy tobacco planters in Maryland. Continued importation through the 19th century led to the notion that all the red fox found here today descend from the foxes brought from England, Ireland and Scotland. This is not so. Indigenous red foxes had been observed and reported prior to 1730. By 1840, Colonel Charles H. Smith, head of the Natural History Society, reported that red fox ranged naturally as far south as the Carolinas. The European reds co-mingled with native foxes. The lack of red fox noted by the earliest settlers is best explained by the fact that fox are happiest in half cleared land, and are not creatures of deep, unbroken forests that greeted immigrants to Maryland and Virginia.

When Lord Fairfax came to Virginia in 1748, he began hunting in the English manner—maintaining a full complement of hounds used for nothing but foxhunting, tended by liveried hunt servants. When the sport was slack around his home, Belvoir, Lord Fairfax would take his hounds into the countryside, bedding down at an inn, and declaring open house and open table for any who appeared to be of "good character and respectable appearance."

Lord Fairfax, it is believed, introduced the father of our nation to foxhunting. George Washington's diaries reveal that he hunted at every opportunity. Washington was very proud of his pack, and tried to hunt them at least three days a week. In one brief report, he noted that his hounds had chased one fox for seven hours. In another, he told of going off to Mr. Robert Alexander's for a foxhunting party that lasted three days. Other famous hunters included Chief Justice John Marshall and President Thomas Jefferson, who balanced their intellectual pursuits with riding and hunting.

The gentry hunted and the clergy hunted and the common man hunted, too. General Washington was always well-mounted and immaculate in a blue coat, red waistcoat, buckskin breeches and black velvet cap. For others, foxhunting amounted to meeting neighbors at a crossroads on a given day at a given hour, each rider bringing his own hound to form a pack.

Because planters had emulated English traditions, foxhunting and racing lost favor for a time after the Revolutionary War. It took an especially long time for the red coats favored by British soldiers (and by today's foxhunters) to return to favor. General Washington did not let such prejudices interfere with his hunting. He returned to foxhunting, his pack strengthened by the gift of magnificent staghounds from Lafayette.

Washington and Baltimore both had hunts and almost everyone who was anyone hunted. A letter published in 1835, written by Mr. John Skinner, publisher of the American Turf Registry, said "I rejoiced to see you out this morning accoutred for the chase, and with you the veteran president of the Washington Hunt, members of Congress, citizens, gentlemen attached to foreign missions, and officers of the army and navy, whose presence gives a sanction to the manly and delightful sport of the field."

The Civil War wiped out almost all the horses, hounds and money in Virginia thus ending hunting for a time. The Piedmont pack, founded in 1840 as the private province of the Dulany family, survived, as did the family fortune. It is agreed that Piedmont, then known as Grafton, is America's oldest existing hunt. After the Civil War, English soldiers stationed in Washington got the sport on the roll again. Within ten years of the war, hunting was back in Washington and Baltimore. As territory in the District became limited, interests moved out to Fairfax and Potomac. Chevy Chase started a club in 1892 with remnants of the Dumblane Hunt, which itself succeeded the Washington Hunt. The club at Chevy Chase experienced ups and downs, but was dealt a death blow when hounds being brought over from England sank with the club's master in the Titanic disaster of 1912.

Washington and Jefferson, diaries and records show, were keenly interested in breeding horses for riding and hunting, as well as racing. Other planters must have held similar interests. A book published in 1775, based on travels in 1759–60, reported that horses in Virginia and Maryland were fleet and beautiful, and that Virginians were exceedingly fond of horses and spared no expense to improve the breed by importing brood stock from England. The fine horses of Virginia made themselves felt in cavalry charges of the Civil War. Soon after, farmers and sportsmen were back in the swing of raising good stock.

In one long and fascinating letter written in 1933, Mrs. Allen Potts of Albemarle County describes leaving the kennel at 4:00 A.M., riding 10 to 15 miles to the meet, hunting all day, then returning home after dark. Mrs. Potts raised and trained her own horses, so that she would have mounts up to the task of a full day's work over challenging terrain, and sometimes at a great pace. Mrs. Potts was the first woman master recognized by the National Steeplechase and Hunt, back in the days when it was the organizing body of formal foxhunting. She was a direct descendant of Dr. Thomas Walker, who was on General Washington's staff and who developed the Walker strain of foxhound, one of America's most famous breeds.

In an account published in 1902, an English visitor on his first American fox hunt praised the Virginia horse, describing it as having bone, muscle, speed and staying qualities and "a gentle and friendly nature not observed in horses in other places." Fine horses were bred not only by landed gentry like Mrs. Potts, but also by ordinary farmers who were invited and encouraged to participate in the sport. Until World War II, many Virginia farmers produced foxhunting horses as an important cash crop, just as they raised other domestic animals.

MASTER OF FOXHOUNDS ASSOCIATION

Morven Park
Leesburg, VA

Contact: Master of Foxhounds Association
Route 3, Box 51
Leesburg, VA 22075

Phone: 703-771-7442

Foxhunting in its present-day form started in the late 1800s when the sport become organized and formal record keeping began. Much of the history of hunting before that time was lost, because it was an informal affair carried on by farmers, each of whom brought his own hounds to a meet. Also, as an early writer explained it, foxes were initially considered vermin, and chasing them was nothing more to write about than chasing squirrels.

The oldest pack in continuous operation in the United States is Piedmont, in Upperville, VA. Pack hunting was mentioned in various diaries and articles from early on, but the less organized side of the sport, still enjoyed on remote hillsides under the full moon, has hardly ever been recorded. It comes to us by oral tradition. As an elderly woman explained it, hunting at the turn of the century was a great social sport. Hunters rode miles to the meet, greeting and hooking up with neighbors on the way. After the hunt, the host's house was opened up to fellow hunters, and the hospitality continued until all finally had their fill, some staying the night. The "night hunters" then, as now, did not ride to hounds, but rather turned the hounds loose and sat around campfires with their companions, passing the jug and listening for the voices of their own hounds to ring through the forest.

To this scene of early informality came, around the turn of the 20th century, men of wealth from the North, some of whom had first become acquainted with the stunning open land of Virginia during the Civil War. Virginia was put squarely in the middle of the foxhunting map in 1905, when the Match took place. In Virginia, one speaks of The War (the Revolutionary War), The War of Northern Aggression (Civil War), and The Match. The Match was conceived by Harry Worcester Smith,

Harry Worcester Smith and his pack of hounds crossed the Potomac at White's Ferry in approximately 1906.
Credit: Courtesy of Dr. Joe Rogers

MFH from Worcester, MA, who organized a face off between himself, hunting what is now the Piedmont Hounds (then called the Grafton), and his arch-rival, New Yorker A. Henry Higginson, hunting the Middlesex pack. The packs were hunted on alternate days in the Piedmont territory around Upperville, to prove the comparative worth of American style foxhounds (Smith's) vs. English foxhounds (Higginson's). After two weeks of hunting, neither pack had killed a fox, but the judges declared

Smith's American hounds victors, because of their speed. By the final days of the match, 70 to 85 hunters from 26 different hunts had come to witness the legendary contest. In 1989 and 1992, a similar match pitting the Midland Hounds of Columbus, GA, directed by one of the present day's most colorful masters, Ben Hardaway, against the Piedmont Hounds took place in the same area. There were even larger mounted fields of riders and much fanfare.

Following the first great Match, northern money started pouring into the area. Members of the Orange County Hunt in New York bought the Skinner pack, based near The Plains at the same location the current Orange County kennels occupies, and started hunting on land that was claimed by Piedmont. Piedmont asked the National Steeplechase and Hunt (NSHA), at the time the sanctioning body of organized foxhunting, to call a halt to this intrusion. The NSHA threw up its hands and refused to deal with the warring factions. As a result, in 1907 foxhunters formed the Master of Foxhounds Association (MFHA), which to this day is the ultimate authority in settling boundary disputes and keeper of the foxhound stud book. In some states, hunting is so limited there's little to arbitrate. However, throughout Virginia, Maryland and Pennsylvania the hunt countries often butt up against one another. In 1992, the MFHA was once again arbitrating another major boundary dispute in the Middleburg area, this time between two rival groups laying claim to the Middleburg Hunt's country.

For most of its life, the MFHA was based in Boston; it did not move to Virginia until 1991. The association now has its offices in the carriage house at Morven Park, the home of the late Westmoreland Davis, who was one of the founders of the MFHA, master of the Loudoun Hunt and former Governor of Virginia. The association shares its quarters with a carriage museum, and the Museum of Hounds and Hunting occupies the adjacent manor house. In addition to its most important task of recording hounds and hunts, the association publishes a number of handbooks and manuals on foxhunting. Beyond names and addresses of hunts, it does not have any particular information about them, so for specifics one must get in touch with the secretaries of the hunts. You will find them listed in Appendix B of this book.

The MFHA is a repository of knowledge and information, but can't be of much help to the uninitiated. Clerk of the MFHA John Glass said his office was inundated with calls when *Gentlemen's Quarterly* ran his phone number in connection with an article on foxhunting. People wanted to know where they could go to learn more about foxhunting, but the MFHA is not set up to deal with that type of thing.

Foxhunting is not much of a spectator sport. You might catch a glimpse of a hunt while traveling down a back road of Maryland or Virginia hunt country on a winter Saturday. It really is a pretty sight to see, as the hunting prints and lamp shade designs confirm. But to view a fox hunt properly, you have to be on the back of a horse, and you *must* be an experienced rider for foxhunting is a very dangerous sport even for skilled riders.

EARLY SPORT

Foxhunting in America came first to Virginia and Maryland, and not much later to Pennsylvania. Eleven hunts, sharing contiguous boundaries, stretch from Manassas to the Blue Ridge Mountains, almost blanketing Fauquier and Loudoun counties in their scope.

Thirty four states have recognized hunts; some have only one hunt, and some of the hunts in some of the states are not overly subscribed. Yet in the densely concentrated hunting areas of Virginia and Maryland there are plenty of members to go around. Fields on a clement Saturday can easily draw 70 mounted followers. Big joint meets can field well over 100 riders. This metes out to the potential of 700-plus able hunters thundering across the fields of Fauquier and Loudoun on a sunny Saturday. In a 1938 issue of *The Chronicle of the Horse* (published in Middleburg) it was reported that a total of 513 horses had been counted in the hunt field of 4 of the 11 local hunts over that weekend. What is most impressive to those who do hunt, and who have hunted in many parts of the country, is how good the sport is here, how professional the staffs, how beautifully prepared the country, how competent the bulk of the riders and how magnificent the horses! The same is said of the hunts in the Charlottesville and Maryland areas, too.

The standard joke in the rest of the country, made by those with hunters to sell, is that if a horse were shipped to Virginia and sold from there, its price could be doubled. One soon learns that the worth of hunters from Virginia derives not from the address but from hundreds of years of selective breeding. In 1828, a stallion standing in Roanoke that traced its bloodline to the famous race mare Selima was advertised as an "amazing and exceptional animal fit for the dray, wagon, coach, as well as the turf, the field and the road." An article written by J. Blan van Urk and published in *Town and Country* in the '30s calls Virginia the eye of hunting in America, and compliments "the country folk who are all interested in horses, and most deal in them, bringing about a harmony in the community more usual in Virginia than in any other section of the United States." What's thrilling to those who love horses is to see the products of the long years of careful breeding proved in the hunt fields and show rings of today. One can see this by visiting such shows as Upperville and Warrenton and observing the strapping yearlings with dispositions and physiques for riding and hunting.

HUNTER TRIALS AND SPECIAL CLASSES

The hunt field is where the finest horses of the area perform. People who don't hunt can get a look at such horses, however, at a number of other places, such as hunter trials and special classes for foxhunters. Though hunter trials present a rather pale equivalent of actual hunting conditions, the horses and riders are bona fide regulars from the hunt field.

Jumps at hunter trials are of the sort encountered in the hunt field. The performances generally lack the polish displayed by show ring hunters accustomed to cantering over eight carefully set and measured obstacles. The obstacles at a hunter trial are spread across wide meadows, and competitors may be asked to perform standard maneuvers necessary in the hunt field, such as trotting over a fence, galloping strongly, then stopping sharply. The Orange County Hunter Trials, and some of the others as well, come even closer to simulating hunt field conditions, by sending out and judging competitors in teams of two to four. This permits judges to observe how horses behave galloping in a group.

A partial listing of hunter trials is included with the specific information about area hunts in Appendix B. Anyone on a road trip to the country can certainly pack a picnic and fill a few hours watching a hunter trial. The trials are staged in the actual hunt territories, usually down some intriguing back roads that permit spectators to see some areas they would not encounter on ordinary commutes.

Classes for field hunters are also included in the programs of the Warrenton and Washington International Horse Shows. (See Chapter IX for further details.) The show conditions are much more contrived from the standpoint of the average field hunter than hunter trials. Even so, the classes are favorites of hunt members who turn out in large numbers to cheer on riders from their hunts. At a recent Warrenton Show, the show grounds were filled with bedraggled spectators who stood in the rain and dark for hours to see the hunt teams. At Washington International the same year, 32 teams representing hunts from all over the east, almost one fifth of all recognized hunts, exhibited on Hunt Night.

VIRGINIA FOXHOUND CLUB SHOW

Horses are only part of the hunting scene. To see hounds, lots of hounds, one can enjoy an absolute feast for the eyes at the annual hound show. The Virginia Foxhound Club, according to its constitution, promotes interest in improving the breed and holds an annual show. The show includes as many as 40 packs. Hunts come from Virginia, Maryland, Pennsylvania, West Virginia, and 18 from other states.

The setting in recent years has been Oatlands, one of the beautiful historic properties in Loudoun County near Leesburg. If the hound show remains there [in question because of planned expansion of guest facilities], it offers yet another reason to hurry up and visit Oatlands, and to enjoy the house and gardens as well as the unique event.

Foxhunters from all over meet, greet, cheer for their own club's entries and admire the best from other packs. White-coated kennelmen step hurriedly from one ring to the next leading entries for the different classes. In most classes, divided by sex, age, type, and pack size, the hounds are led round and round, so judges can observe them in motion. Hounds are then stood up in a line, with handlers encouraging them to stand up straight, tails at full height, stomachs in. Don't slouch, do look proud and regal.

Specifications for the hounds are laid out in the standards for the American Foxhound, as adopted by the Foxhound Club of North America. According to standards, necks should rise light and gracefully from shoulders, strong and clear, free from folds of skin. Shoulders should be sloping, clean yet muscular, conveying strength and freedom of action.

Types of hounds shown are English, American and Crossbred. All must belong to packs recognized by the Masters of Foxhounds Association. Entered hounds must be listed in the stud book of the MFHA, and unentered hounds, born after January 1 of the year of the show, must be eligible for registration. Classes are for single hounds, and for couples—or two hounds shown together and judged as a unit. The pack classes, shown in the big meadow in front of Oatlands that borders on Route 15, provide a visual treat.

MUSEUM OF HOUNDS
AND HUNTING
Morven Park
Leesburg, VA

When: The museum, like the mansion, is open April through October

Time: NOON–5:00 P.M. It is closed Mondays except on holidays

Contact: Morven Park
Route 3, Box 50
Leesburg, VA 22075

Phone: 703-777-2414

Directions: From D.C., take Route 7 through Leesburg. Do not take the Route 7 by-pass. Just west of Leesburg, turn right on

Morven Park Road, then left on Old Waterford Road. Turn right through the second set of gates into Morven Park.

The Museum of Hounds and Hunting is a special feature of the handsome main house at Morven Park. Morven Park was the home of Thomas Swann, Governor of Maryland, and Westmoreland Davis, Governor of Virginia. The museum is operated by the Westmoreland Davis Foundation. Davis was a founding member of the Master of Foxhunter's Association and a master of the Loudoun Hunt.

Current Master of the Loudoun Hunt Joe Rogers helped create the museum. He figures Davis would have approved. The Museum serves as a repository for memorabilia related to foxhunting. Rogers said it was important to find a permanent home for the valuable collection, a compendium of relics collected by foxhunters, most now deceased.

The museum opened in 1985. It contains a number of paintings and hunting horns, one used by Col. John Mosby, who used the horn not only for hunting but also for signaling his men when they set out on their daring middle-of-the night attacks during the Civil War. Letters and artifacts of interest to the aficionado are included. Mannequins, dressed in appropriate attire, are staged in various poses to form tableaus of hunt scenes. A 20-minute film traces foxhunting from the colonial period to the present. The tack, including sidesaddles, is of interest to those who wonder how women-of-old managed.

The house itself was begun as a fieldstone farmhouse in 1781. It has been remodeled and enlarged through the years. Now, an impressive Greek Revival portico added in the earlier part of the 20th century graces the house. Parts of the 1,200-acre estate are open for picnics and nature walks. The estate is used for horse trials in the fall and steeplechases in the spring and fall. A number of riding clinics are also staged at Morven Park, which once housed a year-round riding program to train riding instructors.

Admission: A $4 fee covers a guided tour of the mansion, hunting museum, and boxwood gardens. Visitors may take a self-guided tour of the Victorian carriage museum, which features the 100-carriage collection of the late Mrs. Robert Winmill of Warrenton.

HUNTER CHAMPIONSHIP OF AMERICA
Glenwood Park
Middleburg, VA

When: First week in October. A fair test of foxhunting horses and an enjoyable week for participants, ending in the finals the first Sunday in October. The finals serve as the first act for the second day of the Virginia Fall Race program.

Time: Finals at NOON

Contact: Virginia Fall Races
P.O. Box 2
Middleburg, VA 22117

Phone: 703-687-5662

Directions: I-66 west to Route 50 west. At Middleburg turn right at the only traffic light. The course is about two miles farther on the right.

Participants hunt four days with four different area hunts, as part of the competition. Mounted judges ride along, taking notes and picking out their favorites. One hundred to 150 can turn out in the field for these hunts. Scores are tallied and the top horses are selected to perform on the Sunday of the Middleburg Fall Races. After a run across the race course behind the Middleburg Hounds on a drag line, the number is further reduced. Finalists perform additional tests, more like those in hunter trials, right in front of the race crowd, just before the first race. This is an easy way to see a snapshot of foxhunting and enjoy a day of steeplechasing to boot. (See Chapter VII for more details).

VIRGINIA FIELD HUNTER CHAMPIONSHIP

Sorry not to be more exact, but the Virginia Field Hunter Championship is usually held in October or November, sometimes December, on a Saturday or Sunday, usually, around NOON or 1:00 P.M. The event varies from year to year, because it is planned by the previous year's winner and hosted by the winner's hunt. When the event was hosted by Orange County and by Old Dominion, most of the course was visible to spectators. At Loudoun even less of the course could be seen from the start-finish area.

Because this, like hunting, is for participants, not spectators, it would not warrant a special trip to see. Having said that, one has to add that if you happen to be in the area anyway, it would be interesting to watch.

Each hunt in Virginia is invited to send two representatives to the competition. Unlike the Field Hunter Championship of North America, which is contested in the actual hunt field over the period of a week, this competition lasts just an hour or two, under simulated conditions. The previous year's winner sets the course and leads the field, as the body of riders on a fox hunt are called. The group is required to gallop over fences, trot over fences, and stand quietly, as horses must do on an actual hunt. Mounted judges single out six or so of their favorites, and these are asked to perform further tests, in full view of the spectators. The treat here is to get to look at some of the best field hunters in the state. There are not many spectators so those who do come have plenty of opportunity for an up-close look. While the situation is contrived, the fact that the horses gallop along in a large group make it more of a test for an authentic field hunter than most hunter trials and horse shows.

POINT-TO-POINTS, OLD FASHIONED AND HUNTER RACES

Many hunts sponsor point-to-points. They are an important source of income for the hunt and provide racing experience for both riders and horses and fun for the community. Several sections of this book are devoted to the details of these spring events.

Hunts often hook hunter paces onto their point-to-points to give non-racing hunters a chance to ride. Such events are most often held the day after the races, but may be held the morning of or day before. Riders, usually in pairs, charge around a marked course through the countryside. Awards are given to the pair who comes the closest to an unannounced, predetermined time that has been esoterically chosen by Ouija board or a test ride. Prizes are also given to the fastest pair and to the best team of riders under 18.

For the most part, this is a participatory sport, though one can get a bit of a feel for the hunt country by watching for a while. Riders have an opportunity to win prizes, but most are probably drawn by the opportunity to lark around the hunt country, either in support of their own hunt or in the interest of seeing and riding round the country of another pack.

Old-fashions are usually independent of the point-to-points. These are very like the earliest steeplechases, literally going from one point to another. The format is generally to start and finish in the same area, circling around two or more points in the countryside. There is not a set course, other than rounding appointed spots, and this may be done in any order. The races are not for the fainthearted, for the winner almost certainly is the rider bold enough to jump the big line fence, rather than sneaking down the row to find a low spot. The events are open to members of recognized hunts, but the home team has a decided advantage, for knowledge of the countryside and the quickest route and shortcuts between points is all important. Of the old-fashions, Orange County's is outstanding because the public can easily see the action. The start and finish are perched on a picturesque hilltop several miles from Middleburg, so at least one third of the course should be visible to spectators. Just one event is held, so beginning to end the whole thing lasts less than 30 minutes. For those who make the effort, however, the scene is something to take home and dream about.

HUNT TRAIL RIDES

If riding to the hounds, not simply standing on the sideline, is your goal, this is your chance to get your feet wet. Hunt trail rides are held in the spring after hunt season and through the summer until around Labor Day. This is the prime chance for those who enjoy riding over different territory at a slow, controlled pace. Further, it gives riders of modest ability, advanced age or tender years a chance to ride around with foxhunters. These rides draw members of the sponsoring hunt, friends and landowners from the area, and visitors from other hunts. They also provide a great opportunity for riders who hope to hunt some day to measure their own ability within a group of horses. Most rides are divided into several groups, ranging from the slowest, which may not break out of a walk, to the most ambitious who jump and may canter some. The weather may be warm, and the pace is generally leisurely for all riders. Most have a bring-a-dish or pay-to-participate meal after.

HUNTING SEMINARS

Some hunters are born to the sport, participating first on ponies and carefully supervised by parents, teachers or grooms. Others have the opportunity to hunt while young as part of the Pony Club, a youth organization devoted to developing horsemanship and sportsmanship. Foxhunting is one of many horse activities taught through the Pony Club. Clubs may have mock hunts, in which members take the role of hounds, fox and hunt staff. Or members may be invited to ride with the local hunt on a special occasion, for which Pony Clubbers are carefully schooled and briefed. Members of the Middleburg Pony Club are especially blessed, because the club owns its own pack of beagles, which allows children to ride behind to learn the intricate art of foxhunting at a slightly slower pace. For more information on the Pony Clubs, please see Chapter XII. For the Middleburg-Orange County Pony Club, the contact is Mrs. Peter Hapworth, Route 1, Box 54-A, Middleburg, VA 22117, 703-687-5449.

Those who take up foxhunting after the pony club age must run the gauntlet, so as to be safe and competent when the occasion arises. A good mount and instruction in top riding skills are absolute prerequisites.

Though competence in riding is important, adhering to long-preserved social mandates is also necessary. Foxhunting in the formal English fashion has been going full bore since the late

1600s. Through the years, layer upon layer of social and practical considerations have built up a thick veneer of hunting etiquette. The why of some of these rules has been lost, but the common sense behind some of the traditions is easy to understand. One example are stock ties—long, white strips of material tied ascot fashion and secured with plain gold (never ornate and flimsy!) pins. Should an emergency arise, these stock ties can be used as slings or bandages. Other traditions regarding behavior in the field assure the best possible sport by keeping riders out of the way of the hounds and huntsmen.

Books, such as the standard *Riding to Hounds in America*, are a good source of information about what one does and doesn't do on a hunt. In this highly horsey area, one can also attend seminars to learn about the idiosyncrasies and foibles of foxhunting. These seminars feature excellent programs and for the most part are free.

Capitol Hill Equestrian Society (CHES) holds an annual hunting seminar, usually in September. The seminar is a three-phase affair. The first session is held at the meeting room used by CHES in the Sam Rayburn Building. Two to five speakers form a panel to banter about foxhunting from a particular point of view. Each year, the session begins with a 20-minute discussion to hit the high spots of hunting. The panel discussion takes a slightly different tack every year, because some CHES members have attended the seminar for years. The second session is generally hosted by seminar organizers George and Heather Humphrey, who get down to the nitty gritty of preparing attenders to hilltop with the local hunt. Hilltoppers follow the hunt but do not jump. The third session, for those deemed ready, involves hilltopping with the Loudoun Hunt. The hunt, based in the Leesburg-Hamilton, VA area, maintains two packs of hounds, an American and an English-Crossbred. The packs hunt slightly different areas. CHES members go one year with one, the next year with the other, so as not to overtax either group or territory. More about the CHES organization may be found in Chapter XII. For details on the hunt seminar, contact Capitol Hill Equestrian Society, 1199 Longworth House Office Building, Washington, D.C. 20515. Phone: 202-828-3035.

Horse Country, a saddle shop in Warrenton, sometimes schedules a hunting seminar. This event, when held, takes place in August, just before the club hunting season starts in earnest. Speakers generally include huntsmen. Proprietor Marion Maggioli said most were fox hunters—a few even masters. Some attendees were preparing for their first season as active hunters. The event, when held, is free and open to the public. For more information, write Horse Country, 60 Alexandria Pike, Warrenton, VA 22186, or call 703-347-7141.

XI

OTHER HORSE SPORTS

Coach-and-Four and Days of Yore

In addition to flat racing, steeplechasing, polo and point-to-point races, which are major spectator sports, and horse showing and hunting, which are major participatory sports, the area enjoys any number of other equestrian endeavors. Chief among these are combined training, dressage, driving, trail riding and jousting. All these disciplines have competitors of international prominence living and competing in the area. Each sport can provide an entertaining afternoon for the casual spectator or an engaging opportunity for the true devotee.

COMBINED TRAINING

The most difficult thing about combined training is to explain what it is. It was once sufficient to say that it is what Princess Anne and Mark Phillips do, but it has been a long time since the Princess Royal was European Champion and a member of the British Olympic squad. Then, too, the couple has fallen victim to the rash of royal divorces, so who hears much any more about Mark Phillips, once Britain's best combined training event rider? Phillips, whose reputation is undiminished in the horse world, now busies himself designing event courses around the world, including one at Montpelier in Virginia.

In driving competitions, all competitors, even those with pony carts, are accompanied by a navigator. Here Wayne and Sybil Humphreys compete in the Piedmont Driving Club Show at Foxcroft School in Middleburg.
Credit: Mary Lind

Combined training events once proved the prowess of the cavalry officer. Events are held in three phases. Sometimes these phases are held in one day, sometimes in two, when the volume of entries demands. On occasion, the phases are multiplied in difficulty to form a full three-day event, in which one phase is held on each day of competition. Points from all three phases are combined to determine the winner. To win, a competitor must complete all three phases.

The first phase or day is dressage, a French term for a program ride performed individually in a small arena. The test demonstrates a horse's obedience to its rider's signals. Throughout history, a well-schooled horse was a credit to its cavalry unit on the parade field. The test can be likened to the mandatory phase of figure skating. Each competitor performs the same required figures, which are assigned scores of zero to ten by one to three judges. Ideally, the horse does its work in good balance with a light and forward gait. Riders are meant to be in such good rapport with their mounts that signals are indiscernible. All scores in combined training are negative, so points are added up, subtracted from a perfect score, then multiplied by a variable. The lowest score wins.

Phase II is the cross country test, in which riders face a challenging array of jumps in a natural setting, on a course from 1½ to 4 miles in length. In cavalry days, this equated with the challenges faced by a messenger rushing across the country, jumping whatever obstacles appeared in his path. In this, as in other phases, the perfect score is zero. Penalty points are assigned if a horse refuses to jump, if the time allowed on course is exceeded, or if the horse or rider falls. In a full three day, the test includes two stages of roads and tracks, covered at a trot, and a steeplechase phase, in which riders gun it against the clock over jumps that equate with a steeplechase. Riders later face a cross country course of 2½ to 4 miles.

Phase III is stadium jumping, which features a course similar to those seen at horse shows. Penalties are given for the same items listed in Phase II, along with minus 10 for knocking down a fence. In the cross country phase, knock downs are not counted because jumps are constructed in such a way as to be solid enough not to topple with a stiff breeze or even a hard rap. The purpose of Phase III is to prove that the horse, following the test of cross country, is still sound and fit enough to continue to perform.

Virginia events attract so many competitors that several phases are usually going on at once, permitting a spectator an opportunity to experience an event from soup to nuts in just a few hours. Not many spectators find their way to combined training events, and more's the pity. These events are exciting and the vast majority are free to the public. The horses are beautiful and well-trained, and many Olympic-level riders operate from this area. United States Olympic team members and medal winners may be seen competing in many levels of competition.

The programs won't tell you who's who, but we are willing to name names. Former Olympic medal winning event riders who call Virginia home include Jimmy Wofford, who trains a large number of young riders and horses at his spread in Upperville; Torrence Watkins, who operates out of The Plains, and Tad Coffin, who now lives in Haymarket. Bruce Davidson, twice World Champion and Olympic Gold Medal winner, makes regular forays down this way from his home in Unionville, PA. Recent USET members Phyllis Dawson and Stephen Bradley can be seen in Virginia events. Karen Lende O'Connor, another successful international rider, is based in Virginia when not in England competing. Bradley is one of only two Americans to win Burghley, co-star of England's event circuit. O'Connor is the only American to win Leopardstown, Ireland's biggest event. She comes back to teach regular clinics. The entire Canadian Olympic three-day team has spent part of each spring in recent years training at Morven Park in Leesburg, VA.

Tips for watching a combined training event begin with a caution to dress for the weather. Events are not canceled, but merely delayed in case of thunderstorms that produce an abundance of lightning. Watching can be fun for those who have worn sunscreen, brought bug spray and a large floppy hat if it's hot, or Wellington boots and a wax raincoat if it's rainy.

Dogs seem to enjoy moseying around events, but must be kept on leashes. A few organizers, who have been "bitten" by loose dogs who interfere with competitors, will not allow dogs on the grounds. Young children can be brought out for a romp, too, but parents must keep them out of the path of horses, cars, etc. This shouldn't need saying, but too often little tykes are allowed to wander into hazardous areas. At events, courses often cut through the middle of an unmarked meadow, which makes judgment about safe zones important. There will be plenty of pleasant spots where you can spread out a blanket, lay the baby down for a nap and watch beautiful horses gallop by.

First order of business when attending an event is to find a program and/or a time schedule. This can be tricky, because the event is oriented toward the competitor, not the general public. This is not to say the public is not welcome, only that arrangements, such as putting programs within easy reach, have not been addressed. Unlike most horse shows, events do run on time barring natural disaster. If the program lists Bruce Davidson riding dressage at 8:04 in Arena I, that is where Bruce Davidson will be at that time. It must be noted that he was where he was meant to be at a recent Middleburg Horse Trials but he was not riding. He was holding horses for substitute riders, having bruised some ribs in a fall one week before. At the same event the following year, Davidson competed on eight horses.

Cross country is the most exciting event, especially for spectators who like to walk. Those who are out for the exercise can walk from jump to jump, watching a few horses clear each. Those who prefer less walking can usually see the majority of jumps from a few vantage points on course. Binoculars help, if this is the strategy. The more advanced the division, the more challenging and breathtaking the obstacles.

Divisions in level of difficulty, starting with the highest, are advanced, intermediate, preliminary, training and novice. Three-day events, with a longer endurance phase for cross country, is offered at the three highest levels. International events, like Fair Hill in Maryland, push the difficulty level up the scale even more. However, even in the lowest levels one will see beautiful horses with plenty of promise, sometimes guided by the most skilled riders. At the Rolex Three Day in Lexington, KY, 25,000 plus turn out for cross country. Rolex has been heavily promoted since the World Championship in 1978. At Badminton, England's biggest event, 125,000 fans come for cross country day, rain (which is usual) or shine. In the U.S., the tradition of spectating at events is not so well established. Maybe a hundred curiosity seekers came to the new advanced horse trials at Morven Park. Those who came saw a top-notch show. Even fewer came to the intermediate (second highest level) horse trials at Middleburg. But those who came saw some fine performances. Almost every jump at Middleburg can be seen from one spot. The spectators at some events consist entirely of family and friends of competitors. Because national standards are maintained and competition is good, a visitor will see a good show.

Stadium jumping is held in an arena or a fenced area. More spectators seem attracted to the jumping phase. At some, not all, events, riders compete in this, the final phase, in reverse order of standings, heightening the interest and very effectively spotlighting division leaders.

The first phase of the day is dressage. This is a bit more difficult for the uninformed to fathom, but certainly worth watching for a time to get the hang of what's going on. Sometimes it's fun to study the program (if you found one) and pick out a few riders who sound interesting to watch. Since you will know to the minute what time they are due, you can follow their progress through the other two phases.

Dates for events move a bit from year to year, depending on the schedule of season championships. Events tend to stay in the same season, however. A few outstanding events will be highlighted, but two organizations can provide a complete listing of combined training events planned for the area.

Nationally recognized events are sanctioned by the United States Combined Training Association. USCTA, 461 Boston Road, Suite D6, Topsfield, MA 01983-1295. Phone: 508-887-9090. The USCTA plans to move to Morven Park in Virginia.

Local events in Virginia are sanctioned by the highly active Commonwealth Dressage and Combined Training Association. The CDCTA publishes a monthly newsletter, which lists all events, USCTA included, in Virginia and Maryland. For details, write CDCTA, P.O. Box 1743, Middleburg, VA 22117, or call 703-476-5929.

LOUDOUN HORSE TRIALS
Morven Park
Leesburg, VA

When: Spring, usually the last week in March. Dressage and stadium jumping is generally held on Saturday, with cross country on Sunday.

Contact: Margaret Good
Route 2, Box 117C
Leesburg, VA 22075

Phone: 703-777-8776

Directions: See Morven Park, later this section.

Loudoun Horse Trials are held at Morven Park, an historic property maintained by the Westmoreland Davis Trust. Morven Park is worth a visit for a picnic and the scenic beauty, and the horse trials make just one more incentive to go. Divisions of competition include open intermediate, open preliminary and open training. By the combined training rules, advanced level horses (the highest designation), may enter open intermediate, so many of the best international level riders choose this event as a season opener because of Loudoun's excellent turf and organization. Loudoun is a mega-event, with dressage and jumping lasting from dawn to dusk on Saturday and on Sunday.

BLUE RIDGE HORSE TRIALS
White Post, VA

When: Late summer, usually the first weekend in September. Dressage is held Saturday, with some cross country and stadium held Saturday and Sunday.

Contact: Mary Ellen McMillen
Route 1, Box 30
White Post, VA 22663

Phone: 703-459-5145

Directions: From D.C., travel west on I-66, then exit on Route 50 west through Middleburg and Upperville, over the Blue Ridge and across the Shenandoah River. Approximately two miles past the river, turn left on Route 624. Turn right on Route 626 at the T. The show grounds will be one mile on the left.

Blue Ridge now offers divisions up to and including Open Preliminary. Competition is pretty heavily filled by top riders who are bringing on inexperienced horses, probably because it is the gateway to the fall season. The event is far out in the country, but is in a spectacularly beautiful part of Clarke County hunted by the Blue Ridge Hunt. Before Blue Ridge hunted this land, long before, it was in the center of Lord Fairfax's favorite hunt country. The vestiges of Lord Fairfax's farm and kennel complex are located in nearby White Post. The management is especially nice at Blue Ridge, and the outstanding and adorable members of the local pony club serve as mounted messengers for cross country. There are a fair number of spectators around the stadium jumping ring, which is located in the center of an extravagantly beautiful natural bowl.

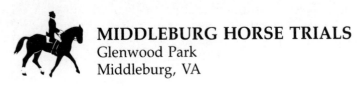

MIDDLEBURG HORSE TRIALS
Glenwood Park
Middleburg, VA

When: Fall, the final weekend in September. Dressage and stadium jumping on Saturday, cross country on Sunday.

Contact: Isobel Zilaca
　　　　　Rt. 1, Box 38F
　　　　　Upperville, VA 22175

Phone: 703-687-6395

Directions: From D.C., take I-66 west to Route 50 west. At the light in Middleburg turn right on Route 626 to Glenwood Park, about 2 miles on the right.

Middleburg held its first intermediate level horse trials in 1992. A number of preliminary divisions are also held in the well-subscribed horse trials. Top riders use the competition to add seasoning to preliminary horses. The course was designed by Jim Wofford, winner of three Olympic medals, and Nina Fout, from the famous riding and racing family and no slouch herself on event horses. Of all horse trials, Middleburg has perhaps the best turf, and its cross country is almost entirely visible from the race grandstands. Those who come to Middleburg for an outing in the country owe it to themselves to spend a few hours watching this fine event.

MORVEN PARK HORSE TRIALS
Morven Park
Leesburg, VA

When: Fall. The first Saturday in October, with cross country on Sunday.

Contact: Morven Park
Route 4, Box 43
Leesburg, VA 22075

Phone: 703-777-2890

Directions: To reach the stadium and dressage from D.C., take Route 7, Leesburg Pike, to the Leesburg by-pass. Head north. Shortly after Route 15 narrows to two lanes, turn left on Route 740 to Tutt Lane. The stadium jumping, stabling and dressage are held behind the steeplechase course, which is located on the left. To reach the cross country: instead of following by-pass, drive through Leesburg on Route 7. Just west of the city, turn right on Morven Park Road, then left on Old Waterford Road, following signs to second entrance to Morven Park.

A new event, the jumps, designed by Bruce Davidson, Olympian, are outstanding. So is the level of competition with rider after rider boasting international experience, many on the Olympic level. Spectator appeal is heightened by the running commentary of knowledgeable British announcer Nigel Casserly. The cross country is held in front of the mansion, which was once the home of Westmoreland Davis, former Governor of Virginia, and former Governor of Maryland, Thomas Swann. The mansion, its gardens and the Museum of Hounds and Hunting, located there, are open during the event.

FAIR HILL INTERNATIONAL
AND FESTIVAL IN THE COUNTRY
Fair Hill, MD

When: Fall. Generally, the event is held the fourth week of October, with dressage and cross country on Saturday, stadium jumping on Sunday. Several other national-level horse trials are held at Fair Hill through the year.

Contact: Fair Hill International
P.O. Box 279
Churchville, MD 21028

Phone: 302-428-4253

Directions: From D.C., travel north on I-95 beyond the Baltimore Beltway to Exit 100, Rising Sun. Turn left off ramp. Take Route 272 to Route 273, turn right. Fair Hill will be on the right, in approximately 5 miles.

The Fair Hill International is the Capital region's only three-day, and its only international event. Though Fair Hill is a lot closer to Pennsylvania and Delaware than it is to Washington or Virginia, there's a lot going on at Fair Hill for those willing to make the trip, or who include the event as part of a fall weekend away.

Beside the event itself, a classic car expo is held, along with a country fair featuring shops, arts, crafts, entertainment, food and the Coors six-horse hitch. The country fair included some 80 shops in recent years and crowds exceeded 10,000. In Lexington, KY, where the Rolex Three Day started the World Championship in 1978, more than 25,000 people attend on weekends. Badminton, England's biggest three day, attracts 125,000 or more on the weekends. In all likelihood, Fair Hill will draw ever-increasing galleries.

One of the most popular and exciting attractions of this three-day event is a full-fledged driving competition. It is described in the section on driving later in the chapter.

Admission: General admission costs $6 per day, with several deluxe packages offered for the span of the event. For $45, one receives two tickets to each day's doings, along with preferred parking, admission to the VIP tent, where lunches may be purchased. Patrons, at $75, receive the Friends benefits, along with two invitations to the pre-event sponsor's party and two passes to "Tea at Dressage" held on dressage day. For $150, one receives the previously listed perks, along with gourmet lunches each day and VIP parking.

WAREDACA-HOWARD IRON BRIDGE
Laytonsville, MD

When: Fall, usually in mid-October. Also, in spring, late May. The fall event has hosted the Area II Training Championships and the team championships. All three disciplines may be seen each day at this large, well-attended event. Divisions include Preliminary, Open Training, and a number of Novices.

Directions: From D.C., take the Baltimore-Washington Parkway to Georgia Avenue, Route 97 north, to Route 650. Right on Route 650, Damascus Road for one mile.

VIRGINIA HORSE TRIALS
Virginia Horse Center
Lexington, VA

When: Fall, usually the last Saturday in October. Also spring, first weekend in June. The fall event has hosted the Area II Preliminary Championship. Divisions ranged from novice to preliminary. Dressage and stadium jumping is held on Saturday, with cross country and more stadium jumping on Sunday.

Directions: From D.C., take I-66 west to I-81 south to I-64 west to the first exit on Route 11 north. From Route 11, take the first left onto Route 39. The Virginia Horse Center is one half mile on the left.

Like Commonwealth Park, the Virginia Horse Center is one of those places horse enthusiasts will want to visit at some time or other. The cross country course at the Virginia Horse Center really rolls up, down and around a natural bowl, making it a good place for viewing. Jumping and dressage are held in rings that have permanent bleachers. The Lexington area is interesting to visit and fall colors, likely to arrive at the time of the horse trials, add to the already impressive beauty of the area. Those who wish to be in Lexington the weekend of the fall trials should book early, because the area fills up with leaf lookers, and visitors to special events at area colleges.

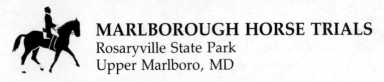

MARLBOROUGH HORSE TRIALS
Rosaryville State Park
Upper Marlboro, MD

When: Fall, generally second Sunday in November.

Contact: Edward Coffren, III
2817 Crain Highway
Upper Marlboro, MD 20772

Phone: 301-627-2298

Directions: From the Washington Beltway, take Route 4 east to Route 301 south to Rosaryville State Park, which will be on the right, just past Osburn Road.

A new event in 1992, held at Rosaryville State Park near Upper Marlboro, MD. The park is a thousand-acre tract surrounding Mt. Airy Mansion, the 18th-century hunting lodge of George Calvert, 3rd Lord of Baltimore. In its first year, the event offered novice and training divisions. The cross country course was designed by Roger Halter, who designed the Rolex course for the World Championship in 1978. Plans are to add a preliminary course as soon as funding can be arranged.

DRESSAGE

In America, dressage hasn't been much of a spectator sport. Those with an affinity for speed and daring liken attending a dressage event to watching paint dry. Dressage is appreciated by large crowds in Europe, where audiences are more sophisticated about the discipline.

Dressage has been described as ballet on horseback. It may be defined as the training of the riding horse through a series of school movements. In its highest form, dressage reaches the levels seen at the Spanish Riding School in Vienna (Austria, that is). Like ballet and figure skating, dressage is an athletic discipline based on correct form and grace. Like a prima ballerina, a grand prix level dressage horse must be both strong and flexible. The horse must also be completely disciplined to the wishes of his rider. Dressage riders, especially in the upper levels, display classically correct style. In jumping and other equestrian disciplines, one occasionally finds a maverick who can accomplish amazing feats in an unorthodox style, but this doesn't seem to play through in dressage, where ten years of concentrated work is needed to bring a horse and rider to the topmost levels.

Each competitor in each class performs the same test (except in the case of free style and musical rides). As in the compulsory figure phase of skating, certain movements must be performed at each level, and each of these is given a score of one to 10 by one to three judges. The ride is performed in an arena, usually 20 meters by 60 meters, or about 66 feet by 195 feet. In some lower level tests, a small arena, which is 20 meters by 40 meters, is used. The arena is delineated by large, visible letters along the sides, so that the accuracy of each movement may be gauged.

Horses of any age, breed, sex, color or national origin may compete. Riders are equally unrestrained by discriminatory classifications. Classes may be restricted to riders under 21, or to riders or horses who have not won a certain number of competitions. Otherwise, restrictions are based on previous experience. For instance, a horse that has excelled in third level dressage may not be dropped back to a first level.

The levels of dressage performed begin with training level, a very simple test in which the horse is asked to walk, trot, and canter on a straight line and around 20 meter circles (the width of the arena). The carriage of the horse is relatively natural at this stage. In each successive level, second through fifth, an increasing degree of collection and extension is required at all three gaits, and the tests are composed to take account of the increase in difficulty.

International level tests are frequently performed at shows in the Capital area. They include Prix St. George, Intermediate, and the most rigorous of all, Grand Prix. In the upper level tests, besides the basic gaits, the horse is asked to perform the passage, a very concentrated, elevated trot, and the piaffe, an adaptation of the trot which is actually done in place. These movements and the pirouette, in which the cantering horse plants his hind feet and pivots around in a full circle, resemble movements one would see at the Spanish Riding School.

Dressage in America has received boosts as a spectator sport from several quarters in recent years. For one, the level of riding at shows has so improved that the American team earned a bronze medal in the 1992 Olympics, wresting it from a field of nations including Russia, Germany, Switzerland and Denmark that have dominated since the founding of the modern Olympics. On the final night of the 1992 Washington International Horse Show, a crowd of 10,000 was transfixed by the performance of Carol Lavell and Gifted, bronze medal winners in 1992 and the most successful American dressage combo in Barcelona. Even those spectators who had never seen dressage before could appreciate the balance and musicality of the pair. A nice side note about Lavell, 49, and her mount is that they started together on the lower levels and reached the pinnacle together.

Some of the top riders are European and some, like Lavell, have come up through the national ranks. Those who live in or make forays to the Capital area include Felicitas von Negmann-Cosel, Mary Alice Malone, Gretchen Verbonic, Todd Bryan, Allison Head, Linda Zang, Wendy Carlson and Lendon Gray.

Further, more shows include classes that are fun to watch, like the musical free style that so delights audiences at Washington. In the musical free style, each competitor choreographs his own performance to the music of his choice. These tests are judged on artistry and choreography, as well as technical achievement. Certain movements must be included and there are time limits. The Pas de Deux follows the basic format, except the musical ride is performed by two horses. The horses are generally matched in appearance and in stride, and this influences the final score. Depending on the whim of the choreographer, the movements of the horses may mirror one another, oppose one another, or be performed in lock step as in a ballet.

The discipline has been given a real leg up by the Washington International Horse Show, which features dressage as a special exhibition. The Washington show keeps both competition and spectator interest in mind. Spectators should be advised that the majority of shows in the area are almost all free to the public, but they are geared to the competitor and lack the most basic amenities such as sound systems and announcements of scores that would give the neophyte viewer any clue as to what's going on. So spectators will have to take dressage as they find it.

Specific information about shows and dates may be obtained from area dressage associations. These associations are manned by volunteers and have the largest memberships of any regional dressage organizations in the country. Membership in the Potomac Valley Dressage Association easily tops 1,000 members, with 500 more in the northern Virginia branch of the Virginia Dressage Association. Between them and CDCTA, described earlier in this chapter, the Capital area boasts a density of dressage shows unmatched anywhere else in the U.S.

WASHINGTON INTERNATIONAL HORSE SHOW
USAir Arena
Landover, MD

Contact: Washington International Horse Show
9079 Shady Grove Court
Gaithersburg MD 20877

Phone: 301-840-0281

Washington's support of dressage goes back more than a decade. During most of that time, dressage was limited to exhibits in which one rider put on an abbreviated display while the ring was reset or the crowd took a stretch. Now, however, the show has been tapped to host the North American finals for the Volvo World Cup Dressage Championships. The show also hosts a qualifier for the World Cup Jumping Championships. Class sponsors are reportedly very pleased with the arrangements at Washington and the audience response. In Europe, jumping and dressage are often hooked together at the same event and draw large crowds. In spite of this history and tradition in Europe, few indoor facilities there can match the capacity of USAir Arena (formerly the Capital Centre). Dressage in Washington is thus performed for one of the largest crowds assembled anywhere for an indoor show. The audience for Washington's World Cup qualifiers is enlarged even more by the fact that these classes are shown over ESPN International, beamed not only to audiences in this country, but also in such dressage-literate places as Great Britain and Germany.

The Washington International Horse Show and New York's National Horse Show are the only two international competitions held indoors in the U.S. The fact that Greg Gingery, president of the WIHS, is committed to including both world-class jumping and dressage makes the Washington show a bonanza.

A dressage class is held the final Saturday and Sunday night of the show. Top jumping classes are held every night of the show, with the World Cup qualifier on the final Sunday night. Other nights of the show, a dressage exhibition is offered. Directions to the show, ticket prices and expanded details about the schedule may be found in the chapter about horse shows.

VIRGINIA DRESSAGE ASSOCIATION

Contact: Darlene Jenkins
Route 12, Box 830
Sterling, VA 22107

Phone: 703-430-0154

The Virginia Dressage Association (VADA) sponsors 40 or more dressage shows each year. Both schooling shows and larger recognized shows (those registered with the American Horse Shows Association and the U.S. Dressage Association) are found on their schedule. VADA is organized by chapters, with the NOVA chapter serving northern Virginia.

Many competitions are clustered in northern Virginia, along with important shows at the Virginia Horse Center in Lexington, VA, at the Virginia State Horse Show in Richmond at Strawberry Hill and at Commonwealth Park in Culpeper. Other important dressage shows are held at Foxcroft School in Middleburg, at Morven Park in Leesburg and at Frying Pan Park in Herndon.

Competition at Foxcroft goes up to the fourth level. International level tests are offered at other shows listed. Most include musical rides. NOVA-VADA can tell you what's being held when. Local tack shops and newspapers usually list dressage events, too.

VIRGINIA STATE HORSE SHOW: Generally, Strawberry Hill hosts a dressage competition in mid-April and mid-July. See Chapter IX.

MORVEN PARK hosts a number of schooling shows, along with big AHSA shows in May and September. The schedule of recognized dressage events stretched to four with the big Potomac Valley Dressage Association show moving there in the face of construction at Prince George's Equestrian Center. Morven Park is a beautiful backdrop for anything, including a picnic.

VIRGINIA HORSE CENTER in Lexington also hosts multiple major dressage events. These occur in May and October, with the Ljungquist Memorial Finals in September. The Ljungquist Memorial is an important regional competition, with championships in all levels, training through Grand Prix. The late Col. Bengt Ljungquist lived in the D.C. area for over ten years. During that time, he coached the U.S. Olympic Team that won the bronze medal at Bromont and was instrumental in the careers of Robert Dover, Kay Meredith, Linda Zang and Elizabeth Lewis, some of America's best competitors and now excellent teachers and judges. The Ljungquist Finals have been paired with the American Horse Shows Association Regional Dressage Finals.

It is about a three-hour drive from D.C., but competitors consider it the finest facility of its kind, with an excellent indoor ring and other covered arenas.

FRYING PAN PARK, an extensive horse facility near Herndon, hosts a major dressage do, generally in mid-July.

Directions: From D.C., take the Dulles Toll Road to the Herndon/Chantilly exit, Exit 2, to Route 675. Turn left on West Ox Road, approximately 1.6 miles. Turn left to Frying Pan Park, one block on the left.

FOXCROFT SCHOOL hosts a recognized dressage event in August. Competition goes to fourth level, with a predominance of lower level tests. The show has been minus niceties like a loudspeaker system, but has a particularly handsome backdrop. Located only two miles from Middleburg, Foxcroft is ideal for inclusion on a day trip to one of Virginia's most charming villages.

Directions: From D.C., take I-66 to Route 50 west. Take Route 50 to Middleburg. Turn right at the light onto Route 626. About 3 miles north of Middleburg, turn right on Foxcroft School Road. Turn right onto school grounds. This turn is generally marked with a competition sign, in addition to the school sign.

POTOMAC VALLEY DRESSAGE ASSOCIATION

Contact: Carol Schwartz
6500 Sweetwater Drive
Derwood, MD 20855

Phone: 301-869-2504

The Potomac Valley Dressage Association is one of the largest in the U.S. Like VADA, it is divided into chapters. It hosts numerous schooling events, stages major spring and fall shows as well as chapter championships later in the fall. The PVDA Fall Show dates back to 1985. It has been held at the Prince George's Equestrian Center in Maryland, the Maryland Horse Center and at Morven Park. The big spring and fall shows are free to the public, feature musical free styles and proper awards ceremonies. A Pas de Deux and even a Quadrille, for four riders, have been added. Another popular PVDA show that features excellent hospitality and a unique setting is the Eastern Shore Dressage Show in Hebron, MD.

DRIVING

Before there were Cadillacs, there were carriages, carts and covered wagons. Through much of the 20th century, horse-drawn vehicles were stored in barns or displayed in museums. Now, suddenly, they are back on the road again in increasing numbers. In fact, where you see one horse-drawn carriage, you are likely to see a cadre of carriages. That is because there is safety in numbers, according to members of carriage driving societies.

Many of the activities of carriage societies are for participants, not spectators. Two popular activities are pleasure drives and picnic drives. On pleasure drives, members meet at appointed spots and times for a drive on lightly traveled roads through the countryside. On picnic drives, all of the above is true, but a picnic is held, perhaps along the way.

Passers-by who witness this spectacle at the very least stop and gawk. Those with a real interest are invited to come to the spot where horses are "put to" or hitched up. Driving society members say the public does not often accept this invitation, but it is one sincerely made. The scenery alone is worthy of a visit. Not only is there the activity of putting on harness and hitching horses to carriages and carts, but during the time-consuming process, most members are happy enough to discuss their carriages, horses and driving experiences.

Some of the clubs hold driving shows and most are free and open to the public. The driving shows, like horse shows, feature ring classes in which competitors are matched against one another. Gaits performed in driving classes are the walk and collected walk, as well as the trot, collected trot and extended trot. Some classes are open to women, some to men, others to novices, ponies, horses, pairs and so on.

The most demanding driving competition is the combined driving event. The first phase, or day, in the case of a three day, is devoted to dressage. Rather than riding the horse through a series of patterns, the horse or pony is driven. The gaits displayed are the walk and various speeds of the trot. The movements, such as cutting across the diagonal of the ring, may sound simple until one realizes that making it all come out accurately and smoothly, especially with a four-in-hand, is a feat akin to making a right-hand turn in traffic with an 18-wheeler.

The dressage arena is 40 by 80 meters for the lower levels and 40 by 100 meters for the upper levels, compared to 20 by 40 meters and 20 by 60 meters in dressage tests that are ridden. The aids or signals to the horse available to the driver are the voice, whip and hands. The whip and voice of the driver provide forward motion just as the seat and legs of a rider do. The driver, in fact, is traditionally referred to as the whip. In ridden dressage tests, the voice may not be used and penalties of up to minus 2 are meted out for each offense. In driving, the voice may be used "discretely and subtly." It has been observed that the hushed tones of the driver in the dressage ring can give way to more raucous encouragement during the marathon phase outdoors.

During the marathon, phase two, drivers urge their horses onward through streams and other difficult hazards. The competition consists of a trot phase, a walk phase and a hazard phase, for an overall distance of about five miles in the training division to a maximum of about 15 miles in the advanced division. In the marathon phase, horses are required to keep to a trot and are penalized for breaking to a gallop, except when negotiating the hazards. Time penalties are given to those who do not finish within a set time for the course. Each hazard is timed as well; these may be taken as swiftly as the driver dares.

The marathon phase leads to the death-defying photos one sees of the carriages careening through water hazards and of wide-eyed grooms gawking at a large oak as the carriage is maneuvered through a haze of trees. Every carriage, even the smallest pony cart, must have a groom aboard. Should the horse and carriage encounter difficulty along the way, the groom dismounts and assists as needed. Should the groom, who is sometimes referred to as navigator, need to step down within the flagged area of an obstacle, a penalty is incurred. If whatever correction is required is made outside the zone, penalties are not incurred. One whip cheerfully offered that her husband, who serves as groom sometimes runs beside the rig making adjustments between obstacles, outside the penalty zone. If a carriage turns over within the obstacle, the competitor may continue if the vehicle is righted within the time limit. The most usual task performed by the groom, however, is that of navigator. The navigator keeps time for the course, reminds the whip which way to turn after each obstacle and also of the test to be faced as they approach each obstacle. The navigator on one husband/ wife teams shouts instructions to the horses, a task usually performed by the driver, in what must be the ultimate example of back seat driving.

The third phase is the cones, in which horses are driven through a series of cones crowned with tennis balls. The width between the cones is gauged to the width of the carriage wheels plus 50 centimeters for the training division, down to 20 centimeters, or about eight inches, for the advanced division. Penalties are meted out for each ball dislodged. Time penalties are also assessed against horses that exceed the time allowed on course. In this phase, upper level competitors often travel at a gallop.

In addition to these three phases, scores are given for presentation. This started as a safety check to make certain the driver had a whip and spares—a kit containing replacements in case of breakage in the marathon, such as a spare rein. Nowadays, everything is also subjected to a white glove test. Extra marks go to outstanding turnouts (as the horse or horses, vehicle and driver are called) with attention paid to such details as the appropriateness of the dress of the driver to the style of the carriage. In dressage and in the cones, the driver is required to wear a hat, gloves and lap robe or apron and to carry a whip capable of reaching the hind quarters of the lead horse.

One step down from combined driving in terms of difficulty are pleasure driving marathons. Though less demanding that the open driving competitions, they feature all three phases. In these, even in the marathon phase, a driver is expected to wear a hat and apron (covering the knees if the whip is a woman) over conservative clothing. A whip is always carried and a spare kit must be in the carriage. The horses or ponies must be kept to a trot. The overall impression should be that the whip is having a grand ole time driving around the course. Even the "posture and dress of the grooms and passengers" are judged.

AMERICAN DRIVING SOCIETY

P.O. Box 160
Metamora, MI 48455

Phone: 810-664-8666

The American Driving Society or ADS is the national rules-making society for driving, as the NSHA is for steeplechasing. The following area events are listed in the ADS schedule.

Fair Hill, MD: April, a full three-day driving event and, in October, an advance championship open driving event, held in conjunction with the international three-day event.

Stratford Hall, VA: Generally, every fourth year in April. An invitational pleasure drive, with a fantastic display of carriages and four-in-hands.

Commonwealth Park, VA: Driving event, new in '93. For directions and contacts at Commonwealth, please see the combined training section of this chapter.

Woodlawn Plantation, near Mt. Vernon, VA: A coaching drive, mid-May.

My Lady's Manor Driving Club sponsors a pleasure driving show and three-phase event in Monkton, MD in June.

Rose Hill Manor, Frederick, MD: A pleasure drive in conjunction with special events at the museum.

Steppingstone Museum: A pleasure show at the annual opening of the museum in Havre de Grace, MD.

Plantation Driving Club: Clinics and picnic drives throughout the year.

 **FAIR HILL INTERNATIONAL "DAY IN THE COUNTRY"**
Fair Hill, MD

Contact: Pat Shipley
P.O. Box 172
Middletown, DE 19700

Phone: 302-378-4520

Directions: Found in this chapter under combined training

Fair Hill Driving is the biggest and best this side of Gladstone NJ. (Gladstone, traditional home of the U.S. Olympic Team, was the site of the World Championship Pair Driving Event in 1993. The United States won the right to host this competition by winning the World Pair Driving Championship in Europe in 1991). Fair Hill holds several driving events during the year, the most important of which are the Fair Hill Three-Day Driving in April and the Fair Hill International Advanced Driving in October. In April, preliminary and advance events are offered. In October, advanced competition is offered, with championships held for single ponies and single horses. Pairs and four-in-hands also compete at Fair Hill. Drivers from as far away as California and Canada have competed at Fair Hill, since it first started hosting big-time driving events in 1989.

232

MORVEN PARK
Leesburg, VA 22075

Contact: Morven Park
Route 3, Box 50
Leesburg, VA 22075

Phone: 703-777-2414

Morven Park has the biggest and best carriage collection in the area, thanks to the late Mrs. Viola Winmill. Mrs. Winmill, one of a long list of New Yorkers who became enchanted with the area in the early part of the century, lived in Warrenton, VA, where she served as master of the Warrenton Hounds for years. Mrs. Winmill hunted six days a week, and rode cross country on the Sabbath. In her spare time, between horse shows and dog shows, she took up coaching. She mastered the art of driving a four-in-hand, a feat of strength and skill for this slight if very fit woman. She finally retired from that activity after several disastrous crashes. The coup de grace came when her team geed when it should have hawed (went left, not right, in mule skinners' jargon) on one of the steep streets in Old Town Warrenton. The mistake made matchsticks of her magnificent coach, and didn't help her husband, a passenger, either. Mrs. Winmill took home the pieces and made the wheels into tables and incorporated other parts into furniture for her Whiffletree Farm. (Whiffletree is the portion of harness through which the traces are run.)

Mrs. Winmill had plenty more carriages, many of which were purchased when she and her husband, who founded the stock brokerage firm of Gude Winmill, traveled to Europe. Perhaps her best remembered rig is a miniature coach, which was hitched to four Shetland ponies, named Happy Boy and Happy Girl, Dapples and Dimples. Through the years Mrs. Winmill accumulated quite a collection, and in her declining years, she pondered over where to leave the carriages. She selected Morven Park, and built a carriage house there, which now houses her collection of 100 carriages.

A tour of the carriage museum is given as part of the tour of the historic house and gardens. Aficionados will be interested in Morven Park's extensive library of carriage books.

For directions to Morven Park, please see the Morven Park listing earlier in this chapter under the heading of Combined Training.

ROSE HILL CARRIAGE SOCIETY
Frederick, MD

Contact: Ms. Colin Clevenger, Curator
Rose Hill Manor Park
1611 North Market Street
Frederick, MD 21701

Phone: 301-694-1648

The Rose Hill Carriage Society holds picnic and pleasure drives on a regular basis. The club organizes a large carriage drive on Sunday early in October as part of Farm Weekend at Rose Hill Manor Park. The public is cordially invited to come watch members hitch up and get ready for the parade. Members are dressed in costumes appropriate to the time period of their carriage. The carriages circle the mansion, then proceed through the historic district of Frederick.

Rose Hill Manor, which was the home of Thomas Johnson, the first Governor of Maryland, has a carriage museum and a children's museum, which features lots of activities to give a hands-on opportunity to learn about earlier times.

PIEDMONT DRIVING CLUB

Contact: Piedmont Driving Club
P.O. Box 206
Boyce, VA 22620

Phone: 703-955-2659

The Piedmont Driving Club, which attracts members from across northern Virginia, holds regular picnic and pleasure drives. Passers-by who happen upon the handsome gathering of carriages this club can assemble are in for a treat. The line of carriages on parade can be long, and Piedmont member Charlie Matheson regularly drives his quartet of handsome homebred Cleveland Bays.

Piedmont has been sponsoring a delightful pleasure driving show annually since 1981. The event generally is held in September at Foxcroft School. The stately facade of the exclusive hunt country girls' school, century-old oaks and the Blue Ridge Mountains form a sumptuous background for the competition, which itself is a feast for the eyes. Only a double handful of spectators attend the show, though it is free to the public.

A pleasure driving show is held on Saturday, featuring standard driving classes along with turnout classes for several categories of vehicles. The two-wheel division is open to Meadowbrooks, Long Island, Tub, Norfolk, Village and road carts, or any two-wheel country vehicle driven to a single pony or horse. The sporting or park vehicles class is open to two- and four-wheel vehicles such as traps, gigs, dog carts and phaetons put to singles, pairs, or tandems. "Antique vehicles" must contain no more than 50 percent of replacement parts. The concours d'elegance is strictly a beauty contest, in which the winner is the turnout judged to present the most elegant picture. Finally, there is the open ride and drive, in which entries drive, after which they are unharnessed and saddled for the riding phase.

On Sunday, dressage, obstacle driving or cones, and a pleasure marathon are held. The different phases are set up fairly close in time and distance. The dressage lasts all morning and can run past noon. The cones have started long before dressage has finished, so a spectator can see both phases within a short period of time. The pleasure marathon starts shortly after noon and lasts most of the afternoon. The course is three to five miles with four hazards. Drivers pop in and out of view of the central area near the dressage rings and secretary's stand. The obstacles form four corners around this central area, so spectators can move from one to the other quickly and easily.

The aim of a pleasure drive is to make everything look pleasurable. The scene is surely one to please, with attractive, smartly trotting horses, ponies, and pairs transporting nattily dressed ladies and gents out for a drive.

MY LADY'S MANOR DRIVING CLUB

Contact: Joyce Clayton
2026 Garrett Rd.
Manchester, MD 21102

Phone: 410-239-7607

My Lady's Manor sponsors an annual driving show and combined driving event in the Monkton, MD, area, generally in June. The club also sponsors clinics and pleasure drives through the year.

LADEW TOPIARY GARDENS
Monkton, MD

When: Open mid-May

Contact: Ladew Topiary Gardens
3535 Jarrettsville Pike
Monkton, MD 21111

Phone: 410-557-9570

Directions: From D.C., take I-95 north to I-695 toward Towson. Take Exit 27B, north on MD 146 about 14 miles to Ladew Gardens (signs on the right).

There are many reasons to visit Ladew Gardens: its carriage museum is just one. The topiary gardens feature fanciful sculptures, including a rider leaping over a fence in pursuit of a pack of boxwood hounds. The house is open from mid-April through October 31, Tuesday through Sunday. Other horsey activities include polo on Sundays from mid-May through the summer and early fall. Please see the chapter on polo for details. Ladew is the beneficiary of the My Lady's Manor Race Meet.

Admission: $7 for tour of house and gardens, $5 for self-guided tour of gardens.

DRIVING FOR THE DISABLED BENEFIT

Contact: Sybil Dukehart
4246 Madonna Road
Jarrettsville, MD 21084

Phone: 410-557-7163

Ever wondered what it would be like to travel in one of those beautiful carriages seen in movies and museums? These primo vehicles are being restored and moving onto the roads in increasing numbers. Mrs. Dukehart, a champion of Driving for the Disabled and herself a renowned driver, assembled the best collection she could find for this special event, which began in 1992. For a fee of $100, contributors climb aboard a four-in-hand or unique unicorn, in which a single horse is hitched in front of a pair. The drive goes up the Northern Central Railroad Trail in Gunpowder Falls State Park. The package includes a reception at a private carriage barn, and lunch and tour at Ladew Topiary Gardens. The benefit is held on a weekday in October, when the fall foliage is at its peak and the public path can be temporarily cleared.

STRAWBERRY HILL STEEPLECHASE
State Fair Grounds at Strawberry Hill
Richmond, VA

Contact: Sue Mullins
P.O. Box 26805
Richmond, VA 23261

Phone: 804-228-3238

The Strawberry Hill Steeplechase incorporates a major carriage drive with its steeplechase each April. A large and impressive collection of carriages from a wide geographic area are invited to participate in pre-race activities. Participating carriages are parked along the steeplechase course the evening before the race so that patrons can view them at their leisure. The carriages then parade around the inside of the large stock barn which is converted into the site of the black-tie dinner dance for patrons. On race day, drivers trek over to the state capitol for a brief reception, then carriages turn back to the race course for a special exhibition at the steeplechase.

For ticket information and directions to the course, please see the chapter on Steeplechasing in Virginia.

ENDURANCE RIDING

Endurance rides, like most horse events, are for competitors. Two formats are used. In one style ride, competitors are required to finish a course of 25 to 100 miles in a pre-designated window of time, and are judged also on recovery rates of vital signs—the heart rate and respiration—and general soundness and conditioning of the horse. The other style ride is an actual horse race, in which the winner is the first horse to finish. Each horse in these races must also meet standards of soundness and recovery. In both styles of rides, veterinary checks are held before and after the rides, and at a number of points along the trail. Several of each style of ride are held in Virginia, along with the Old Dominion 100 mile, one of the three most prestigious and difficult rides in the United States.

 OLD DOMINION 100-MILE RIDE
4-H Center
Front Royal, VA

When: second Saturday in June

Contact: John Crandell III
Box 216
Galesville, MD 20765

Phone: 410-867-2145

Old Dominion rates up there in terms of difficulty with the Tevis Cup, held in the rugged mountains in the West. The Virginia ride starts at 5:00 A.M. at the 4-H Center in Front Royal, and crosses the Shenandoah at historic McCoy's Ford, used for thousands of years by the Indians and later by Daniel Morgan, who built military roads for George Washington. Much of the ride takes place in the George Washington National Forest. The winners usually finish around dark, with the 30 or so finishers coming in by 5:00 A.M. the following morning, the cut off time for the ride. The winning horse must pass, in addition to a vet check Friday and frequent checks along the trail, a final check one hour after finishing.

The ride is occasionally used by veterinary researchers to study some particular aspect of equine anatomy. Matthew Mackay-Smith, D.V.M., long associated with the ride (which dates from 1974), said that the competitors are most cooperative when such research is conducted. The ride once had a fair number of spectators of an unusual sort—human competitors in the 100-mile race. These long-long distance runners held their own against the horses for the first 50 miles. In fact, the number of runners has increased to the degree that the running event is now held on a separate weekend.

Spectators not wishing to run the 100 miles but willing to put forth an effort can see something of this interesting event. The veterinary inspection Friday afternoon is one opportunity; the other may be found on the trail itself. Hikers can incorporate a portion of the ride into their outing, with hopes of seeing the competitors pass by. Another interesting and busy spot to stake out is a veterinary check on the trail. Here, competitors clock in to have their mounts' heart rate, respiration, and general condition checked, and re-present them to inspectors when a sufficient recovery is met. While they wait, support crews work on the horses, sponging them off, offering man and beast alike water and nourishment, checking shoes and gear. A leader board is also kept at the vet checks, so that one can follow the progress of the ride. Watching this event has been compared to watching a golf tournament. You will not see every player at every hole, but you can have a fascinating time if you're willing to walk. Trophies and prizes are presented at the 4-H Center the next day. Prizes include coveted completion awards to all who cross the finish lines within 24 hours and meet the veterinary requirements.

JOUSTING

Jousting, which, to many urbanites is associated only with medieval knights in shiny, 200-pound armor on chargers that weighed a ton, is the Official State Sport of Maryland. Only two or three states have state sports, and jousting became Maryland's by an act of the legislature in 1962. Jousts dot the countryside from April to October, predominantly in summer.

Jousting in its contemporary form, namely with competitors trying to hook small rings, not fellow knights, with a lance, came to Maryland with the first load of horses in 1634. Poking lances at knights was banned in England in 1599. With the advent of gunpowder, lances lost their effectiveness on battlefields. Going for the rings, like those used today, sharpened skills and entertained knights.

The English settlers landed with an interest in hunting, racing and jousting. The annual joust at Rose Hill Manor in Frederick, MD, celebrated its 200th anniversary in 1993. A number of other jousts on the Maryland schedule are well over a century old. These could claim to be much older still, had it not been for the Revolutionary War, during and after which colonists lost their tastes for traditional English sport. Jousts were back in vogue by the time of the Civil War; and after, jousts were used as fund raisers to build war memorials and cemeteries for the war dead.

For a joust, participants bear some fashion of a keenly pointed stick—generally about seven feet in length, made of wood or metal—and ride horses or ponies of any description. The jousting field is 80 yards long with three sets of rings suspended six feet off the ground at 20 yard intervals. The course, almost the length of a football field, must be covered in eight seconds in Virginia, nine in Maryland. Metal rings used in the first round are one-half inch in diameter. All participants make three runs. Those who hook all nine rings proceed to a tie-breaker with rings that are one-quarter of an inch in diameter.

Lacking television, drive-in movies and video games, rural communities would liven up the summer season with an occasional joust. Even today, jousts are often part of family gatherings in the country, though one participant said his family now uses cars to traverse the course.

In Virginia, fewer jousts seem to have survived, but the state does have its own special jousting story, repeated in a recent biography of Turner Ashby. One of the daring Confederate cavalry leaders, Ashby is reported to have burst out with the first Rebel Yell at a joust at Green Gardens Farm near Upperville. (The big brick house is located on Green Gardens Road, which turns north off Route 50.) Local historians figure the jousting course was located in a flat field just after the hump-back bridge. By the time of John Brown's raid, the yell was well known. Ashby and his men used the high-pitched squeal to communicate from the ridges overlooking Harpers Ferry. Next time you hear a Rebel Yell, think of Ashby letting his horse loose down a jousting course.

HUME RURITARIAN JOUST
Hume, VA

When: Held annually the second Saturday in August

Contact: Emley Buikstra
Route 1, Box 311B
Hume, VA 22639

Phone: 703-364-1700

Hours: 3:00 P.M. through dinner

Directions: From D.C., travel west on I-66 to the Markham exit. Travel south on Route 688 about 6 miles to the old school grounds on the right just as you enter the village of Hume. Don't blink or you'll miss Hume. Do admire the post office, which is the size of a good sized kitchen pantry. That and a renovated country store are the long and short of Hume. On your way there, you will pass Leeds Episcopal Church, founded in 1769, the oldest church in Leeds Parish of Lord Fairfax's original land grant.

The joust at Hume is not old by area standards. It has been sponsored by the local Ruritarians for about 30 years, but par-

Jousting remains a popular sport in Virginia and Maryland. Sir Michael of Leeds goes for the rings at the joust in Hume, VA.
Credit: Betsy Branscome

ticipants who were born and raised in the area agree that jousts have been held there for generations.

Crowds saunter in around mid-afternoon, coming in family groups and bearing coolers and blankets. This is definitely the way to go if you come to a joust. Spectators lie contentedly on the hillside, idly watching participants roar down the jousting course. They cheer for their favorites, and if they have come without a champion, most will have picked one before the final awards are given.

Children adjourn to the playground equipment at will, and local politicians work the crowd. Should a sudden summer shower blow by, all huddle under the picnic shelter where the barbecue dinner is served after the athletic competition is completed and when the meat, which has cooked overnight in pits, is deemed ready.

The dinner itself is worth the drive out from D.C. Not only does the barbecue feature locally grown beef and pork, but also corn and tomatoes, picked from nearby gardens at the peak of ripeness. To the bounty of nature, local Ruritarian wives add to the feast with their finest homemade desserts.

After dinner, drawings are held for door prizes. The prizes are quite good, and may include a healthy young pig; so if you're feeling lucky, you might drive out in your pickup truck. The drawings last into the night, but those who use the event as a family homecoming settle into contented groups, catching up on news and renewing acquaintances as dusk falls.

Admission: $5, a $12 ticket includes barbecue dinner.

MARYLAND JOUSTING

Contact: Maryland Jousting Tournament Association
328 Bush Chapel Road
Aberdeen, MD 21001

The Maryland Department of Economic Development, Office of Tourism, produces and distributes a jousting schedule annually.

The earliest jousts take place in mid-April, the latest in the final weekend in October. Almost invariably these events are sponsored by civic organizations, including 4-H clubs, riding clubs, and churches. A number are held as competitions or exhibits at special festivals at historic properties and parks. Highlights of the Maryland schedule typically include:

- **Rose Hill Days Festival Joust**
  Rose Hill Manor Park
  Frederick, MD

  When: Mid-May

  Phone: 301-694-1648

- **Steppingstone Museum Joust**
  Steppingstone Museum
  Quaker Bottom Road
  Havre de Grace, MD

  When: Final weekend in July

  Phone: 410-592-8918

- **Dutch Picnic Joust**
  Deer Park Road
  Westminster, MD

  When: First weekend in August

  Phone: 410-795-9625

- **Calvert County Jousting Tournament**
  Christ Church
  Port Republic, MD

  When: Final weekend in August

  Phone: 410-586-0565

- **Prince George's County Fair**
  Prince George's Equestrian Center
  Upper Marlboro, MD

  When: First weekend in September

  Phone: 301-505-0103

- **Frederick Fair Exhibition**
  Frederick, MD

  When: Tuesday of the fair, third week in September

  Phone: 301-834-7488

- **Pemberton Colonial Fair Joust**
  Pemberton, MD

  When: Last weekend in September

  Phone: 410-482-6029

- **Prince George's Farm & Heritage Festival**
  Exhibition Prince George's Equestrian Center
  Upper Marlboro, MD

  When: Final weekend in September

  Phone: 301-884-3390

XII

ODDS AND ENDS

From Tales to Trails

Precise information about the events in this book can be obtained from the contacts listed for each. However, there are other sources for information about specific events that are easy to access. Should your interest in horse events or in the beautiful horses themselves deepen, libraries and special book collections listed here will enable you to read more about the subject. Also included are descriptions of tours offering unique opportunities to see where horses and horse people live. In short, this is the section where you find the "dis" and "dats" not covered elsewhere.

NEWSPAPERS

The Washington Post: Besides baseball, football and basketball, *The Washington Post* sports section does a very acceptable job of covering horse sports. The paper devotes a page or two daily to area racing, chiefly the Maryland tracks, Rosecroft Harness Track and Charles Town Races. The reporters on the beat, Vinnie Perrone and Andrew Beyer, are excellent, and editors put major race stories on page one of sports. On Saturdays and Sundays during spring and fall, readers will find steeplechasing accounts by Laurel Scott on the racing page. Scott's articles, held to several paragraphs, hit the high points of the jump races, but the paper often carries full results on the "Scoreboard" with other box scores. The paper also offers daily coverage with stories and lists of winners during the Washington and Upperville horse shows. Horse shows, trail rides, public riding stables and other

Trail riders course through Washington's Rock Creek Park.
Credit: Courtesy of Rock Creek Park Horse Centre

horse events find their way into the Friday "Weekend" section, under the "On the Move" heading.

Arundel Publications: Newspapers owned by Nick Arundel, chairman of the Virginia Gold Cup, give generous coverage to horse events. The *Fauquier Times-Democrat,* especially, devotes three or more pages weekly to what's going on in the horse community. Coverage includes a full column of upcoming events, excellent photos, previews of the weekend's events and results and in-depth analyses of the previous weekends do's. Reporters Hilary Scheer Gerhardt and Betsy Burke Branscome were recognized by the Virginia Horse Council for the state's most outstanding horse coverage.

Articles by Branscome are picked up by other newspapers in Arundel's chain. The *Loudoun Times* usually offers generous coverage in their sports section, and papers that serve smaller communities, like the *Rappahannock News,* may place a photo of their local point-to-point on top of the fold on the front page. This generous coverage stems from more than the publisher's interest—these papers serve heavy concentrations of horsemen, as witnessed by the extensive lineage of paid classified ads devoted to horses and horse-related goods and services.

PERIODICALS

Besides newspapers, there are a number of nationally distributed periodicals produced in the area, along with scads of broadsheets and smaller local magazines. Some of these are free for the asking, others are available by subscription. Local libraries usually keep several of these publications in their magazine section. The list of small, independently produced advertising tabloids that are glued together with horse news and features is too long to list, but these are free and can be found in stacks in local saddleries and other spots where horsemen gather.

Chronicle of the Horse: Published weekly from the heart of Hunt Country—Middleburg, VA—the *Chronicle* covers steeplechasing, horse shows, hunting, youth activities and most of the sports described in Chapter XI of this book such as dressage, combined training and endurance riding. It was founded in 1937, and back then was filled with delicious details about marriages and other social goings-on among the sporting set, along with their comings and goings, especially who was in Middleburg to hunt. Now its coverage is national in scope, and it is America's equivalent to the British publication *Horse and Hound*. For subscription information call 703-687-6341.

Equus: Published in Gaithersburg, MD, *Equus* is a monthly with a wide national following. The magazine is devoted to horse health features, along with some horse management tips.

Polo: Published by the folks who bring you *Equus*, *Polo* is the national news and life styles magazine of the polo gang. Both *Equus* and *Polo* carry full color photos and charts, and offer a good blend of features and news items. For information about *Equus* and *Polo*, call 301-977-3900.

Middleburg Life: Middleburg's monthly newspaper, also Middleburg's only newspaper. It is long on photos of hunt country folk at play, but also carries some good columns, including an outstanding, if extremely satirical, feature about foxhunting. This is free and can be picked up in many locations around Middleburg and in some surrounding villages as well.

Horse Country: A Warrenton, VA, saddlery, Horse Country now produces a very good bi-monthly newspaper which carries its name. *Horse Country* is sent free to their extensive mailing list and distributed free around Warrenton and surrounding burgs. The publication draws from a bevy of local writers who provide a variety of entertaining and informative features. The newspaper also carries an extensive listing of upcoming events. Call 703-347-3141 to be added to their mailing list.

LIBRARIES

Public libraries and bookstores can, of course, provide further information about horses. The Washington area is especially blessed to have several special libraries that house rare books and extensive collections about horses.

Bowie Branch of Prince George's Public Library

15210 Annapolis Road
Bowie, MD 20715

Hours: Monday–Thursday: 10:00 A.M.–9:00 P.M.; Friday: 10:00 A.M.–6:00 P.M.; Saturday: 10:00 A.M.–5:00 P.M.; Sunday (October–May) 1:00 P.M.–5:00 P.M.

Phone: 301-262-7000

Bowie Library houses the Selima Room, a large reading room stacked high with horse books. The collection is weighted toward racing books and references but contains a first-rate range of equine topics. Further, it features file cabinets bulging with clips and magazine articles. Some of its reference works are treasures such as the complete set of the *British Racing Calendar*, which started in 1743 before there even was a thoroughbred breed registry.

The Selima Room was envisioned when the Bowie library was in its formative stages, out of the belief that it would be good for the library to house a special collection. The specialty was a natural, because the library was built on the grounds of the former Belair Stud, and was near Bowie, formerly a race track, now a training track. (At one time, Pimlico Race Track was said to have had an excellent library; it burned with the clubhouse years ago.) Bowie librarians are helpful and cooperative to those wishing to use the collection. The Selima Room is open during regular library hours.

National Horse and Field Sports Library

301 West Washington Street
Middleburg, VA 22117

Hours: Monday–Friday: 10:00 A.M.–4:00 P.M. It is suggested one call ahead to make certain one of the members of the very small staff is in.

Phone: 703-687-6542

The National Horse and Field Sports Library, formerly the National Sporting Library, is run by a private, non-profit foundation and is open to the public. The new name of this library, founded in 1954, gives a clue to its collection. Mr. Alexander Mackay-Smith, the library's curator, said that when George Ohrstrom, Sr. had the idea for the library, he insisted on including "National" in the name because of his ambitions for the collection. The more general term "Sporting" was initially used because the founders were unsure of the exact direction the collection would take. The bent is toward horses, and hunting with hounds and beagles; but some of the current directors hope to see the shooting and fishing sections of the library expanded.

The collection currently is housed in the basement of the *Chronicle of the Horse,* located on the main street in Middleburg, VA. Plans for expansion include moving the *Chronicle,* the weekly news publication, to another location, allowing the library to take over all of the charming old brick house. This will permit expansion of the collection, along with creation of a comfortable reading room.

Some of the works in the collection are very valuable. It is not out of the ordinary to pick up leather-bound volumes dating from the 1850s that contain hand-tinted lithographs. In addition to numerous fine books, the library contains entire collections of various sporting magazines. With a grant from a local benefactor, *The American Turf Registry and Sporting Magazine,* a fine guide to the sporting scene of the 1800s, has been fully catalogued. Other collections of magazines have not yet been catalogued, but are on microfiche for ease of handling.

National Agricultural Library
10301 Baltimore Blvd.
Beltsville, MD 20705

Hours: Monday–Friday: 8:00 A.M.–4:30 P.M.; stacks close at 4:00 P.M.

Phone: 301-504-5755

The largest agricultural library in the world, this collection contains books, journals, reports, patents and audiovisuals about equine subjects, including stud books that date back to the 1700s. The public may use the library, but not browse through the stacks. The library has closed stacks, meaning librarians fish out materials on request. The library also houses the Animal Welfare Information Center.

HUNT COUNTRY TOURS

Horsemen in Maryland and Virginia annually open up their houses, stables and gardens to interested strangers for the benefit of local causes.

Trinity Episcopal Church Annual Stable Tour

Trinity Church
Route 50
Upperville, VA 22176

When: The tour is always held Saturday and Sunday of Memorial Day weekend. Hours are 10:00 A.M.–5:00 P.M. except at Middleburg Training Center, where one may watch young race horses exercise from 7:00 A.M.–10:00 A.M. on Saturday only.

Phone: 703-592-3343

Trinity Church is sometimes referred to as Paul Mellon's church because he and his wife gave the current building to the community as a gift. Sometimes, it is known simply as "that beautiful church in Upperville." Its first annual stable tour was held in 1959.

Horsemen should not miss this one. Eventually neighbors may get to visit every farm on the list, but this tour lets one get the job done in a day or two. Other tourists come from all over, some by the busload, to enjoy the beautiful countryside and magnificent animals and to get a peak at the private lairs of several prominent scions. Paul Mellon's Rokeby Farm is noted for its architecture and grounds, and will be especially appreciated by horsemen for the grandness of bloodstock the owner has produced through generations of selective breeding. Mellon has won the Arc d'Triumph, the Epsom Derby and, with one of the last crops of horses bred and raised at Rokeby, the 1993 Kentucky Derby.

About 12 farms open annually. Some, like Rokeby, have been on the tour every year. Others are dropped and added. The most recent addition is Newstead Farm, residence of Mr.

and Mrs. Bert Firestone, who have added a major show hunter and jumper training grounds. Demonstrations are part of the program annually. In recent years, these have included performances by Katie Monahan Prudent, one of the country's most successful Grand Prix jumper riders, and demonstration games by Middleburg Polo.

Proceeds go directly into Trinity Church's outreach budget. Recipients include the local rescue squads and fire departments and the "So Others May Eat" program, which feeds the hungry and needy in Washington, D.C.

Admission: Tickets, good for both days, are $13 in advance, $15 the day of the tour.

Historic Garden Week in Virginia

Contact: Garden Week Headquarters
12 East Franklin Street,
Richmond, VA 23219

Phone: 804-644-7776

First held in 1933, Historic Garden Week features on its tours at least a few homes of significance to the riding community. These opportunities occur with regularity in Fauquier County on the Warrenton tour, and in Loudoun County on the Middleburg or Leesburg tour. Any of the venues in the provinces of northern Virginia are possibilities for important horse properties, and if this is a goal, you'll also want to eye carefully the list of homes and gardens open in the Orange and Keswick, VA, areas. One year, the Warrenton Hounds were paraded at one of the hunt country venues open on the tour. Another, the Middleburg tour took in a residence which included extensive training grounds for young family members who had ridden on the Olympic level. The Leesburg tour visited one of the largest, most modern boarding stables in the area, and one that housed international level dressage horses.

Both houses and gardens are open on this tour. At the very least, one will see valuable works of equine art, charming photos of the family hunting or at horse shows and sleek thoroughbreds punctuating the beauty of the surrounding grounds.

Admission: Tickets are $12 per tour, or $4 per house. These can be purchased at the individual homes, or in advance by mail.

Maryland House and Garden Pilgrimage
1105A Providence Road
Towson, MD 21286

Phone: 410-821-6933

Sometimes, but not every year, the Maryland House and Garden Pilgrimage will include horse farms. A staff member says that Maryland is a small state with lots of horses, so the odds are that horse properties will be included. Tours in northern Baltimore County and Harford County almost invariably include horse farms. As an example, ABC race commentator Jim McKay's farm near My Lady's Manor has been on the tour. Call the garden tour office after the first of the year and you can find out if the upcoming tour will be especially gratifying to horse buffs.

Maryland Million Horse Country Tour

Contact: Maryland Million, Ltd.
P.O. Box 365
Timonium, MD 21094

Phone: 410-252-2100

As part of its celebration of, and build-up to, the Maryland Million Day of racing, a whole calendar of events has been developed. Calling it Maryland Million "week" is something of an understatement. Events actually begin four weeks before the Maryland Million goes to the post at Pimlico Race Course on the final Sunday in September. See Chapter VI for details on the race itself.

Horse farms in Baltimore, Carroll, Cecil, Harford and Howard counties have opened their gates to visitors. Besides thoroughbred farms, tourists have had an opportunity to visit an Egyptian Arabian stud farm, a miniature horse farm, Ladew Topiary Gardens and several vineyards.

Admission: Tickets, good for two days, cost $15 for adults, $7.50 for children.

Other events include a special polo match at Ladew Gardens and a Grand Prix jumping competition in Columbia, MD. Events designed to please insiders include a race writer's crabfeast, a Gala Reception, a golf tournament and Breakfast of Champions to announce entries.

BED & BREAKFAST IN HORSE COUNTRY

This listing is not meant to be a tour guide to bed and breakfasts, but a few such establishments in horse country bear mentioning, either for historic significance or other intriguing equine ties. Three B & Bs in Virginia offer riding as well as lodging.

Welbourne

Nathaniel H. Morison III
Middleburg, VA 22117

Phone: 703-687-3201

Welbourne, between Upperville and Middleburg, VA, takes the cake for the most historic lodging in the hunt country. Many, many fox hunters have crossed its well-worn threshold. It can be said fox hunters have been in residence there since the house was built. The Piedmont Hunt, the nation's oldest, began as the private pack of Col. Richard H. Dulany, who built the farm. Col. Dulany also founded the Upperville Horse Show, imported outstanding stallions to upgrade horses bred in the area, and led a cavalry charge at Gettysburg, to name a few of his accomplishments. Direct descendants of Col. Dulany still live at Welbourne, and have welcomed guests into their bed and breakfast since the '30s, when feeding and housing all comers and their horses gratis no longer seemed feasible. The house is well lived in and, like many old places, eccentric. It fascinates Civil War buffs with its stacks of valuable and obscure leather volumes about the war and family memorabilia, as well as fox hunters, with its history and tradition.

Red Fox Inn
2 East Washington Street
Middleburg VA 22117

Phone: 703-687-6301

Red Fox Inn, which sits in the middle of Middleburg at its only traffic light, has been in operation since 1728 and has been the most visible landmark since the village was formed years later. The inn, first known as Chinn's Ordinary, was located between Alexandria and Winchester. No one knows when the first fox hunters stopped there but Lord Fairfax, whose favorite hunt country lay beyond at White Post in Clarke County, might have stopped on his way there. Lord Fairfax, taken by the beauty of the land and its potential for foxhunting, hired young George Washington to survey his western holdings. Washington, Chinn's cousin, was also a visitor.

In modern times, the Middleburg Hunt has long held an annual meet here, in recent years its opening meet. Stirrup cups and country ham are served, after which the riders move north to the fields of Homewood Farm. It certainly provides a photo op and chance for the public to get a glimpse of a real-life fox hunt. Even before there was a Middleburg Hunt, fox hunters visiting Piedmont Hunt hung their hats here, and the Red Fox continues to be a favorite place for the ever increasing legions of hunters to hang their spurs while in town.

You don't have to be a hunter to appreciate the charming accommodations, both in the main inn and in the converted cottages offered for overnight stays. The Red Fox is most English in mood and appearance and serves three meals a day. The back room is especially pub-like in appearance, with its big fireplaces and low ceilings. An ever changing collection of sporting art, for sale down the street at the Red Fox Gallery, graces the walls. As much as you would expect to see fox hunters raising mugs

257

and bursting into song here, you must go down the street to Mosby's Tavern, also operated by Red Fox management, to see the hunt and jump crowd at play.

Conyers House
Sandra & Norman Cartwright-Brown
Slate Mills Road
Sperryville, VA 22740

Phone: 703-987-8025

Conyers House, which began life as Conyer's Old Store in 1810, offers romantic lodging, gourmet dinners on Saturday nights to suit the most discriminating palate and an option to participate in weekend trail rides. The rides meander through the Rappahannock Hunt Country and the nearby Blue Ridge Mountains. Visitors may board their own horses, and qualified riders can hire hunters for a day with the Rappahannock Hounds. The fee for a two-hour ride on one of the Conyers House horses is reasonable. The Conyers House is a short drive from some of the area's best hikes, for those wishing to counterbalance the luscious meals.

Jordan Hollow Farm Inn
Route 2, Box 375
Stanley, VA 22851

Phone: 703-778-2285

Jordan Hollow is located on the western slopes of the Blue Ridge, about 100 miles from Washington.

Jordan Hollow Farm Inn, a 28-room inn, offers three-hour trail rides at a reasonable per hour fee. Beginners ride in western saddles, more advanced riders have a choice of English or western. The trails cover both private and Shenandoah National Park land, and terrain ranges from wooded and mountainous to open meadows. Riding is available daily, and six riders represent an average-sized group. Like other such establishments, Jordan Hollow attracts couples looking for a romantic getaway, but some couples, drawn by an opportunity to ride, bring their children.

The inn has been in business for over 10 years. Reasonably priced breakfasts and dinners are available.

Lavender Hill Farm
RR 1, Box 515
Lexington, VA 24450

Phone: 703-464-5877

Lavender Hill Farm near Lexington, VA, offers a horse lover's package that includes two full days of riding, with lunch on the trail, a full country breakfast each morning, a trout dinner, and, of course, comfortable lodging. Trail rides go through the George Washington National Forest, and in separate packages one can sign up for riding lessons and an introductory course on foxhunting.

TRAIL RIDES
You don't have to buy into the B & B route to hop on a horse for a trail ride. You can enjoy nature from the back of a horse well inside the beltway, or at a number of area parks. Some parks lease horses, others permit riders with their own horses to use marked trails. Those with their own horses looking for new horizons see Chapter X for information about hunt trail rides.

Rock Creek Park Horse Centre
5100 Glover Road NW
Washington, D.C. 20015

Phone: 202-362-0117

Rock Creek Park, coursing through the heart of northwest Washington, still permits horseback riding from Colorado Avenue north to East West Highway and Meadowbrook Riding Stable (see more about Meadowbrook in Chapter IX). Meadowbrook offers riding lessons and boarding, but does not lease horses. Rock Creek Park Horse Centre, south of Military Road, does lease horses for trail rides. Riders must be at least 12 years old. The speed of the one-hour guided rides is held to a walk, which, with the gentleness of the mounts, makes this an activity in which beginners can participate. Riding lessons are also offered. Both Meadowbrook and Rock Creek will board privately-owned horses. Rock Creek holds summer camps and is also the site of the National Center for Therapeutic Riding.

Trail rides out of Rock Creek are offered at 3:00 P.M. Tuesdays through Thursdays, and at least three times a day on Saturdays and Sundays. Weekday rides may be reserved by phone, no later than one hour before the ride. Weekend rides are first-come, first-serve, or by pre-paid reservation—phone reservations not accepted. Cost of a one-hour ride is $17.

Virginia Public Horse Trails

The Virginia Horse Council (more about them later in this chapter) offers a map and list of public horse trails in the state. The trails are organized under national, state and regional headings. The chart lists an address and phone number for each, along with the length of each trail, and a description of the terrain and facilities. Unfortunately, these do not give much of a clue as to whether or not rental horses are available; one must call the parks to find out.

Trail Riders of Today
TROT
Box 75
Brinklow, MD 20862

Phone: 301-588-TROT

The Maryland Horse Council (more about it later in this chapter) does not list information about state trails in its annual directory, but not to worry because the highly active Trail Riders of Today (TROT) offers a monthly newsletter that lists scads of trail riding opportunities. These are almost entirely on the Maryland side of the line. TROT's spring ride schedule includes rides every Saturday, some to regional and state parks, some along the C&O canal. Many start on private farms, and many have a trail leader.

Marriott Ranch
Route 1, Box 113
Hume, VA 22639

Phone: 703-364-2627, 703-364-3741

The folks who bring you Marriott Hotels also offer trail rides on the family ranch near Hume, VA. The rides cross the rolling meadows of the Blue Ridge foothills, and offer glorious vistas of the nearby mountains. The guided trail rides are suitable for beginners. Western saddles are used. Rides are offered daily at 10:00 A.M., NOON and 2:00 P.M., except Mondays. The 1½ hour ride costs $20 on weekdays, $25 on weekends. Phone for reservations.

PUBLIC STABLES

The Washington Post's "Weekend" section lists public riding stables that offer trail rides, both in Virginia and Maryland. Capitol Hill Equestrian Society (CHES), offers its own list of a dozen or so public stables. CHES schedules special rides for its members on a regular basis and even provides the names and numbers of members who are willing to trailer horses for others who lack transportation. (See Club section below).

Equestrian Enterprises

Phone: 703-759-2474

Rides through Great Falls Park on the Virginia side of the Potomac are offered aboard comfortable Tennessee Walking Horses and fox trotters. Special all-day and moonlight rides are offered, as are riding classes.

CLUBS AND ORGANIZATIONS

Clubs offer opportunities for like-minded individuals to come together. The chapters on foxhunting, horse showing, polo, steeplechasing and other horse sports abound with lists of specialty clubs. There are still other clubs for those with more general interests in horses. Such clubs can be springboards to fun and fellowship, as well as sources for knowledge about horses.

Virginia Horse Council
P.O. Box 72
Riner, VA 24149

Phone: 703-544-7471

In a state with as many horses as Virginia, it seems appropriate that the Virginia Horse Council should also be big and active. The Virginia Horse Council lists itself as the spokesman for the Virginia horse industry, devoted to education, legislation, recreation, communication, health and research. They sponsor youth programs, seminars and a yearbook. The Horse Council was incorporated in 1971, two years after the Governor's Task Force recommended the establishment of a modern horse center.

The Horse Council newsletters are informative, and the fat Virginia Horse Industry Directory is chockfull of useful information, including leads to yet more horse organizations and activities. The Horse Council holds a yearly convention, not expensive to attend, and other educational seminars through the year. Membership in the Horse Council is a reasonable $10 per year.

Maryland Horse Council
P.O. Box 4891
Timonium, MD 21093

Phone: 410-252-2100

The Maryland Horse Council was formed in 1984 to represent the common interests of all horse-related organizations in Maryland, as well as to serve as an industry information source. In 1991, the Horse Council published its first comprehensive list of horse organizations. As a newer publication, Maryland's book is not so thick and full of advertising as Virginia's, but it is well laid-out and full of horse organizations to suit all tastes and ages.

The booklet begins with a chapter full of fascinating facts about horses in Maryland, where horse-related businesses represent the third largest industry in the state. In a 1990 horse census, it was estimated that 75,000 horses occupied the state. Thoroughbreds prevailed in terms of numbers, with 28,000 registered animals. That figures out to 2.7 thoroughbreds per square mile.

To supplement the booklet, the Horse Council produces a monthly update of horse events in the state, with dates and contact numbers.

Capitol Hill Equestrian Society

Attention: Debby McBride
1199 Longworth House Office Building
U.S. House of Representatives
Washington, D.C. 20515

Phone: 202-225-3261, 202-828-3035 (voice mail)

Back in 1977, a number of Capitol Hill types, who would rather be riding than working late, formed Capitol Hill Equestrian Society (CHES). The club's purpose is to bring together people with an interest in horses—English, Western, trail riding, or any other horse activity—with a goal of having fun. The group of horse lovers has grown from the initial 11 women and one brave man to 300 members. The ratio of males to females is now almost balanced. Unlike most other such organizations, horse ownership and riding proficiency are not prerequisites to membership or participation.

Monthly programs are well thought-out, varied and interesting. These are generally held the third Tuesday of each month at the Sam Rayburn House Office Building at Independence Avenue and South Capitol Street. Speakers and programs are previewed in the monthly newsletter. An example of speakers include *The Washington Post* ace racing writer Andrew Beyer, retired publisher of *The Chronicle of the Horse* Peter Winants, and talented hunter/jumper rider and trainer Kathy Newman.

The monthly newsletter lists CHES activities along with other area horse events. It is full of interesting odds and ends, such as a review of Dick Francis mysteries, listing of horse flicks and events on television, bits and pieces from the local, national and international horse news. Beside the newsletter, members receive a membership directory, and lists of riding stables and tack shops that give CHES members 10% discounts.

CHES activities range from trail rides to farm visits to driving clinics to practice fox hunts to trips. On one trip to Rosecroft Harness Track members received a demonstration, then got to try driving a racing sulky. In recent years, CHES has planned excursions to major horse events like the World Pair Driving Championship. Special rides have included a trip to Gettysburg Battlefield and Jordan Hollow Farm for a weekend horse fest.

4-H

Contact: County Agricultural Agent

Many 4-H clubs in the Capital area offer horse projects. In Maryland alone, 44 clubs offer projects. Programs, headed by

Pony club and the 4-H teach youngsters valuable lessons about riding, caring for horses, sportsmanship and friendship.
Credit: Roselie Malone

adult volunteers working with county extension agents, emphasize horse care and management. Children are given opportunities to learn how to show project animals. Leadership and sportsmanship are emphasized at all levels. More so than most clubs, the 4-H makes ways for children who don't own horses to participate. The cost of membership is little or none.

United States Pony Club
Kentucky Horse Park
4701 Ironworks Pike
Lexington, KY 40511

Phone: 606-254-7669

The Pony Club was founded in Great Britain in 1928. The first club in the United States received a charter from the British club in 1954, and the United States Pony Club (USPC) was formed in 1956. US membership has grown to 10,000. The USPC is divided into 28 regions, four of them in or near Washington.

The club is open to youths 21 and under. Programs vary with the size and sophistication of the club, but instruction on riding and horse care is always given. Sportsmanship is promoted through the emphasis of team competition, and leadership through a system by which older members assist younger and less experienced members. The goal of the club is "a happy confident child on a happy comfortable horse."

Clubs in Virginia and Maryland are among the oldest, biggest and best in the USPC. As such, they offer high level instruction and competition in eventing, dressage and show jumping. Members proceed to the highest levels of national and international competitions after graduation from pony club. Such advanced skills can leave the horse-loving child that does not own a horse out of many programs. However, with the proliferation of boarding barns in this area, horses can often be leased for mounted lessons. Activities like summer camps, mounted games, and trail rides can help bring the less experienced into the fold. Every club, offers a long list of unmounted activities, including movies, lectures and demonstrations. These give those not bound for the Olympics opportunities to participate.

Capital Region
Kathleen Dougherty
9350 Bessie Clemmon Road
Union Bridge, MD 21791

Phone: 301-898-5994

Delmarva Region
Mrs. Robert E. Read
1537 Old Coach Road
Newark, DE 19711

Phone: 302-737-2499

Maryland Region
Howard M.Skipper
2605 Green Briar Lane
Annapolis, MD 21401

Phone: 410-268-3840

Old Dominion Region
Dorothy B. Renfro
1908 Benefit Road
Chesapeake, VA 23322

Phone: 804-421-2546

Virginia Region
R.C.Howard
202 N. Mooreland Road
Richmond, VA 23229

Phone: 804-740-8352

Appendix A

HORSE SHOW COMPLEXES

A number of large, impressive facilities throughout Virginia and Maryland are designed for horse shows. These complexes stage numerous competitions throughout the year, mostly for the benefit of the riding community. The shows are about perfecting form, earning a record that makes an animal more saleable, achieving enough points to win a year-end championship or the right to enter one of the prestigious indoor shows.

Though, for the most part, the program is not designed with entertainment in mind, spectators are welcome and most often admission is free. One will almost certainly see top horses and very good performances, because of the vast number of excellent horses raised and trained in Maryland and Virginia.

STRAWBERRY HILL EQUESTRIAN COMPLEX

Virginia State Fair Grounds at Strawberry Hill
Richmond, VA

Contact: Atlantic Rural Exposition, Inc.
P.O. Box 26805
Richmond, VA 23261

Phone: 804-228-3238

Directions: See Virginia Horse Shows of Atlanta Rural Exposition, Inc., Chapter IX.

The Virginia State Fair Grounds includes three horse show rings, one of which is covered, extensive stabling and niceties for competitors like paved parking lots and restrooms with flush toilets. There is plenty of seating for spectators: 900 seats in the covered arena and 2,000 at the main ring outside.

Besides the horse show associated with the State Fair, a Virginia State Horse Show is held at Strawberry Hill, along with more than a dozen other shows. Most are for single breeds, such as quarter horses, Arabians, Shetland ponies, mules, draft horses, and hunters and jumpers.

The State Horse Show has been a three-phase affair, held at three different times of the year. However, in 1993, the annual "A" rated show for hunters, jumpers and dressage horses was held in late June, followed by an all-breed show through the 4th of July. Quarter horses and 4-H members get their chance in their segment of the Virginia State Horse Show in August. The middle phase of the State Show, the all-breeds show, like the center of a sandwich, provides the tastiest morsel for the general public. The June segment of the show is like shows of the old style, featuring numerous breeds of horses and styles of competition. This format provides variety, which adds to the spectator appeal of the show.

Arabians, Morgans, saddlebreds, hackneys, roadsters, palominos, and walking horses share the spotlight with pleasure driving horses. Classes start at 8:00 A.M. daily, with night sessions in all three rings.

Admission: Most segments of the state horse show are free to the public. A ticket for the championship segment of the all-breeds show costs around $5 per person in advance, more at the door. The cost depends in part on the special entertainment on display along with a varied horse show program. The most glamorous group booked was the Royal Lippizaner Stallions.

VIRGINIA HORSE CENTER
Lexington, VA

Contact: Virginia Horse Center
P.O. Box 1051
Lexington, VA 24450

Phone: 703-463-2194

Directions: From D.C., take I-66 west to I-81 south. Turn west at Exit 191 (I-64) to Exit 55, Route 11 north. Turn left on Route 39 west, just ¹⁄₁₀ mile from I-64. The horse center is one mile on the left.

Recognizing the worth of the horse to the history and economy of Virginia, the Virginia Horse Center was established by an act of the legislature. The act culminated 21 years of discussion and consideration. Once committed, the state began a search for the best location. In 1985, 400 acres near the juncture of I-81, a major north-south highway, and I-64, a major east-west highway, was purchased. With a combination of state funding and private donations, phase one of the horse center includes a large indoor ring with 3,800 seats for spectators, real bathrooms and concession areas. There are three outdoor arenas; two are lighted, one has grandstands. Other competition areas include four dressage arenas, a cross country and an outside hunter course and wooded trails. Plans are on the drawing board for a steeplechase course. Stabling is available for almost 600 horses.

A partial list of events includes 75 events and 200 days of competition. It is safe to say that almost any weekend between February and November something will be going on at the Horse Center. Motel space can be scarce when large shows couple with special doings at Virginia Military Institute, Washington & Lee or Southern Seminary, the three institutes of higher learning in Lexington.

Many of the events are free to spectators or feature a very modest admission charge. A sampling of the schedule includes horse trials and dressage shows, draft horse pulls and Jack Russell terrier races, hunter and jumper shows, breed shows for Arabians, walking horses, quarter horses, Morgans, Ponies of America and miniature horses.

For spectators the high point comes with the Virginia Horse Festival in April. The Horse Festival is booked as a showcase for the Virginia horse industry, sponsored by the Virginia Horse Council and the Virginia Horse Center. Included are 80 trade booths, 25 breeds on display and shown in performance demonstrations, a draft horse pull, stallion row to give mare owners a chance to eyeball potential suitors, an equine art show, a foxhunting demonstration, wagon rides, musical entertainment and an old-fashioned barbecue. The festival is held over a weekend, from 9:00 A.M. to 9:00 P.M. Saturday and 9:00 A.M. to 5:00 P.M. Sunday.

Besides the Rockbridge Regional Fair, the Horse Festival is about the biggest spectator draw at the Horse Center. Southern States Feed in conjunction with Virginia Tech has been sponsoring a two-day Equine Seminar at the Horse Center. The first day of the seminar is devoted to breeding and nutrition. On the second day, veterinary and training issues are addressed. The

Arabian and saddle horse shows draw appreciative crowds. More about combined training and dressage events at the Horse Center may be found in Chapter XI.

COMMONWEALTH PARK
Culpeper, VA

Contact: Showday
Route 4, Box 78
Culpeper, VA 22701

Phone: 703-825-7469

Directions: From D.C., travel west on I-66 to the exit to Warrenton via Route 29 south. Continue on Route 29 to the second Culpeper exit, Route 3, Mineral. Proceed to the left on Route 3 (away from Culpeper) for ¼ mile, turning right on Route 522 south. The show grounds is 3 miles on the left.

Commonwealth Park lists about 30 events a year, predominately shows for hunters, jumpers, and dressage, along with two horse trials. The level of competition is good and for most events, the admission is free. Commonwealth, in its out-of-the-way location, does not draw many spectators.

Nine major hunter/jumper shows are held annually at Commonwealth. Traditionally, a significant jumper stakes occurs mid-day Sunday in conjunction with these shows. These events are beyond a three-ring circus, at most times four rings are going full-tilt. Jumping competition, horse trials and dressage shows almost always attract Olympic-level riders who stable in the area.

All in all, Commonwealth has eight rings for competition and 900 stalls for competitors making it one of the largest horse facilities in the nation other than race tracks. Creature comforts for humans include two restaurants, in operation during shows, including one in a pavilion overlooking the main show ring. Another, cafe-style, features an attractive shaded deck.

Events, besides those listed, include a show for walking horses, tractor pulls, and two rodeos. The majority of events at Commonwealth are free to the public. More about combined training and dressage events at Commonwealth may be found in Chapter XI.

FRYING PAN PARK
Herndon, VA

Contact: Frying Pan Park
2709 West Ox Road
Herndon, VA 22071

Phone: 703-437-9101

Directions: From D.C., take I-66 west to Route 50 west. Turn right on Centreville Road (Route 645). Travel 3.3 miles to the traffic light, turn right on West Ox Road to Frying Pan Park, ¼ mile on the left.

Over 20 years ago, Fairfax County officials became concerned that space for equine activities was disappearing and remedied the situation by creating Frying Pan Park. Besides a complete equestrian complex, Fairfax County government also developed an historic site which features a working farm, simulating living and working conditions between 1920 and 1940. The model farm is open daily from 8:00 A.M. to 6:00 P.M. In addition to attending horse events at Frying Pan, one can see cows, sheep, rabbits, chickens and ducks, making this a nice outing for a family with younger children. Kidwell Farm includes a house, blacksmith shop, country store, schoolhouse and Baptist church.

The equestrian complex includes a large indoor ring and two outdoor show rings, along with a schooling ring and outside jump course. Horse shows, clinics or schooling shows are held almost every week of the year.

Cutting horse and quarter horse shows at Frying Pan draw a fair number of spectators. Of particular interest are the cutting horse events, including the semi-finals for the East Coast Cutting Horse Association, a national event that draws competitors from as far away as Texas. These events feature about 100 horses and 150 cows. The name of the game is to separate or "cut" a designated calf away from a group of cattle, just as cowboys in the Ole West did when animals needed veterinary attention or branding. Competitors are judged on the skill of the rider and the savvy and training of the horse. Good cutting horses are said to be on automatic pilot when they understand which calf is to be singled out. Unlike some rodeo events, the cows are neither roped nor wrestled, only re-directed.

PRINCE GEORGE'S EQUESTRIAN CENTER
Upper Marlboro, MD

Contact: Prince George's Equestrian Center
14955 Pennsylvania Ave.
Upper Marlboro, MD 20772

Phone: 301-952-4740

Directions: From D.C., take East Capitol Street to Pennsylvania Avenue (Route 4) to the center, located seven miles beyond the Beltway (Exit 11 A-Upper Marlboro), near the intersection of Route 4 and Route 301.

Prince George's Equestrian Center includes a race track and extensive stabling for a thoroughbred race horse training facility. Its indoor exhibition hall seats 5,000 for horse shows and concerts, even more for conferences and trade shows. Outdoors, the center has two show rings along with 250 stalls for exhibitors.

Events include a variety of small shows sponsored by local associations, along with larger shows for miniature horses, quarter horses, Arabians and hunters. The biggest horsey events of the year are the Marlborough Races (for details, please see Chapter VI). Other events at Prince George's Equestrian Center include Girl Scout jamborees, auto shows, kennel club shows, and a Farm Heritage Festival. Special exhibits and the races have admission fees. Plans for the indoor complex include spectator-oriented horse shows.

McDONOGH SCHOOL SHOWS
Owings Mills, MD

Contact: Gary Baker
P.O. 2122
Middleburg, VA 22117

Phone: 703-687-3455

Directions: From D.C., drive north on I-95 to the Baltimore Beltway (I-695). Travel toward Towson to Exit 20N, Route 140, Reis-

272

terstown Road. Turn left on McDonogh Road to the school, which is on the right.

McDonogh School, located in the midst of Owings Mills, MD, near Baltimore, hosts several schooling shows, as well as the Boumi Temple Horse Show. The Boumi Temple Show, founded in 1940, claims to be Maryland's oldest horse show. It is held at the end of May. The 50-acre show ground at McDonogh School includes three all-weather show rings, and a wide complement of jumps.

TRAINING STABLES

A number of large public stables across Virginia and Maryland offer horse shows throughout temperate months. These are for boarders and locals. They are not fancy, but can feature very fine young horses and riders destined for greatness. Because such outstanding horsemen live in the Capital area, it would not be unheard of to see an Olympic-level rider at one of these shows, schooling a new or inexperienced horse.

These shows are invariably free. Spectators are welcome to stop in and watch for a while. Those who are seeking a place to learn to ride, to sign up their children for lessons or to board a horse can also get an idea of what the facility is like.

PAPER CHASE FARM
Middleburg, VA

Contact: Paper Chase Farm
P.O. Box 448
Middleburg, VA 22117

Phone: 703-687-5853

Directions: From D.C., take I-66 west to Exit 15, Route 50 west. Follow Route 50 for 21 miles to Paper Chase Farm, located two miles east of Middleburg.

One of the easiest farms to find is Paper Chase Farm, two miles east of Middleburg, VA on Route 50. Almost two dozen shows are held annually at Paper Chase, appropriately named for a farm managed by the daughter of the head of *USA Today*.

Appendix B

FOX HUNTS IN THE CAPITAL AREA

The following is a list of area hunts recognized by the Master of Foxhounds Association. A brief history of the hunt, description and location of the hunt country, policy on visitors or "cappers" and contact are included for each.

BLUE RIDGE HUNT
Clarke County, VA
Established 1888

Contact: Mrs. A. R. Dunning, Jr., Honorary Secretary
Caveland Farm
Boyce, VA 22620

Phone: 703-837-1719

Blue Ridge is by any standards an old hunt, established in the pre-history of modern-day pack hunting. Its country in Clarke County, VA, has been used for even longer than the 100-plus years of the current Blue Ridge Hunt. In fact, it was discovered and hunted regularly by two of the nation's most famous fox hunters: Lord Fairfax and George Washington. Clarke County was in Lord Fairfax's original grant, and it quickly won favor with him. Legend has it that great herds of buffalo grazed the Shenandoah Valley, and that Indians burned it periodically to create natural grassland. Lord Fairfax built Greenway Court near the current village of White Post, VA, and used it as a hunting center. His friend George Washington, who drove the original white post there when surveying the area, frequently joined Lord Fairfax for the sport. The house at Greenway Court long ago burnt down and was rebuilt. Descendants of the family who inherited Greenway Hall from Lord Fairfax live there to this day, and the land is hunted still, now by the Blue Ridge Hounds.

Greenway Court is not the only famous fixture on the Blue Ridge card. The hunt gathers at Carter Hall annually for its opening meet. This is perhaps the most photographed of all hunt scenes in America, and certainly one that telegraphs to people who haven't been here yet what hunting in Virginia is like.

Carter Hall was built by Nathaniel Burwell in the late 1700s. Around 1980, it passed out of private hands when its owners willed it to Project Hope, an international humanitarian mission that trains and sends medical teams to underdeveloped countries. The Blue Ridge Horse Show, which celebrated its one hundredth birthday in 1992, was held at Carter Hall for many years. The show, sponsored by the hunt, now is held at Foxcroft School in Middleburg. Besides the horse show, the hunt sponsors a point-to-point, a hunter pace, a horse trials, and a spring trail ride. The hunt country includes portions of Warren, Clarke, and Jefferson counties, about 70 miles west of Washington and beyond the Blue Ridge Mountains and Shenandoah River. Visitors are permitted to hunt.

BULL RUN HUNT
Haymarket, VA
Established 1937

Contact: Thomas Hafer, Honorary Secretary
14692 Stratford Drive
Woodbridge, VA 22193

Phone: 703-878-0271

Visitors are permitted to hunt. The hunt sponsors a point-to-point and a number of hunter pace events. The country lies near Manassas and Haymarket, VA. The hunt now also uses country in Madison, Greene and Culpeper counties.

CASANOVA HUNT
Casanova, VA
Established 1909

Contact: Mrs. Edward Shelton, Honorary Secretary
P.O. Box 105
Casanova, VA 22017

Phone: 703-371-4749

The hunt sponsors a point-to-point and hunt trail rides, both spring and late summer. The hunt kennels are located at

Weston, a historic property near the charming village of Casanova. Opening hunt meets on Casanova's village green. Weston, one of the oldest homes in Fauquier County, was built on land granted to Giles Fitzhugh. In 1859, the house and land was bought by Charles J. Nourse, whose daughters Charlotte and Constance lived there until their deaths in the 1950s. Charlotte was an avid horsewoman and master of the Casanova Hunt. Weston is opened for tours by appointment. Call 703-788-9220 to see this interesting property, in the heart of the Casanova hunt country.

The hunt country is located not far from Warrenton, VA, in central and eastern portions of Fauquier and southeast Culpeper counties. Hunters who formed the Casanova club once rode over to hunt with Warrenton. The group then established its own hunt, dividing up territory with its neighbor Warrenton.

Visitors may cap a maximum of three times per season. Cap, the fee paid by non-members, should be paid the day of the hunt. Grooms may hunt only by special permission of the MFH and are expected to pay cap.

DE LA BROOKE FOXHOUNDS W
Leonardtown, MD
Established 1961

Contact: Mrs. William Gallagher, Honorary Secretary
Rocking Horse Ridge
401 Farmington Road West
Accokeek, MD 20607

Phone: 301-292-5957

Foxhunting in America began on land now hunted by De la Brooke. The club draws its name from the ancestral home of Robert Brooke, who in 1650 imported the first pack of hounds to America. Brooke's home has long since been destroyed, but another manor house by the same name still exists and is an annual fixture of the hunt. The "W" was added to the name De la Brooke because the group first sought to register itself under the name of Wicomico, for the river that courses through its territory. Another group had reserved the name with the Master of Foxhounds, so De la Brooke included an intriguing W in memory of what might have been. Their hunt country is located in the tidewater area of Maryland, south of D.C. Visitors are permitted to hunt. The hunt sponsors a hunter pace event in April and an annual trail ride.

DEEP RUN HUNT
Manakin-Sabot, VA
Established 1887

Contact: Jt. Master Coleman P. Perrin
Dover Green
955 Dover Road
Manakin-Sabot, VA 23103

Phone: 804-784-5702

Deep Run hunts a territory in the eastern end of Goochland County, northwest of Richmond. Its territory extends to Rock Castle, the ancestral home of Dr. Thomas Walker, who served on the staff of General George Washington and who developed the Walker foxhound, one of the most famous American strains of foxhounds. The Deep Run Race Association long hosted a steeplechase, and built the race course now used by Strawberry Hill, which has taken over management of the race through the Atlantic Rural Exhibition Association. The Deep Run Hunt Cup, probably the oldest continuous race in Virginia, is offered annually at the Strawberry Hill races.

The hunt club maintains almost 200 acres, which include the hunt kennels, homes of the professional hunt staff, a horse show grounds, stabling for special horse events, a swimming pool and tennis courts. Through the Deep Run Horse Shows Association, the hunt is able to invite the public into its private club a number of times each year. Deep Run itself hosts an annual "A" rated show each June. It permits other organizations to host horse shows there in the temperate months. The hunt itself hosts a fall hunter trials. The show grounds are special because the arena and jump courses are on turf, rather than all weather surface, which can be dusty or muddy, depending on weather conditions. The Deep Run Pony Club holds its annual week-long summer camp there.

ELKRIDGE-HARFORD
Monkton, MD
Established 1878

Contact: MFH Mrs. John Shapiro
Tally-Ho Farm
3500 Hess Road
Monkton, MD 21111

Phone: 410-771-4852

Hunting in the Baltimore area, which existed before the War, was formally established with the Elkridge Fox Hunting Club in 1878. This group hunted southwest of the city. Unlike other groups, ladies were welcomed to hunt, and never permitted to pay subscription. They were considered "an honor and ornament to the field," according to accounts in early journals. Not so long before the Elkridge Hunt was founded, articles in sporting journals proclaimed, "Women are suited for the sofa not the saddle, and their presence in the hunting field would be an abomination."

From 1906, the Harford Hunt frequented the verdant Green Spring Valley north of Baltimore. In 1934, Elkridge and Harford merged to form what is now the Elkridge-Harford, an event of significant social importance to warrant a headline and prominent placement in the Baltimore newspaper.

Elkridge-Harford hunts territory north and east of Baltimore in the picturesque Monkton area which, with Glyndon and Middleburg, form three of America's most famous hunting boroughs. With the exception of its neighbor, Green Spring Valley Hounds, Elkridge-Harford boasts the most substantial fences fox hunters encounter in these parts. The hunt hosts the annual Elkridge-Harford Point-to-Point Races on the grounds of its hunt club. My Lady's Manor Races are held in the nearby hunt country. It also hosts an annual hunter trials and an old-fashioned point-to-point.

Visitors hunt only by permission of the master.

FAIRFAX HUNT
Loudoun County, VA
Established 1927

Contact: Ms. Steffanie H. Burgevin, Honorary Secretary
43882 Laburnum Square
Ashburn, VA 22011

Phone: 703-729-5928

The Fairfax Hunt bears the name of Lord Fairfax, who un-doubtedly encouraged or perhaps originated "hunting in the English fashion" in the colonies. From early on the county of Fairfax was hunted, and as Washington, D.C. lost its territory, Fairfax usurped more and more of the area's hunters. Today's Fairfax Hunt was founded by A. Smith Bowman in 1927. Bow-man's own estate of 7,000 acres was the nucleus of the hunt country. He gave the hunt 10 acres and a old log cabin clubhouse.

Like its forerunner in Washington, the Fairfax Hunt has suffered in recent years from encroaching population. Sunset Hill, Bowman's estate, became the town of Reston. Then Dulles Airport claimed a lion's share of the hunt territory. Fairfax Master of Foxhounds Randy Rouse remembers hunting from fixtures all over Fairfax County, including Wolf Trap, a popular meet. The hunt has been pushed into Loudoun County, and as their ter-ritory in eastern Loudoun builds up, the hunt is turning its attention to a historic patch of Loudoun County north of Mid-dleburg that was once hunted by legendary Master Joe Thomas.

The hunt sponsors a point-to-point, a steeplechase and a fall hunter trials. It holds a glittering charity ball every year on the Mall in Washington, most recently at the Department of Agricultural Building. MFH Rouse said that one of the nicest opportunities it offers for spectators to get the flavor of fox-hunting is the annual Blessing of the Hounds on Thanksgiving Day. This ceremony, conducted by an Episcopal cleric, was held until 1992 at Belmont, the site of the point-to-point. Then it was moved to historic Huntland, the fabulous old house of Joe Thomas, since purchased by Roy Ash. The hunters, who are mounted, are formally attired in top hats or hunt caps with "pink" coats for male members, black coats for women and vis-itors. All draw near for the ceremony, with the hounds right at the feet of the priest, who blesses the hunters, the hounds, the foxes and other game, and the land and farmers.

FARMINGTON HUNT
Charlottesville, VA
Established 1929

Contact: Gloria Fennell, Honorary Secretary
P.O. Box 5562
Charlottesville, VA 22905

Phone: 804-823-5018

Farmington Hunt members are involved with the highly popular Foxfield Steeplechases. They also put in winning appearances annually at the Washington International Horse Show. The pack hunts on rolling to slightly hilly land near Charlottesville, VA.

GLENMORE HUNT
Middlebrook, VA
Established 1930

Contact: MFH Frederick Getty
Route 1, Box 498
Bold Stream Farm
Middlebrook, VA 24459

Phone: 703-886-1701

The territory hunted by Glenmore is described as rolling to steep hilly land. It is located on the other side of the Blue Ridge south of Staunton, VA.

GOSHEN HUNT
Olney, VA
Established 1957

Contact: Ellen S. Miller, Honorary Secretary
3660 Daisy Road
Woodbine, MD 21797

Phone: 301-854-6104

Goshen hunts over rolling farm land west/northwest of Baltimore. Its territory is becoming built up, but the hunt still enjoys good sport. It shares its huntsman, extraordinary horseman and steeplechase rider Bay Cockburn, with the Loudoun Hunt.

GREEN SPRING VALLEY HOUNDS
Glyndon, MD
Established 1892

Contact: Michael D. Hankin
13820 Longneck Road
Glyndon, MD 21071

Phone: 410-833-5166

The Green Spring Valley Hounds hunt the verdant valleys north and west of Baltimore. The sweeping valleys, broken by Piedmont ridges, have long been a favorite of fox hunters. In the beginning, the Green Spring Valley itself was hunted. As suburbanization of this area became a problem, the kennels moved to the Worthington Valley, which, along with adjacent valleys, Green Spring continues to hunt. Glyndon, the seat of Green Spring hunting, and nearby Monkton and its Elkridge-Harford Hunt are akin to Middleburg, in that these areas revolve around horses and hunting. In this part of Maryland the players never seem to change. The same families stay generation after generation, pursuing the same beloved activities, hunting and racing.

Visitors are permitted to hunt with Green Spring, but are advised this hunt's territory is considered the most rigorous in America in terms of jumps. The Maryland Hunt Cup course is located in the hunt's territory and the hunt regularly crosses the line fences that are jumped in the race. The race itself has been likened to the English Grand National and is a prize sought after by the best horsemen in the world. The charge is always given that none but very competent riders should consider foxhunting. Here, none but the fittest, best mounted, most experienced fox hunters should consider participating. Before the day is done, the hunter will face four-board fences. Those who accept the challenge get to hunt behind an excellent pack.

281

HOWARD COUNTY-IRON BRIDGE HOUNDS
Ellicott City, MD
Established 1930

Contact: Dr. Patricia A. Straat
830 Windy Knoll
Sykesville, MD 21784

Phone: 410-442-1582

Howard County country lies west of Baltimore. Its territory adjoins Green Spring on the north, and it shares a portion of Frederick County with the New Market hunt. Howard County hosts a point-to-point in the spring, the first of the Maryland races. Visitors are permitted to hunt.

KESWICK HUNT
Keswick, VA
Established 1896

Contact: Jt. Master John J. Carle II
P.O. Box 261
Palmyra, VA 22963

Phone: 804-589-3012

Keswick hunts southern Rapidan and Orange County east and north- east of Charlottesville. Visitors are permitted to hunt only by invitation.

LOUDOUN HUNT
Leesburg, VA
Established 1892

Contact: Mrs. Mary Ball Pitz
Route 2, Box 135
Leesburg, VA 22075

Phone: 703-338-4477

Loudoun Hunt has been served by a long illustrious line of masters, including two founding fathers of the Master of Foxhounds Association, Harry Worcester Smith and Westmoreland Davis. Smith, from Worcester, MA, was a colorful, controversial character, and as much as any man responsible for turning the attention of the foxhunting fraternity to the prime hunting territory of Loudoun and Fauquier counties. In a nice turn of fate and sympathetic planning, Morven Park, the home of the late Westmoreland Davis, now houses the Museum of Hounds and Hunting, and also the MFH Association. Another interesting master was E.B. McLean, publisher of *The Washington Post* and owner for a brief time of the Hope Diamond.

Loudoun owns two distinct packs of hounds and operates two kennels. Their hunt country occupies a 25-by-18 mile swath of Loudoun County, neighboring the Middleburg Hunt on the south. Basically, the country lies both north and south of Route 7. The southern portion of the country is in the Hamilton, VA, area, and centers around land farmed for 200 years by the family of the current joint-master, Joe Rogers. Loudoun sponsors an annual point-to-point and provides technical support to steeplechases held spring and fall at Morven Park. From time to time, the hunt puts on hunter trials and trail rides.

 MARLBOROUGH HUNT
Upper Marlboro, MD
Established 1936

Contact: Jt. Master Edward Coffren, III
2817 Crain Highway
Upper Marlboro, MD 20772

Phone: 301-627-2298

Marlborough hunts in Rosaryville State Park, located east/southeast of Washington, D.C. Included in their territory is Mt. Airy Plantation, the hunting lodge of George Calvert, the third Lord Baltimore. Hunt members have joined the Rosaryville Conservancy, which holds a long-term lease with the Maryland Department of Natural Resources, assuring that the state park will remain open for riding activities, including popular fall horse trials. Other user groups in the conservancy hold field trials for bird dogs there. The hunt has a clubhouse called the Patuxent

Rod and Gun Club, an old hunting lodge originally used by duck and rail bird hunters.

Marlborough sponsors a large and successful point-to-point at Roedown, and is now involved with the horse trials at Rosaryville State Park. A unique event that would give even non-riders a glimpse at what hunting's all about is the annual Hunt Bowl, held in the fall. A dozen hunts from the area come to compete in a day-long competition. The first phase is a bench show, or beauty contest for hounds. Next, the hounds are "roaded" on foot. Hounds are roaded to get fit in the summer, and to get from place to place in hunt season. They are trained to stay well together and travel in a mannerly style. Next, they are roaded on horseback. Finally the hounds are turned loose on a drag line, which is laid by dragging fox scent over the desired path. Master Ed Coffren says that after being held at tight check the entire day, the hounds are more than ready to go when put on the drag line. Visitors hunt by invitation of the joint masters.

 ## MIDDLEBURG HUNT
Middleburg, VA
Established 1906

Contact: Jt. Master Jeffrey Blue
P.O. Box 2030
Middleburg, VA 22117

Phone: 703-687-3770

Middleburg Hunt was in the headlines in 1992 when two rival groups within the hunt locked horns in a land and leadership dispute. Territorial controversy is not new to the hunt. Middleburg, in fact, was born out of a boundary dispute already being waged by its current neighbor to the west, Piedmont, and its current neighbor to the south, Orange County. Orange County had its hand in the formation of Middleburg, enlisting large land owners to keep Piedmont in check to the west. Reports indicated that bad feelings and political peccadilloes followed for years to come. New Yorker Daniel Sands was the master of

Middleburg, then he wasn't, then he was again. Unlike some Yankees who passed through, Sands settled in to take an active part in the community. Through his leadership of the hunt, Middleburg gained a reputation for excellence in the hunt field, as well as on the bench at hound shows.

Bound on all sides by other active hunts, Middleburg's territory lies north of the village of Middleburg. The bulk of the registered territory of the hunt is still held by the family of S.R. Fred through his daughter Dorothy Smithwick. Middleburg hosts an annual point-to-point.

NEW MARKET-MIDDLETOWN VALLEY HOUNDS
Middletown, MD
Established 1963

Contact: Mrs. Steven Spector
1749 Thurston Road
Dickerson, MD 20842

Phone: 301-831-8175

New Market and the Middletown Valley Hounds merged in 1981. Their territory consists of almost all of Frederick and Washington counties north and west of Frederick, MD. Visitors are permitted to hunt.

OLD DOMINION HOUNDS
Orlean, VA
Established 1924

Contact: Jt. Master David H. Semmes
P.O. Box 203
Flint Hill, VA 22627

Phone: 703-635-2652

Old Dominion hunt territory bumps up against the Blue Ridge Mountains in western Fauquier County and in parts of

Rappahannock County. The land hunted is to this day sparsely populated and consists mainly of rolling grassland; the sudden and unexpected views of the mountains are magnificent. The territory was claimed in the early 20th century by Joe Thomas, one of the legendary masters of the area, with Major Louis E. Beard, commanding officer of the Front Royal Army Remount Depot as his joint master. When Thomas moved on to other areas and formed other hunts, Sterling Larrabee hunted the territory, changing the name to Old Dominion in 1931. The Hume area, in the center of Old Dominion's country, has produced some fine huntsmen over the years, including the Poe family. Albert Poe currently serves as huntsman for Middleburg; his brother Melvin first served as huntsman of Old Dominion and later as huntsman for Orange County. In earlier times, the Chadwell family of Hume produced Ned Chadwell, also huntsman for Old Dominion and Orange County, and William Chadwell, huntsman for Essex, in New Jersey. The Ballard family, related to the Chadwell family by marriage, raised hounds that served as some of the foundation stock for the Orange County Hounds.

Old Dominion devoted itself solely to hunting until the late William Brainard signed on as master in 1966, when other activities were added, including an annual point-to-point and hunter pace. The hunt has begun holding a hunter trial in the fall and sponsors occasional trail rides in the summer.

Hunting is by invitation only. Guests wishing to hunt must obtain permission of one of the joint masters.

ORANGE COUNTY HUNT
The Plains, VA
Established 1900

Contact: Mary Southwell Hutchison, Honorary Secretary
Route 1, Box 18
Middleburg, VA 22117

Phone: 703-687-6885

The first detail that must be cleared up is that Orange County is not to be found in Orange County, VA. Its name is drawn from the original location of the hunt, Orange County, NY. When word of the hunting Shangri-la in Fauquier County reached him, New Yorker A.L. Harriman purchased a private pack of hounds from William Skinker, who lived two miles south of The Plains. The kennels were located just about where the kennels are today. The northern invaders were not looked upon with favor by Harry Worcester Smith, who himself had come down from Massachusetts and joined forces with another local pack, that of Col. Dulany, whose Piedmont Hounds harked back to 1840. Smith had duly registered Piedmont's territory with the National Steeplechase and Hunt, which interested itself in hunting for the sake of approving horses for hunter races. When it became a shoving match between powerfully connected and vocal forces both claiming the right to hunt the territory in The Plains, the NSHA refused to become involved. To establish an avenue for solving such a dispute, Smith founded the Master of Foxhounds Association. Orange County stuck to its new-found land, and the Atoka Road was drawn as a boundary. Some say the Cobbler Hunt, commanded by General Patton, was carved out of an area around Delaplane and Rectortown, just to keep opposing sides separated.

Starting as early as 1903, New Yorkers were traveling to The Plains for weekend hunts. Harriman had a fitted railroad car, which carried his horses and provided him lodging. Other members stayed in a large clubhouse, across the street from the current Piedmont Lumber. They did not own property, nor did they blend into the community, nor would they have won any popularity contest. When Fletcher Harper was chosen master, that all began to change. Members bought farms and improved them with deluxe chestnut-railed fences, so that the hunt could gallop through unimpeded by wire or gates.

So popular and prime was the country, that the hunt was and is to this day limited to landowners and their house guests. Hunting is by expressed permission of the master. Don't call him, he'll call you.

Orange County does have a number of events open to the public, including both a point-to-point, and an old-fashioned point-to-point, a hunter pace, all in the spring, and highly successful hunter trials in the fall.

PIEDMONT HUNT
Upperville, VA
Established 1840

Contact: Jt. Master Erskine Bedford
Old Welbourne
Route 1, Box 145
Bluemont, VA 22012

Phone: 703-592-3493

The Piedmont Hunt has a legitimate claim to calling itself the oldest hunt in America. The current hunt stems from to the private pack of the Dulany family. It was Col. Richard Henry Dulany, master of the pack until the 20th century, who founded the Upperville Horse Show, and it was Col. Dulany who headed the Confederate cavalry at Gettysburg. The Dulanys, prominent and prosperous planters, hosted visitors from around the nation and the world to hunt across the beautiful bluegrass fields in the Middleburg/Upperville area. When in 1898 Harry Worcester Smith came to visit from his home in Worcester, MA, it was love at first sight love of the land and the hounds he found here. He wanted to make Middleburg the Melton Mowbray of the U.S.—patterned after England's most famous hunting village—and he wanted the world to come and enjoy the sport. To put the place on the map, he staged the famous hunting match of 1905, which did indeed draw attention to that little dimple of Virginia. Smith had joined Col. Dulany as joint master of Piedmont and had registered their hunt country everywhere he could think to register it. That didn't stop the New Yorkers of the Orange County Hunt who came to The Plains from hunting some of Piedmont's territory. The turf battles that followed eventually were ended by the Master of Foxhounds Association, formed for the purpose of settling such disputes.

Piedmont today, as then, offers world class sport, witnessed by the long and steady stream of visitors who come to pay homage. Visitors in recent years have included Princess Anne of Great Britain and her cousin, Michael, the Prince of York and his wife the Princess.

Though visitors are restricted by some of the hunts, Piedmont welcomes skilled riders with suitable, well-mannered horses. Riders should also be especially fit, because Piedmont, now as always, goes long and hard.

The hunt sponsors a point-to-point and hunter pace each spring. Some visitors may wish to see Welbourne, the Dulany family home, where the Piedmont Hunt was founded. It is now operated as a bed and breakfast, by descendants of the Dulany family. When the concept of the Great Hound Match was revived in 1989 and 1991, Ben Hardaway, who came from Georgia to challenge Piedmont, used Welbourne as his headquarters. More details on Welbourne may be found in Chapter XII.

POTOMAC HUNT
Dickerson, MD
Established 1910

Contact: R. Thomas Hoffman, Honorary Secretary
4800 Hampden Lane
Bethesda, MD 20814

Phone: 301-656-7603

As Washington grew, hunting moved from there toward Fairfax and Potomac. Some authorities claim the old Washington Riding and Hunt Club is a direct antecedent of the Potomac Hunt. Potomac MFH Irving Crawford thinks it was more a case of members of the one joining the other. In any case, Potomac has relocated any number of times, due to the burgeoning population of the area. The hunt club and kennels are now located in Barnesville, and Crawford hopes that agricultural zoning of the area will assure the hunt can remain there. Their current country is located in Montgomery County, reaching from their point-to-point course near Seneca all the way to Sugarloaf Mountain. The Potomac River forms its western boundary.

Potomac runs a clubhouse that is used for meetings and social events, and is also offered for community activities. Besides their annual point-to-point in May, the hunt also hosts a spring hunter pace event, and a fall hunter trials.

PRINCESS ANNE HUNT
Williamsburg, VA
Established 1927

Contact: Jt. Master Elias Lyons Guy
112 Falling Creek Circle
Williamsburg, VA 23185

Phone: 804-253-1688

Princess Anne Hunt territory includes open fields and woodland along the James River near Williamsburg.

RAPPAHANNOCK HUNT
Sperryville, VA
Established 1926

Contact: Peter F. Weslow, Honorary Secretary
RR 1, Box 440
Warrenton, VA 22186

Phone: 703-347-5533

Rappahannock hunts a patch of 30 square miles in Rappahannock, Madison and Culpeper counties. One of the largest hunt countries in the U.S., it would be enormous if flattened with a steamroller. The country starts at the foot of the Blue Ridge Mountains and works its way north where the hills are very steep. Visitors, who are jokingly advised to bring their own parachutes, should make contact with the honorary secretary for information about hunting. The hunt sponsors an annual point-to-point, hunter pace, and several trail rides. A horse show, with special classes for hunt members, is held each summer at Hay Day Farm in Culpeper. The hunt also sponsors a special two-day mounted clinic each August for riders who wish to sharpen up skills before the hunt season. The clinic is taught by Rappahannock huntsman Oliver Brown, who is also a top horse show and point-to-point trainer.

Brown's father was a good horseman, and his brother Charlie is huntsman at Old Dominion. The brothers grew up listening to legends of the early hunters. Hunters owned several hounds, which they merged with their neighbors to form a pack. Though the stories may have been embellished, Alexander Mackay-Smith, author of *The American Foxhound,* devotes an entire chapter of his scholarly book to the hounds of the Rappahannock valley, 1799–1887. His research convince him that these hounds formed the foundation stock of most of the great packs of American foxhounds. The land, he points out, is not so well suited for riding as it is for producing hard-running, hard-working hounds.

ROCKBRIDGE HUNT
Glasgow, VA
Established 1947

Contact: John T. Jesse, Honorary Secretary
Route 1, Box 163-1
Glasgow, VA 24555

Phone: 703-463-7089

The Rockbridge Hunt is located in the Lexington, VA, area, bound by the Appalachian and Massanutten Mountains. The territory is in a very handsome part of the very pretty state of Virginia.

SOUTHHAMPTON FOXHOUNDS
Franklin, VA
Established 1979

Contact: MFH S.W. Rawls, Jr.
P.O. Box 777
Franklin, VA 23851

Phone: 804-562-3115

Southhampton's territory skirts the border of Virginia and North Carolina. Visitors may hunt by invitation of the MFH only.

WARRENTON HUNT
Warrenton, VA
Established 1887

Contact: Mrs. Julian W. Scheer
Route 2, Box 24
Catlett, VA 22019

Phone: 703-347-3816

Warrenton was one of the original hunts recognized by the National Steeplechase and Hunt Association. The NSHA sanctioned hunts for the purpose of overseeing races for bona fide hunters, and Warrenton had a long history not only of hunting, but of steeplechasing, as well. The history of the Warrenton Hunt claims that the area was hunted as early as 1790. Certainly its current territory was hunted in the early 1830s, when the hounds were kenneled at the current Fauquier Springs Club, which then boasted a hotel. A hurdle race was run there in 1838, which organizers claimed to be the first such race held on a public race course.

After the Civil War, the area was "discovered" by a succession of Englishmen who found the fertile, gently rolling land perfect for foxhunting, their favorite pastime. The sport was enormously popular, almost from the first. An article in the Fauquier Democrat, 1908, gushed that the Warrenton Drag Hunt crossed "the prettiest country that ever dawned in a poet's dream." Such hyperbole would hardly make it to a newspaper of today, though one account of a day with Warrenton in 1934 was described in *The Washington Post* as being held on "an October day just too perfect for words." This account and other early reports of the hunt listed those in the field [mounted body of riders]. *The Post* reported: "Mr. and Mrs. Winmill arrived for the hunt in their miniature coach and four, just like Cinderella."

Warrenton's fame was due in great part to the long tenure as huntsman of H.D. "Dick" Bywaters, a member of the famed Bywaters family. The Bywaters, who settled in the Culpeper area in 1740, were among the first to master the art of pack hunting. They excelled at both hunting and raising hounds, and sold hounds as well as horses at premium prices. Through the years, the Bywaters were associated with most hunts and every famous master in Virginia.

Mrs. Maximillian Tufts, one of Warrenton's current joint masters, also claims a long family association with Warrenton. Both her father and stepfather served as MFH's.

A charter member of many groups that recognized hunts, Warrenton from the earliest days has sponsored racing. Currently it sponsors a point-to-point. (It originally sponsored the Virginia Gold Cup.) It claims its current point-to-point is the oldest continuous race on the Virginia point-to-point circuit, reaching back to 1941. Back as far as 1900, though, Warrenton held races, and in the '30s it was the ring leader for old-fashioned point-to-points, which gave impetus to the current craze for this type of racing in Virginia. The hunt also sponsors an annual fall hunter trials, as well as an informal horse show circuit, held in the heart of their hunt country on Wednesday nights in the summer. Their trail ride on Memorial Day at Wildcat Mountain is one of the area's most enjoyable and best attended.

Much of Warrenton's prime territory in recent years has fallen prey to development. The hunt still holds the nucleus of what was once one of the great hunting dukedoms of America. It stretches in a narrow swath through the fabulous old farms south and west of Warrenton, through Fauquier County towards Culpeper. Visitors may hunt.

WICOMICO HUNT
Salisbury, MD
Established 1929

Contact: Carolyn C. Senter, Honorary Secretary
Route 1, Box 590
Salisbury, MD 21801

Phone: 410-546-5253

The Wicomico country is situated at the tip of the Eastern Shore of Maryland, and stretches into neighboring Delaware. Visitors may hunt.

About the Author

Jackie Curry Burke grew up riding and fox-hunting in Alabama. She achieved an "A" rating, the U.S. Pony Club's highest mark, and was state horsemanship champion. She gained an appreciation for steeplechasing, eventing and dressage while living in Tennessee. There she earned an American Horse Shows Association judge's license, and National Steeplechase Association trainer's license.

When Burke moved to Middleburg, she was enchanted by the noble equines and abundant sporting opportunities that greeted her. Her deep appreciation for the fine horses, horsemen and equestrian competitions the area produces led to the idea for *Capital Horse Country*.

Her writing background includes a degree in journalism from Middle Tennessee State University and various posts on the sports, life styles, and business desks of the *Nashville Banner* and Franklin, TN, *Review Appeal*. She has been a regular contributor to a long list of horse, sailing and general interest magazines.